SEARCHING FOR LIFE

SEARCHING FOR LIFE

The Grandmothers of the Plaza de Mayo and the Disappeared Children of Argentina

RITA ARDITTI

Para Pablo:
amistosamente
y por los derechos
humanos!
Rita Arditti
Noviembre 2001

University of California Press
Berkeley Los Angeles London

University of California Press
Berkeley and Los Angeles, California

University of California Press, Ltd.
London, England

All photographs by author unless otherwise credited.

Library of Congress Cataloging-in-Publication Data

Arditti, Rita
Searching for life : the grandmothers of the Plaza de Mayo and the disappeared children of Argentina / Rita Arditti.
p. cm.
Includes bibliographical references and index.
ISBN 0-520-21113-8 (alk. paper). — ISBN 0-520-21570-2 (alk. paper)
1. Asociación de Abuelas de Plaza de Mayo. 2. Children of disappeared persons—Argentina—Family relationships. 3. Missing children—Argentina—Family relationships. 4. Civil rights—Argentina. I. Title.
HV6322.3.A7A74 1999
362.7—dc21 98-46637
CIP

Printed in the United States of America

08 07 06 05 04 03 02 01 00
9 8 7 6 5 4 3 2

The paper used in this publication meets the minimum requirements of ANSI/NISO Z39.48-1992 (R 1997) (*Permanence of Paper*). ∞

For the Grandmothers

and in loving memory of my mother,
Rosa Cordovero de Arditti,

and of Renée Epelbaum,
Mother of the Plaza de Mayo/Línea Fundadora

CONTENTS

ILLUSTRATIONS

photographs follow page 78

ACKNOWLEDGMENTS

Many people in Argentina and in the United States gave me practical help and nourished my spirit. While in Buenos Aires I was fortunate to be able to stay in the home of my sister and brother-in-law, Edith and Jaime Benveniste, and of my cousin Renée Blankleder. They supported me in every conceivable way. Without their help this book would not have happened. Many thanks also to my sister Alicia Arditti, to my cousins Laura and Eduardo Marbach, to Julia and Jan Lichtig, to Sylvia Kossoy, and to my aunt Daisy Wollenberger.

My friend Alicia d'Amico kept me informed of the latest political developments in Argentina and sent me crucial clippings from Buenos Aires newspapers. Her comments were always illuminating. Magui Bellotti and Marta Fontenla from ATEM (Asociación de Trabajo y Estudios de la Mujer) helped me learn about current feminist debates in Argentina and provided the connection with Lita Boitano, from Familiares de Detenidos y Desaparecidos por Razones Políticas, who put me in touch with HIJOS (Hijos por la Identidad y la Justicia, contra el Olvido y el Silencio). Juan Jorge Fariña shared ideas and resources and Esteban Costa provided encouragement and an attentive ear. Graciela Mabel Wolfenson, Ariel Pereyra, and María Adela Antokoletz (daughter) skillfully transcribed interviews. The late Renée Epelbaum and María Adela Antokoletz (mother), from the Mothers of the Plaza de Mayo/Línea Fundadora, were (and are) a constant inspiration. Alejandro Inchaurregui from the Equipo Argentino de Antropología Forense provided detailed information about some of the pregnant women killed after the delivery of their children. Cristina Camusso helped me get access to out-of-print publications. Marcelo Pablo Castillo shared his graphics archive.

María Santa Cruz, Analía Rivadera, and Daniel Bustamante at the Grandmothers' office were invariably helpful. Abel Madariaga kept me informed, electronically, on the latest developments of the Grandmothers' work.

In the United States, I am indebted to Christine Dinsmore for suggesting that I contact the University of California Press and to Becky Thompson, Cynthia Enloe, and Gilda Bruckman for sound advice about publishing. Shelley Minden and Tatiana Schreiber read selected chapters and made many excellent suggestions. George A. Stewart and Janine Baer read the chapter on the right to identity, provided references, and gave me useful and pointed feedback. Elly Bulkin, most generously, read the whole manuscript. Her intelligent and sensitive comments were invaluable. Brinton Lykes introduced me to the work of Ignacio Martín-Baró and Jean Hardisty, and the late Jeanmarie Marshall encouraged me constantly. Elliot G. Mishler provided me with a copy of his book on research interviewing, which helped solidify my approach. Blue Lundgren invited me to give a talk about the Grandmothers at the Women's Village in Sugarloaf Key in Florida. The reception I experienced from the women at the commune greatly boosted my spirits. Marguerite Feitlowitz, while completing her own book about Argentina, generously shared resources. Many thanks to Markéta Freund and Enriqueta Horenovsky, who through their work with Amnesty International provided support to the Grandmothers and organized their trips to the United States.

I owe special gratitude to Victor B. Penchaszadeh and Inés Musacchio, who introduced me to the work of the Grandmothers, and to César Chelala for information, comments, and support. Many thanks to Lawrence Weschler, who provided me with the address of Rev. Jaime Wright in Brazil, and to Bert B. Lockwood Jr. for the address of Theo van Boven in the Netherlands. Eva Fleischner and Susan Zuccotti in the United States and Sabine Zeitoun from the Centre d'Histoire de la Résistance et de la Déportation in Lyon, France, helped me with the Finaly case, and my friend Dick D'Ari, in Paris, sent me Jacob Kaplan's book. My nephew Martín Benveniste, also from Paris, provided me with Irene Barki's book. The Cambridge Public Library staff and their reference desk were always patient and friendly. Also, during the writing of this book I enjoyed the friendship and support of many of my colleagues from the Union Institute.

My son, Federico, his spouse, Naïma Benali, and their daughter, Layla Muchnik, reminded me by their presence of my multiple blessings and helped with sources in French and editing. My *compañera* Estelle Disch thought with me about the organization of the material, encouraged me from the very beginning, and patiently read all my drafts. Her firsthand knowledge and love for the Grandmothers made all the difference.

My editor at the University of California Press, Naomi Schneider, was enthusiastic from the start and unfailingly supportive as the work progressed. Many thanks to Alice Falk for her intelligent and careful copyediting, to Sue Heinemann for demystifying and coordinating the production process, and to Estrella Fichter for her work in publicity and marketing. My heartfelt gratitude to all the people who agreed to be interviewed for the book and who patiently educated me about the various aspects of the Grandmothers' work.

The Thanks Be to Grandmother Winifred Foundation was the sole source of financial support for this project. Their grant helped pay for travel and transcription expenses. The Foundation, which gives grants to women fifty-four years old and over, can be contacted at P.O. Box 1449, Wainscott, NY 11975-1449. I am forever thankful for their support.

ACRONYMS

AAA	Alianza Anticomunista Argentina, also known as Triple A (Argentine Anticommunist Alliance)
AAAS	American Association for the Advancement of Science
ANCLA	Agencia de Noticias Clandestinas (Clandestine News Agency)
APDH	Asamblea Permanente por los Derechos Humanos (Permanent Assembly for Human Rights)
CEA	Conferencia Episcopal Argentina (Argentine Episcopal Conference)
CELS	Centro de Estudios Legales y Sociales (Center for Legal and Social Studies)
CGT	Confederación General del Trabajo (General Workers Confederation)
CI	Cadena Informativa (Information Network)
CONADEP	Comisión Nacional sobre la Desaparición de Personas (National Commission on the Disappeared)
EAAF	Equipo Argentino de Antropología Forense (Argentine Forensic Anthropology Team)
ERP	Ejército Revolucionario del Pueblo (People's Revolutionary Army)

ESMA	Escuela Superior de Mécanica de la Armada (Navy Mechanics School)
FEDEFAM	Federación Latinoamericana de Asociaciones de Familiares de Detenidos-Desaparecidos (Latin American Federation of Associations for Relatives of the Detained and Disappeared)
HIJOS	Hijos por la Identidad y la Justicia, contra el Olvido y el Silencio (Children for Identity and Justice against Oblivion and Silence)
IACHR	Inter American Commission on Human Rights
MEDH	Movimiento Ecuménico por los Derechos Humanos (Ecumenical Movement for Human Rights)
MTP	Movimiento Todos por la Patria (Movement All for the Country)
NN	Nacht und Nabel (Night and Fog)
OAS	Organization of American States
PRT	Partido Revolucionario de los Trabajadores (Revolutionary Workers' Party)
SERPAJ	Servicio Paz y Justicia (Peace and Justice Service)
SIDE	Secretaría de Informaciones del Estado (State Intelligence Agency)
UFER	Mouvement International Pour l'Union Fraternelle Entre les Races et les Peuples (International Movement for Fraternal Union among Races and Peoples)

INTRODUCTION

This book is about the Grandmothers of Plaza de Mayo, a courageous group of women in Argentina who have worked tirelessly to find their disappeared grandchildren and to achieve a measure of justice in their country for more than twenty years. The book is also about the countless human rights violations that the military inflicted on the Argentine people between 1976 and 1983 and how this group of women resisted the worst dictatorship in Argentine history.

Under the military regime's reign of terror, even mild dissent was equated with subversion. All "subversives" were seen as enemies of the state, enemies who needed to be eliminated. In addition, the military believed that the children of subversives should not be allowed to grow up with the families that had produced their parents. They needed to be with "decent" and "patriotic" families, who would save them from becoming the next generation of subversives. These are the children that the Grandmothers are searching for—children who were born in captivity in the more than 340 concentration camps where their pregnant mothers were detained and killed after delivering them, as well as children who were kidnapped and disappeared with their parents.

I first learned about the Grandmothers of the Plaza de Mayo in 1986 when, after responding to a fund-raising letter from the Argentine Information Service Center (AISC) in New York, I received a book about them, *Botín de Guerra*, by Eduardo Nosiglia. I remember looking with amazement at the gray and black cover, which showed a burned baby carriage and what looked like the remains of a building after an explosion. I wondered what the book was about. I was shocked by what I read.

I had known for many years about the repression in Argentina, and I knew that if I had been living there during the military regime I might have disappeared myself. During the years of the dictatorship, every time I went to Argentina I had to go to the federal police to renew my passport (when Argentine citizens living abroad entered the country, their passports automatically expired). These visits to the police always made me nervous—and for good reason. In similar situations, Argentine friends of mine had been held and interrogated, sometimes for hours; and a scientist whom I had met while working at MIT, Antonio Missetich, had disappeared after returning to Argentina.

I knew about the Mothers of the Plaza de Mayo who marched every Thursday at 3:30 P.M. and about the moral leadership they had provided for so many years both during and after the dictatorship, but I had been unaware of the existence of the Grandmothers. It was hard to believe that during the "dirty war" (as the military themselves called the repression) children had become targets, that newborn babies were given away to families who were part of the repressive regime, and that hundreds of children were growing up with false histories and identities.

When AISC called to ask if I would accompany two Grandmothers during their visit to the Boston area, I was delighted to do so. María Isabel Chorobik de Mariani, known as "Chicha" to her friends, and Nélida Gómez de Navajas, the president and the treasurer of the Association, were in the United States for a tour sponsored by Amnesty International that included visits to colleges, universities, churches, and human rights organizations. As I translated their stories for English-speaking audiences, I began to realize the multilayered nature of their work and the complexities of their task. I was very moved to learn that some of the found children had long been suspicious about their origins and that after their initial shock about the truth they rapidly integrated themselves into their legitimate families. I heard about the arguments over the restitution of the children: Would the restitution constitute a second trauma? Would it not be better to leave the children with the people they knew as parents, regardless of the role of those "parents" during the repression? And I heard about the delays of the judicial system that enabled the children to be taken abroad so that their kidnappers could escape justice. I understood the urgency of the Grandmothers' work. Each day that went by was one more day in which the children were growing up with lies and without their histories, deepening the fraudulent socialization to which they were subjected.

As I heard about the many facets of the Grandmothers' work, I was intrigued by the richness of their stories and decided that I wanted to learn more about them. After that visit, every time I went to Buenos Aires to see family and friends I visited the Grandmothers' office. Back in the States I kept in touch by reading their newsletter and occasional news updates. My own work on reproductive technologies had led me to consider issues of identity and personal history and to take part in a larger discussion in the feminist community about the rights of children, identity, and the various definitions of what constitutes a family; I saw many points of connection with their work.

I decided to tell the Grandmothers' story because I wanted to pass on to others what I had been learning from them. In spite of the pain and terror that had been part of their lives, these women radiated an irresistible and contagious positive energy. Their inspiring courage in the face of danger challenged my own stereotypes about women and aging. In 1993, during a sabbatical from my teaching responsibilities and in the spirit of "bearing witness," I wrote to the Grandmothers about doing a book on them. I explained that I wanted the opportunity to present their work to the English-speaking public. The reply was swift and positive. Yes, they would give me the names and addresses of grandmothers who identified themselves as members of the group and any other information that would be useful to the project. I sent a detailed description of the project to twenty women: three declined to be interviewed, but later another three joined in. Each of the twenty Grandmothers I interviewed expressed their desire to go on record with their comments rather than be anonymous.

Most of the interviews took place at the Grandmothers' office in Buenos Aires, in a neighborhood close to the Jewish business section of town. The office stands in front a huge abandoned market, a ghost building. The neighborhood is also known for having once been home to the legendary Carlos Gardel, Argentina's most famous singer. Going up to the fourth floor in the elevator—an elaborate and sinister-looking wrought-iron cage built in the beginning of the century—was an unsettling experience. I often felt a knot in my stomach as I anticipated the dark hall outside the office and then, once the office door opened, the big display with pictures of hundreds of disappeared children and their parents. Posters, international awards, paintings, and photographs on the themes of children and human rights made the mission of the group immediately clear. The Grandmothers' office is a vibrant place: the telephone is constantly ringing, conversations are animated, and visitors from other parts of the country are common. Relatives of the disappeared children stop to inquire about the status of the searches. I had the privilege of attending six of the weekly planning meetings of the Association, at which active members discuss the latest news about each case and scrutinize the political developments on the national scene that may affect their work.

The interviews lasted from one and a half to three hours. I collected demographic information for each Grandmother regarding her age, family situation, class background, and the events that led her to become involved in the group. An interview guide helped start the conversation. In most cases, after one or two leading questions, the guide was put aside and I simply listened to what they wanted to tell me. The interviews were audiotaped and transcribed either by me, by people suggested by the Grandmothers, or by trusted friends and supporters of the human rights movement. Unless otherwise noted, all translations from Spanish are mine. Though I have usually quoted the interviews verbatim, in some cases I condensed the accounts slightly. I also interviewed other people related to the Grandmothers' work: relatives, psychologists, lawyers, the director of the National Genetic Data Bank, forensic anthropologists, human rights activists, and three of the found children.

In December 1993 and again in 1994 I attended the end-of-the-year party held at the Grandmothers' office. I was touched to see some of the found children (now teenagers or young adults) with their legitimate families, chatting with their friends and totally at ease with all who were present. The pride and pleasure of the Grandmothers in being with them was obvious. Since most of the Grandmothers have not yet been able to identify their grandchildren, those who have been found are very special to them. The presence of these children reminds them of their successes, reassures them that their work is not a hopeless dream, and gives them confidence that other children will also be found. The youngsters seemed very much aware of that role as they moved among the various Grandmothers, asking about their work and their families, reflecting the intimate knowledge and bonds that exist among them.

During a trip to Argentina in October–November 1996, my last visit before finishing this book, the unexpected happened. Within forty-eight hours of my arrival my sister informed me that a relative, Reina Waisberg, wanted to talk with me. I had met Reina briefly in my youth (one of her sisters is married to my only living uncle). Over the telephone, Reina said that she had heard about the book I was writing through her work with the Grandmothers' Association. When we met she told me about the disappearances in 1976 of her son Ricardo and his companion, Valeria Belaustegui Herrera, two months pregnant at the time. My family was stunned to learn of Reina's activism; they knew about the disappearance of her son but did not know that his companion was pregnant when she disappeared and that Reina was looking for her grandchild. When I mentioned my connection to Reina to one of the Grandmothers, however, she was not surprised, commenting, "That is why we say that there is no family that has not been touched by what happened here, one way or the other." It was a phrase I had heard several times since I started working on the book, but this time it hit home. Visiting with Reina and her granddaughter Tania (who was fifteen months old when her parents disappeared) was one of the highlights of my trip, and I was particularly happy when they agreed to be interviewed. It brought home how deeply entrenched in Argentina is the conspiracy of silence to which the Grandmothers so often allude, and I felt more determined than ever to help spread the word about the crimes of the dictatorship and the resistance of the Grandmothers.

As I started to work on the book memories of my own childhood reawakened. During the 1940s one of my mother's sisters, Matilde Cordovero, who was living in France, had vanished. From half-heard telephone conversations between my mother and her siblings, I gathered that she had been sent to a concentration camp. We never heard anything else about her. I decided to start my own search for information about her fate. Thanks to the work of Serge Klarsfeld on the deportation of Jews in France, I learned that Matilde had been taken to Auschwitz on March 7, 1944, in a convoy with 1,501 other people and that she had perished there. When I told this to my aunt Daisy, her only surviving sister, she thanked me for giving her the "good news," as she called it. While I had never personally met my aunt, her presence had lingered in the family and there was an inexplicable sense of relief as we finally learned what had happened to her. This experience reinforced my belief in the healing potential of the work of the Grandmothers and the need to establish the truth regarding the fate of their children and grandchildren.

Because kidnapping children and changing their identities are not crimes covered by the amnesty laws and pardons given by the constitutional governments that followed the dictatorship, the work of the Grandmothers has unique significance. The Grandmothers want the past to be remembered and speak often about the importance of collective memory. However, their focus is on the future. They believe that for a *true* national reconciliation to take place, those guilty of atrocities must admit their crimes and accept punishment. Only then will Argentine society have a chance to become fertile ground on which a true democracy may flourish. I join in their belief and I hope that this book will, in some small measure, contribute to their success by increasing the public support and understanding of their work.

ONE

NOT JUST ONE MORE COUP

First we will kill all the subversives; then we will kill their collaborators; then . . . their sympathizers, then . . . those who remain indifferent; and finally we will kill the timid.

General Ibérico Saint-Jean, governor of Buenos Aires (1977)

Here I can do with you whatever I want because I am the lord of life and death.

Colonel Roberto Roualdes, First Command, Army Corps

On October 23, 1975, at the Eleventh Conference of Latin American Armies in Montevideo, Uruguay, journalists asked Lieutenant General Jorge Rafael Videla, commander in chief of the Argentine military forces, about the fight against subversion. "In order to guarantee the security of the state," General Videla replied, "all the necessary people will die." And when asked to define a subversive, he answered, "Anyone who opposes the Argentine way of life."[1]

Five months later, on March 24, 1976—for the sixth time since 1930—the military seized power in Argentina. Lieutenant General Videla, Admiral Emilio Eduardo Massera, and Brigadier General Orlando Ramón Agosti toppled the constitutional government of María Estela (Isabel) Martínez de Perón and proclaimed themselves the new rulers of the country, with General Videla as the new president. This was not just one more coup; the bloodiest and most shameful period in Argentine history was about to begin, during which Argentina became infamous for the atrocities of its government and its striking similarities with the Nazi regime. This period brought the word *desaparecido* (disappeared) into common parlance, forever associating it with the mere mention of Argentina. As a chilling preview of what was to come, Bernardo Alberte, a prominent Peronista leader, was visited in the early hours of the day of the coup by a joint army-federal police unit. As his terrorized family watched, he was thrown out of his sixth-floor apartment window. With this, the first of many acts of terror, the new government took hold.[2]

General chaos and political instability under the government of Isabel Perón had prepared the ground for the takeover. Assassinations, inflation, and deep divisions within the political parties made the coup seem inevitable to large segments of society.[3] A carefully orchestrated campaign by conservative segments of the media, the support of the Argentine landowners and industrialists, and pressure from international financial circles created an image of the generals as reasonable and honest men willing to shoulder the heavy burden of "saving" Argentina. The media presented General Videla and company as "doves" who would prevent the bloodshed that might take place if the other faction, the "hardliners"—like the followers of Augusto Pinochet in Chile—gained power.[4] Prominent intellectuals such as writer Jorge Luis Borges commented, "Now we are governed by gentlemen."[5]

The highest levels of the military had approved the coup in September 1975, shortly after Isabel Perón named General Videla commander in chief of the army; it was to be staged within six months. As the details were planned, the military consulted on economic matters with a member of the landowning Argentine oligarchy—José Alfredo Martínez de Hoz, future finance minister—and on cultural matters with Ricardo Pedro Bruera, future minister of education and culture. They would be among the few civilian members of the new regime.[6]

Almost immediately after the coup the military replaced the constitution with the Statute for the Process of National Reorganization (popularly known as *El Proceso*) giving themselves the authority to exercise all judicial, legislative, and executive powers. Habeas corpus was undermined, censorship was extended to all spheres of life, and trade unions, political parties, and universities fell under the control of the military. The state of siege that had been imposed by Isabel Perón's government was extended indefinitely, and all constitutional guarantees were suspended; 80 percent of the judges were replaced. The military, presenting itself as the defender of "tradition, family, and property," considered any criticism of its rule as a sign of anti-Argentine, subversive behavior that it needed to crush in order to protect the nation. Again, General Videla put it clearly: "The repression is against a minority which we do not consider Argentine."[7]

The "Right of Option," which had allowed prisoners at the disposal of the president to choose between jail and exile, was immediately abolished. A host of newly promulgated decrees and laws both increased the powers of the police and the military and introduced the death penalty for political crimes. Taking over all branches of government, the junta launched one of the Western Hemisphere's most brutal campaigns of repression. Four juntas ruled the country for almost eight years. Only after the debacle of the Malvinas/Falklands war was democracy restored with the election in 1983 of Raúl Alfonsín.[8]

BACKGROUND TO THE COUP

After the military toppled the government of Juan Domingo Perón in 1955, Argentina's economic, social, and political problems continued to grow unabated. Perón and his enormously popular wife, Evita, had instituted extensive social reforms on behalf of the poor and ignited their hopes and their imagination, thus raising their self-esteem and expectations. After his fall, Perón was still very popular among workers who had benefited from his programs and who would not readily accept the rule of his opponents. Although military and civilian administrations succeeded each other, they were unable to stop the country's increasing unemployment, inflation, sociopolitical divisions, and institutional decay.

When General Juan Carlos Onganía took power in June 1966, the coup was heralded as a "new beginning." Presenting himself as a friend of the working class, Onganía launched the idea of a "Peronismo without Perón" to gain the support of workers. However, it quickly became clear that Onganía's goal was to manipulate the labor unions and quell their resistance. He installed a military regime and created an autocracy: changes in society would come from above. He banned all political parties and activities, intervened in the national universities, sent the military to repress workers' protests, and announced his intention to remain in power indefinitely.[9]

In May 1969 the city of Córdoba erupted in what became known as *El Cordobazo,* one of the largest popular protests of that period. Led by university students and automobile workers, it presaged the downfall of the Onganía regime. By 1970 two guerrilla groups appeared on the scene: the Montoneros, which identified with left-wing Peronismo, and the People's Revolutionary Army (ERP), the armed branch of the Revolutionary Workers' Party (PRT). The Montoneros kidnapped and subsequently executed former president Pedro Eugenio Aramburu, one of the leaders of the coup against Perón in 1955.[10] At the same time, clandestine right-wing organizations emerged; they kidnapped students and union militants, who vanished without a trace. In early 1971, one such "disappearance" was occurring every eighteen days.

In 1970, after four years in power, Onganía was overthrown. His successor, General Roberto M. Livingston, lasted only nine months before being replaced by yet another general, Alejandro Lanusse. Lanusse promised elections and tried to isolate the extremists, allowing the labor unions to assume leadership on wage issues. His most important conciliatory gesture—lifting the eighteen-year ban on Peronismo—eventually led to the return of Perón to Argentina in 1973.[11] Perón's homecoming was marked by violence: at the Ezeiza International Airport where his plane was to land, right-wing forces attacked the left-wing factions of the Peronista movement, leaving scores of people wounded or dead. Dissociating himself from the left-wing groups within Peronismo, Perón created alliances with the most reactionary groups and in October 1973 he began his third term as president. Seventy-eight years old and in ill health, he died before his first year in office ended; he was succeeded by his wife, Isabel Perón, who had been his running mate.

During Isabel Perón's government, right-wing death squads launched a campaign of terror against workers, students, and anyone vaguely suspected of leftist tendencies. Declaring a state of siege in November 1974, she gave carte blanche to the military, thus authorizing a bloody campaign to squelch guerrilla activities in Tucumán province. Organized by José López Rega, who was Isabel Perón's right-hand man and minister of social welfare, the sinister Argentine Anticommunist Alliance (or Triple A, as it was commonly called) murdered some seventy of its opponents in the latter half of 1974; by early 1975 the alliance was eliminating leftists at the rate of fifty per week.[12] Among those assassinated were prominent figures like exiled General Carlos Prats, commander in chief of the Chilean army during Salvador Allende's presidency, and his wife, who were killed by a car bomb; lawyer and academician Silvio Frondizi, brother of former president Arturo Frondizi, was kidnapped in midday in the center of Buenos Aires and gunned down in the outskirts of the capital.[13]

When the first junta came to power in 1976, the guerrilla groups in Argentina had been all but wiped out. General Videla himself had declared in January 1976 that the guerrilla groups were no longer a danger. The total insurgent forces probably did not amount to more than 2,000 people, of whom perhaps only 20 percent were armed, while the modern and powerful armed forces numbered about 200,000.[14] The threat of left-wing terrorism was an excuse to take complete control and impose the junta's own brand of state terrorism. The military leaders intended to modify, by any means necessary, the social, political, economic, and cultural structure of the country and to establish themselves as the final unchallenged authority.[15]

THE DOCTRINE OF NATIONAL SECURITY

The Doctrine of National Security, the political cornerstone of the regime, was not a new idea. Under the right-wing rule of General Onganía, the army was already teaching its soldiers that the real threat to Argentina came from within, from "subversives" who sought to destroy the traditional values of Argentine society. Who were these subversives? Anyone who did not adhere to the Christian and military virtues that were supposed to save the world from communism.

Like many other military men in Argentina, Onganía was heavily influenced by U.S. counterinsurgency courses, which had helped spread this doctrine throughout Latin America; indeed, he called it the "West Point Doctrine" in honor of the institution that had given birth to its central tenets. Under the 1947 Inter-American Treaty of Reciprocal Assistance, in 1951 the U.S. Defense Department set up its Military Assistance Program to arm and train Latin American armies. The Latin American officers were trained at centers in the United States such as the Inter-American Defense College at Washington's Fort McNair. U.S. Defense Secretary Robert S. McNamara praised the programs: "These students are hand-picked by their countries to become instructors when they return home. *They are the coming leaders,* the men who will have the know-how and impart it to their forces." In 1969, after a tour of Latin America on President Nixon's behalf, Nelson Rockefeller announced that the military was "the essential force of constructive social change."[16]

In Argentina, French officers who had participated in Vietnam and Algeria were instrumental in training the army. General Ramón Juan Camps, the chief of police of the Buenos Aires province from 1976 to 1979, admired the French approach toward repression; he considered it more effective and complete than the American approach, which relied almost exclusively on sheer force and a militaristic perspective. He prided himself on synthesizing both perspectives and, in the process, creating Argentina's unique brand of repression.[17]

The Doctrine of National Security was a loose set of concepts, some contradictory and poorly delineated; its cohesive power rested in its definition of "the enemy" as communism. A remnant of the cold war, it was designed to protect the economic hegemony of the United States in Latin America. The fear of "another Cuba" drove the United States to fund and train the Latin American armies to obliterate the "menace" of Marxism.[18] The doctrine held that a "third world war" was being waged between the "free world" and communism, a war in which Argentina was a key battleground. As General Luciano Benjamín Menéndez, commander of the Third Army Corps in Córdoba, explained: "On one side were the subversives that wanted to destroy the national state to convert it into a communist state, a satellite in the red orbit, and on the other side, us, the legal forces, which by [the authority of] two decrees of the then-constitutional powers participated in that struggle."[19]

On this account, the internal enemy was more dangerous than enemies from abroad because it threatened the fundamental Western and Christian values of Argentine society. National boundaries became subordinated to "ideological frontiers": the armed forces were to protect the country's ideological purity, not just its geographical borders. The state began to intervene in other countries' internal affairs and joined the Southern Cone's military regimes in fighting "subversion." At the same time, the repressive model was exported to other countries—particularly to Central America, where the Argentine military took an active role in training government forces in Nicaragua, Guatemala, El Salvador, and Honduras.[20]

To coordinate military activities among neighboring countries, General Roberto Viola, a member of the second junta and Argentina's president, proposed the doctrine of Continental Security (*Seguridad Continental*), which created a veritable underground network for the repression. It was open season on political refugees from Uruguay, Bolivia, Chile, Paraguay, and Brazil.[21] Foreigners were told by the authorities that they would be expelled if their presence in any way "affected national security." Recognizing the danger, the UN High Commissioner for Refugees (UNHCR) issued a worldwide appeal to help resettle the refugees in other countries.[22]

In the view of the military, communism's global strategy required that the state respond with a global approach. It followed that the militarization of Argentine society was needed to fight the Marxist "menace." That is how the junta justified launching an undeclared war—a "dirty war," as they called it—against its own people. The inevitability of a third world war was carefully drilled into the minds of the men who ran the day-to-day operations needed to keep the repressive regime in power. Writing of his experiences in the clandestine detention camp where he was held prisoner, Jacobo Timerman, editor of *La Opinión,* recalls weekly courses given by the army on such a war. Timerman reports that "attendance was obligatory for the entire staff of torturers, interrogators, and kidnappers."[23] The message conveyed by this "academy" was simple: Communism needed to be stopped, and Nazi tactics and methods were the only effective tools for fighting subversion. After the classes, Timerman's guards would discuss their lessons with him while he took the opportunity to correct them about their misconceptions regarding Zionism.

Trade union workers were among the main targets of the repression. Argentina's labor movement was the backbone of the Peronista Party, and the workers' demands for social reform and economic justice were seen as part of a "communist plot." Economic policies that disenfranchised the workers were imposed by Finance Minister Martínez de Hoz, who was also president of the board of directors of Acindar (one of Argentina's three steel companies, a subsidiary of U.S. Steel), member of the board of directors of Pan American Airways and ITT, and a personal friend of David Rockefeller.[24] His actions obliged those business interests: freezing workers' salaries while increasing military wages, annulling progressive labor laws, and strongly favoring foreign investors at the expense of local industry. "Deindustrialization" was the result, as enormous credits by foreign banks propped up the economy.[25] Martínez de Hoz made strikes punishable by a ten-year prison term and borrowed over one billion dollars in less than one year. Enchanted with his policies, the International Monetary Fund labeled him the "Wizard of Hoz," while President Ronald Reagan proclaimed him "the architect of what may turn out to be one of the most remarkable economic recoveries in modern history."[26]

In the short run money flowed, and Argentines who could afford it traveled around the world, their pockets full of *plata dulce* (sweet money), but rampant inflation and unemployment soon drove down incomes. As journalist Iain Guest aptly described the result of Martínez de Hoz's right-wing economic policies, "Down came the barriers, up went the peso and in came the loans."[27]

THE DIRTY WAR AND THE METHODOLOGY OF REPRESSION: KIDNAPPING, TORTURE, AND MURDER

The military put in practice a new methodology of repression to enforce the Doctrine of National Security: the kidnapping, torture, and murder of tens of thousands of people. The junta did not invent this particular brand of terror. In 1941 Hitler himself had crafted the Nacht und Nebel Erlass (Night and Fog Decree), aimed at persons "endangering German security": because their public execution might create martyrs, the decree was designed to "make them vanish without a trace into the night and fog of the unknown in Germany."[28] In Latin America disappearances first emerged on a massive scale after 1966 in Guatemala, where paramilitary groups and death squads provided cover for military and police activities against peasants, rural workers, and political organizers.[29]

In Argentina, former policeman Rodolfo Peregrino Fernández has testified that shortly after the 1976 coup, at a meeting of the commanders of the army, a detailed discussion of the doctrine took place. Physical elimination of "unpatriotic subversion" and an all-out "defense of tradition, family, and property" were high on the agenda. They believed that by spreading general terror in the population, the Doctrine of National Security would make it impossible for the guerrilla groups to gain support. Rooted in such politics, the disappearances started to be carried out systematically.[30]

Though there had been disappearances before the coup, the number began to increase dramatically in March 1976. For two murdered bodies found, there were nine disappearances.[31] Nobody was immune. Male and female; young and old, babies and teenagers; pregnant women, students, workers, lawyers, journalists, scientists, artists, and teachers; Argentine citizens and citizens of other countries; nuns and priests, progressive members of religious orders—all swelled the ranks of the disappeared. The term *detenidos-desaparecidos* (detained-disappeared) more accurately describes the methodology of repression than does *desaparecidos*. People did not simply vanish into thin air, or leave the country without alerting their relatives, as the authorities implied. Nor were they kidnapped by fringe groups lacking any direct connection to the government. Use of the former term would directly incriminate the state, ascribing responsibility for the disappearances and reflecting what was *really* happening: people being detained by armed groups acting on orders from the authorities and disappearing into the night and fog of the regime.[32]

The government had learned well the lessons that Hitler had taught. In the absence of physical evidence, it was difficult to organize protests against the regime. The vanishing created terror within the population, but without bodies no one could be blamed. Families were afraid to denounce the abductions, thinking that such actions could endanger the victim and eliminate any chances of their relatives being returned. The silence increased the atmosphere of terror and hopelessness, thereby placing an especially cruel burden on the families of the disappeared. Even worse, they were made to feel in some sense responsible. As Dr. Vicente Angel Galli, director of mental health of the Argentine government, has explained: "To presume the death of people you have not seen dead, without knowing the conditions of their death, implies that one has to kill them oneself. I believe that is one of the more subtle and complex mechanisms of torture for the relatives and for all the members of the community. . . . To accept their deaths we have to kill them ourselves."[33]

The military proclaimed its innocence, stating that it had no knowledge of these events. Emilio Mignone, a founder of the Center of Legal and Social Studies, who met with many members of the military as he sought to learn the fate of his daughter, heard repeatedly: "We are not going to shoot them, like Franco and Pinochet did, because then even the pope is going to ask us to stop it."[34] It was a diabolical plan, and it succeeded for almost eight years in creating a reign of terror unparalleled in Argentine history.

Judicial acquiescence was necessary for the repression to fully take hold. Though not officially suspended, the writ of habeas corpus was rendered ineffective by the complicity of most judges. In Argentina, when a person is detained, a writ of habeas corpus to obtain information about the person's whereabouts may be presented to a judge. The judge is then supposed to make inquiries of the authorities. Refusing to challenge the silence of the military and security forces, the judges rejected almost all the habeas corpus requests presented to them. Mignone estimated that as many as 80,000 writs had been sought, because some families made multiple vain attempts to gain information about their relatives.[35] Division General Tomás Sánchez de Bustamante candidly commented, "In this type of struggle, the secret that must be part of the operations makes it impossible to make it known who has been taken prisoner and who still remains to be captured: There must be a cloud of silence that surrounds everything."[36] Lawyers who presented writs of habeas corpus on behalf of the victims' relatives were themselves at high risk of disappearing. No fewer than 109 lawyers disappeared—90 percent of them between March and December 1976. Twenty-three were assassinated for political reasons, over one hundred ended up in prison, and a countless number went into exile to save their lives.[37]

The repression was the result of a systematic, deliberate plan, centrally organized and directed from above. It was not haphazard and random violence, or simple "excesses" of a war, as the junta proclaimed. A methodology of terror had been developed and it was faithfully followed. The violations of human rights, even in distant parts of the country, followed a set pattern: the same forms of torture, similar kidnappings, even the same grills used to chain the prisoners. In the words of General Santiago Omar Riveros, head of the Argentine delegation to the Inter-American Defense Junta: "We waged this war with the doctrine in our hands, with the written order of each high command; we never needed to have, as we have been accused, paramilitary organizations. . . . This war was conducted by the generals, the admirals, and the brigadiers. . . . The war was conducted by the military junta of my country through its high commanders."[38]

The fundamental instrument of the repression was the Task Forces constituted by the different branches of the military and the security forces. Task Forces 1 and 2 were staffed by the army, Task Force 3 by the navy, Task Force 4 by the air force, and Task Force 5 by the State Intelligence Service (SIDE). Members of the Task Forces were used at different times in different combinations for a variety of "special missions." Often, the participants did not know one another when they met in predetermined places to receive instructions for a specific mission of terror. Once the task was accomplished, the individuals returned to their original groups.[39] A "blood pact" kept the members of the Task Forces bound and loyal to each other. They all engaged in the different parts of the repressive operation—kidnapping, interrogation, torture, and murder—rotating the various activities to ensure silence and complicity.[40]

Most of the kidnappings took place at night or at dawn—primarily in private homes, though sometimes in the streets or at workplaces—usually toward the end of the week. The timing helped delay whatever action relatives might wish to initiate. Heavily armed men dressed in civilian clothes would appear and threaten the victims and their families, and frequently their neighbors. By prior arrangement, the police would make the area near the home safe for the kidnappers. Often it would be "sealed," with several cars blocking access. The number of men involved varied, from six to fifty. Private cars without license plates (often blue-green Falcons), or trucks or vans from the military, would take the blindfolded and handcuffed victims to a secret detention center. Sometimes, before the gang arrived, the electricity would be cut off in the neighborhood where the raid was taking place. Occasionally, a helicopter would circle over the area. The gangs involved in the operations usually looted the homes of their victims.[41]

The kidnappers would throw their prey on the floor of a car or into the trunk and take them to one of the 340 secret detention centers located throughout the country. These centers were small houses, cellars in large buildings, auto repair plants, or military bases adapted for the purpose and complete with double barbed-wire fencing, guards with dogs, helicopter strips, and lookout towers.[42] Financed by the state, they were the foundation of the military's operation. On arrival at a center, each prisoner was carefully identified and registered. The guards filled out forms in quadruplicate and sent copies to the Ministry of the Interior and the Security Services. The forms also recorded which guards were responsible for each prisoner.[43] At these centers, the repressors applied mental and physical torture and deliberately attempted to strip the victims of their identity and their history, to break down their humanity, and to annihilate their sense of themselves as human beings. Prisoners were given a letter and assigned a number in sequence (e.g., M1, M2) and would be brutally punished if they used their names. This system fulfilled two purposes: it heightened their sense of alienation and loss of identity and it kept them from knowing the identity of the other prisoners.

By making every effort to lead the prisoners to feel that their disappearances had wiped them from the world of the living, the repressors left them without hope. A survivor of one of the camps testified:

> The normal attitude of the torturers and guards toward us was to consider us less than slaves. We were objects. And useless, troublesome objects at that. They would say: "You're dirt." "Since we 'disappeared' you, you're nothing. Anyway, nobody remembers you." "You don't exist." "If anyone were looking for you (which they aren't), do you imagine they'd look for you here?" "We are everything for you." "We are justice." "We are God."[44]

Other odious techniques aimed at bringing about the psychic collapse of the victim involved inducing the prisoners to collaborate with their repressors. Once in the camps, the "subversives" who cooperated were offered improved living conditions, the possibility of contacting their families, and, in some cases, the promise of eventual release. Turning a person into an informant was another way of destroying him or her. The repressors chose as targets mostly prisoners who had a certain level of responsibility in their political organizations—much as the Nazis did in their concentration camps.[45] In a few cases, prisoners were even allowed to leave the camps and visit their families. The guards made clear to them that any attempt to escape would cause the death of their family members and other prisoners. Some, after being released from the camps, were forced to engage in slave labor. However, collaboration did not necessarily guarantee their survival.

Physical and mental tortures were designed to humiliate and degrade the victims. Testimonies of survivors of the torture sessions provide detailed information on the methods used. Two prisoners who spent fifteen months in the camps and were able to escape described their experiences vividly:

As regards physical torture, we were all treated alike, the only differences being in intensity and duration. Naked, we were bound hand and foot with thick chains or straps to a metal table. Then an earthing cable was attached to one of our toes and the torture began.

For the first hour they would apply the *picana* (cattle prod) to us, without asking any questions. The purpose of this was, as they put it, "to soften you up, and so that we'll understand one another." They went on like this for hours. They applied it to the head, armpits, sexual organs, anus, groin, mouth, and all the sensitive parts of the body. From time to time they threw water over us or washed us, "to cool your body down so that you'll be sensitive again."

Between sessions of the *picana,* they would use the *submarino* (holding our heads under water), hang us up by our feet, hit us on the sexual organs, beat us with chains, put salt on our wounds, and use any other method that occurred to them. They would also apply 220-volt direct current to us, and we know that sometimes—as in the case of Irma Necich—they used what they called the *piripipi,* a type of noise torture.

There was no limit to the torture. It could last for one, two, five, or ten days. Everything was done under the supervision of a doctor, who checked our blood pressure and reflexes: "We're not going to let you die before time. We've got all the time in the world, and this will go on indefinitely." That is exactly how it was because, when we were on the verge of death, they would stop and let us be revived. The doctor injected serum and vitamins, and when we had more or less recovered they began to torture us again.

Many of the prisoners could not endure this terrible treatment and fell into a coma. When this happened, they either left them to die or else "took them off to the military hospital." We never heard of any of these prisoners again.[46]

Entire families, too, became targets of the repression. The gangs kidnapped whole families, including small children, youngsters, and adults, and often used relatives as hostages for people who were being sought. The relatives of "subversives" were punished because of their blood ties. Their torture was one way to force the prisoners "to talk."[47] Jacobo Timerman, who was kidnapped in April 1977 and held prisoner for thirty months, comments on the torture of families:

Of all the dramatic situations I witnessed in clandestine prisons, nothing can compare to those family groups who were tortured, often together, sometimes separately but in view of one another, or in different cells, while one was aware of the other being tortured. The entire affective world, constructed over the years with utmost difficulty, collapses with a kick in the father's genitals, a smack on the mother's face, an obscene insult to the sister, or the sexual violation of a daughter. Suddenly an entire culture based on familial love, devotion, the capacity for mutual sacrifice collapses. Nothing is possible in such a universe, and that is precisely what the torturers know.[48]

Defying the imagination in its horror were the systematic practices of torture of children in front of their parents. A prisoner at one of the camps reported that one torturer wanted to know: "how much should a child weigh before we can torture him? Vidal (the Doctor) responded 'after 25 kilos you can run electrical charges through their bodies.' "[49] Children were also often made to witness the torture sessions of their parents. Some could not stand the horrors they had to endure. Five-year-old Josefina Sánchez de Vargas was forced to watch the torture of her father so that he would talk. When she was returned to her grandparents' home, she took a gun from her grandfather's drawer and shot herself.[50]

"Transfer" was a euphemism for killing. The physical extermination of the prisoners took a variety of forms. Some prisoners died after their torture sessions or were shot; some committed suicide. Others were drugged, carried into airplanes, and thrown into the sea.[51] Bodies started to show up along the shore of the Río de la Plata. Unmarked NN (*Nacht und Nebel*) graves proliferated in cemeteries. When some of these mass graves were opened after the fall of the dictatorship, another obscene aspect of the torturers' madness was revealed: they contained only pieces of bodies, decapitated and dismembered before burial. They were fragmented, atomized, and spread throughout different parts of the cemetery to ensure not only the disappearance of a person but, after death, the disappearance of his or her corpse.[52]

As one witness recalls:

> On the day of the transfer the atmosphere was very tense. We didn't know whether it would be our turn that day or not. . . . [T]hey began calling prisoners by number. . . . They were taken to the first-aid room in the basement, where a nurse was waiting to give them an injection to send them to sleep, but not kill them. They were taken out by the side door of the basement like that, alive, and put in a lorry. They were driven to Buenos Aires Municipal Airport half-asleep, put into a plane which flew southward out to sea, and thrown in alive.[53]

The mass executions by firing squads also created a problem: bodies requiring disposal. Another witness recounts that the bodies would be put inside pits, sprinkled with gasoline, and burned to ashes.[54] For some prisoners the guards invented "reasons" for their murder, including "armed confrontations" and "escape attempts."[55]

The methodology of repression did not spare women. Women were kidnapped alone or with friends or family members, held prisoner and tortured in the secret detention centers, and eventually murdered. Some forms of torture, such as hanging naked while the guards' dogs were incited to attack, seems to have been used primarily against women.[56] Added to the already intolerable conditions facing all prisoners, women prisoners suffered an extra dimension of sexual violence and rape.[57] Their sexual integrity and physical and mental dignity were directly attacked. The repressors aimed the torture toward the most vulnerable and intimate parts of the female body, the sources of life itself: "With women, they would insert the wire in the vagina and then apply it to the breasts, which caused great pain. Many of them would menstruate in mid-torture."[58]

Martha García Candeloro recalls that after she was kidnapped, she was told: "Oh, so, you are a psychologist? A whore, like all shrinks. Here you'll learn what is good for you." And they started to torture her in front of her husband, so that he would talk. Brutalizing a child in front of his or her mother and torturing a man in front of his wife were favorite ways of trying to make the women talk.[59] Women prisoners were also used as sexual slaves. At the El Vesubio, one of the clandestine detention centers, the chief of the camp used the women—even those who were pregnant—for his sexual gratification. That did not stop him from eventually ordering them killed. On the weekends, when Major Pedro Durán Sáenz left the camp, this "family man" would go home to his wife and five children.[60]

A variety of forms of rape and the constant threat of its occurrence served to humiliate women and to shatter their dignity and sense of self-respect. Children and teenagers as well as adults were raped. Twelve-year-old Zulema Chester, who was tortured and raped in her home when her father was kidnapped, describes her ordeal:

> They stood me up and leaning against the wall they raped me, I do not know with what, because I was blindfolded and they told me I could go and look for my father in the ditch. After stealing everything they could, they went away.[61]

On September 16, 1976, the repressors kidnapped a group of teenagers from their homes in the city of La Plata, in a tragic episode that became known as the Night of the Pencils (both because the students were taken at night and perhaps because the name evoked the Night of the Long Knives under the Third Reich). The young people were high school student leaders who had been actively campaigning to have student transportation fares reduced. The authorities saw them as "subversives in the classroom." Among those kidnapped was sixteen-year-old María Claudia Falcone, who remains disappeared. Only three students were eventually set free; Pablo Alejandro Díaz was one of them. The night before his liberation he saw María Claudia briefly and he reported the following dialogue:

> María Claudia: Thank you for the strength that you give me, Pablo.
>
> Pablo: No, No. You will get out. . . . You will get out soon. When we are out we will see each other.
>
> María Claudia: I cannot give you anything, nothing. They raped me from behind, in front.[62]

PREGNANT WOMEN IN CAPTIVITY

The treatment and torture of pregnant women reveals an almost unimaginable level of hatred and cruelty. After the repression was over, a former official of one of the Task Forces, who had been in charge of the largest concentration camp in Buenos Aires, the Navy Mechanics School (ESMA), recalled that "One of the lovely systems Mengele [the nickname given to the camp doctor] invented to torture pregnant women was with a spoon. They put a spoon or a metallic instrument in the vagina until it touched the fetus. Then they give it 220. They shock the fetus."[63]

Often such torture of pregnant women resulted in miscarriages. Isabel Gamba de Negrotti, a twenty-seven-year-old nursery school teacher, was pregnant when she was abducted:

They took me to another room where they kicked me and punched me in the head. Then they undressed me and beat me on the legs, buttocks and shoulders with something made of rubber. This lasted a long time; I fell down several times and they made me get up and stand by supporting myself on a table. They carried on beating me. While all this was going on they talked to me, insulted me and asked me about people I didn't know and things I didn't understand. I pleaded with them to leave me alone, or else I would lose my baby. I hadn't the strength to speak, the pain was so bad.

They started to give me electric shocks on my breasts, the side of my body and under my arms. They kept questioning me. They gave me electric shocks in the vagina and put a pillow over my mouth to stop me screaming. Someone they called the "colonel" came and said they were going to increase the voltage until I talked. They kept throwing water over my body and applying electric shocks all over.[64]

Two days later she miscarried.

Mónica Brull de Guillén, a blind pregnant woman who was active in the Socioeconomic Union of Disabled People, was kidnapped off the street and taken to El Olimpo, a secret detention center:

Then, "Julián" said that he would take me to the "machine" and two thugs appeared who took me to a room and began to beat me as I refused to get undressed. One tore off my blouse and threw me on to a metal table where they tied my hands and feet. I told them that I was two months pregnant, and "Julián the Turk" replied, "If so-and-so can endure the machine being six months pregnant, you can stand it, and be raped too." Then the torturers became more and more incensed with me, for two reasons: because I belonged to a Jewish family, and because I did not cry, which exasperated them.[65]

She also miscarried after being released.

Ana María Careaga was sixteen years old when she was kidnapped in midday off the streets of Buenos Aires. She was two months pregnant and was one of the few women released who did not miscarry. Her story is particularly gripping because of her youth, because of the amount of torture she endured, and because of the fate of her mother, who had been actively searching for her:

Everything happened very quickly. Two men forced me into a car. I managed to scream; passersby were in shock. At first, I did not tell them that I was pregnant. Only afterward, when it started to show. Once they knew that I was pregnant they tortured me in all sorts of ways. We could not speak or move; we were blindfolded and grilled. They would not take us to the bathroom when we needed, and, if we urinated in the cell, they would torture us. Torture was permanent. They used the electric prod for many hours. They inserted it and threw kerosene and gas in my vagina, in my eyes, in my ears. They hung me down a trestle with my wrists tied to my ankles, head down, and rocked me. I still have the marks on my arm, because of the abscess that resulted from it.

They had a physician that would take my blood pressure and kept an eye on me. They would say, "We are not going to let you die." They knew that that was what one wanted, to die. During the torture sessions, they gave me pills for the heart. While I was tied to a metal table with my arms backward and my legs open.

In the camps, we were totally isolated in very small cells. It is terrible to be pregnant in a camp, but it also was a privilege. Because I was not alone, I learned to speak with the baby, I put my hands over her, I caressed her all the time. The moment that she moved for the first time was very important because somehow I felt that together we had triumphed over the horror. I was tied to the torture table and I started to cry from joy. What better company can one have than a life growing inside oneself? When I got out of the camp I wrote a poem to her saying: "My blood was your life. Your blood was my strength." She survived because my blood nurtured her and, in turn, she nurtured me in a different way.

After I was released I went to Europe. The Europeans could not understand why I had not immediately told to my kidnappers that I was pregnant. They thought it might have helped me. I had to explain to them that in the Argentine camps, they would have used that information to make things worse for me. The Swedish government offered asylum to my parents. My mother refused it. After I was released my mother decided to keep working with the mothers of other disappeared young people. She wanted to continue until "until everybody's children reappeared." My mother was kidnapped in December 1977, while I was in Sweden. When I called to tell her of the birth of my child, I learned the bad news. She never knew that I had delivered safely.[66]

Most of the time pregnant women were not "transferred." Those who did not miscarry under torture gave birth in captivity and were killed afterward.[67] At least three clandestine centers—the ESMA, Campo de Mayo, and Pozo de Bánfield—are known to have had "facilities" for pregnant women. In some cases, physicians and nurses attended to them. The doctors often performed cesarean sections to speed up the births, violating the most basic principles of the Hippocratic oath. In the throes of labor, pregnant women were held down, tied to the beds by their hands and feet, and given a serum to accelerate the birth.[68]

Two survivors from the ESMA described how the pregnant women were misled into thinking that their children would be given to their families:

On our arrival at the Navy Mechanics School we saw many women laid out on the floor on cushions awaiting the birth of their children.... Once the child was born the mother was "invited" to write a letter to her relatives where the child was allegedly going to be taken. The then director of the School, navy Captain Rubén Jacinto Chamorro, personally accompanied visitors, generally senior navy officers, to the place where the pregnant women were being held, boasting that conditions established in the prison were as good as those in the Sarda (the best-known maternity hospital in Buenos Aires). [F]rom the comments made we learnt that in the Navy Hospital there was a list of married couples in the navy who could not have children of their own, and who were prepared to adopt one of the children of people who had disappeared. The man who drew up the list was a gynecologist attached to the Navy Mechanics School.[69]

Medical personnel at the Campo de Mayo Military Hospital later revealed that there were prisoners whose admission to the hospital had not been officially registered; that the prisoners were women in an advanced state of pregnancy who were kept blindfolded or with their eyes covered with black sunglasses; that they were heavily guarded; that, in most cases, they were subjected to cesarean sections; and that after the operation the mothers were separated from their babies. The destiny of the children was unknown.[70] At least one military physician—Dr. Norberto Atilio Bianco, who worked in that hospital—is known to have kept two of the children born from women prisoners and registered them as his own. After many years as a fugitive living in Paraguay he was finally extradited to Argentina in early 1997.[71]

Sometimes pregnant women were taken to regular, civilian hospitals where, heavily guarded by the police, they were not allowed to communicate with the hospital staff. The names of the women would be listed in the birth registry simply as NN. Silvia Isabella Valenzi, seven and a half months pregnant, was taken to a municipal hospital. She managed to cry out her name and that of her relatives, hoping that somebody would alert them to her plight. But the military was not taking any chances: a midwife and a nurse who informed the family of the plight of the young woman were both kidnapped and disappeared shortly afterward. They were reportedly last seen at one of the secret detention centers. The secret of the fate of the pregnant women and their children had to be kept at all costs.[72]

Adriana Calvo de Laborde was one of the few exceptions, a pregnant woman who gave birth in captivity and survived. She was kidnapped when she was six and half months pregnant:

On April 15 I began to go into labor. After three or four hours of being on the floor with contractions that were coming faster and faster, and thanks to the shouts of the other women, I was taken away in an army patrol car with two men in front and one woman behind (the woman was called "Lucrecia" and she used to take part in the torture sessions).

We drove in the direction of Buenos Aires, but my child wouldn't wait and at the crossroads of Alpargatas, opposite the Abbott Laboratory, the woman shrieked that they should stop the car on the verge and there Teresa was born. Thanks to the forces of nature, the birth was normal. The only assistance I received was when "Lucrecia" tied the umbilical cord, which was still linking me with the child as there was nothing to cut it with. No more than five minutes later we drove on, supposedly in the direction of the hospital. I was blindfolded and my child was on the seat. After many twists and turns we arrived at what I later learnt was the building of the Detective Squad of Bánfield (the Pozo de Bánfield). There I saw the same doctor that assisted Inés Ortega de Fossatti. He cut the umbilical cord in the car and took me up two or three floors to a place where they removed the placenta. He made me undress in front of an officer on duty. I had to wash the bed, the floor and my dress, and clear away the placenta. Then, finally, they left me to wash my baby, while they continued their insults and threats.

Her torturers dropped her, ten days after giving birth, near her parents' home in the middle of the night. In a nightgown and slippers, with both herself and her baby covered with fleas, Laborde was a "lucky" woman, one who survived and kept her child.[73]

Far more common is the case of Graciela Alicia Romero de Metz, described by Alicia Partnoy in *The Little School.* Graciela, age twenty-four, was kidnapped when she was five months pregnant and forced to remain

prone, blindfolded and handcuffed like the rest. In the last month of her pregnancy, she was permitted "exercise"—blindfolded walks around a table, holding on to the edge. A few days before giving birth they took her to a trailer on the patio. On April 17 she had a son—normally, but without medical assistance. I persistently asked the guards to let me help her or keep her company, but they didn't allow me. She was helped by the guards. On April 23 she was removed from the Little School and I never heard of her again. She is on Amnesty International's list of disappeared people. Her son, according to the guards, was given to one of the interrogators.[74]

THE CATHOLIC CHURCH: CHURCH OF CAESAR OR CHURCH OF THE PEOPLE?

In a country like Argentina that is 90 percent Catholic, the church has enormous power to influence politics and all aspects of life. Moreover, since the military regime presented itself as a defender of Christian values, criticisms from religious leaders would have created serious problems for the junta. Regrettably, the Catholic hierarchy became an accomplice to the junta.

The night before the March 26 coup, two of the commanders in chief, General Videla and Admiral Massera, met with the leadership of the Argentine Episcopal Conference (CEA), the main body of the

Argentine Catholic Church. The day of the coup, the junta had a long meeting with Archbishop Adolfo Servando Tortolo, president of the CEA and head of the military vicariate who, as he left the meeting, encouraged the population to "cooperate in a positive way" with the new government. Out of the more than eighty priests who belonged to the CEA, only four stood up and supported the human rights organizations: The Executive Commission of the CEA characterized them as "communist and subversive."[75]

The declarations and comments of some members of the church hierarchy regarding the government bordered on the surreal. After the coup Bishop Victorio Bonamín, provicar for the army, asserted "that when a military man is carrying out his repressive duty, 'Christ has entered with truth and goodness,'" and he foresaw a time when "The members of the military junta will be glorified by generations to come." Father Felipe Perlanda López, chaplain of the prison system, told one prisoner who complained about the tortures he had endured: "Son, what do you expect, if you are not willing to cooperate with the authorities who are interrogating you?" During a trip to Italy in 1982, one of the leading members of the CEA, Cardinal Juan Carlos Aramburu, archbishop of Buenos Aires, responded to a question about the disappearances by saying, "I don't understand how this question of guerrillas and terrorism has come up again; it's been over for a long time."[76] Furthermore, in line with the views of the CEA, Argentine Cardinal Eduardo Pironio, who held a very influential post in the Roman curia, never had the time to meet with representatives of the human rights organizations during his frequent visits to the country, although he did meet with Videla and other members of the junta. Similarly, when John Paul II came to Argentina in 1982, human rights organizations were unable to meet with him.[77]

Two of the strongest supporters of the regime were Monsignor Antonio José Plaza, the powerful archbishop of La Plata, and Father Christian von Wernich. Monsignor Plaza identified with the dictatorship at every possible occasion, brought accusations against students (including his own nephew), and accepted the post of chief chaplain of police in the province of Buenos Aires. While receiving as police chaplain a second salary and a second automobile, he visited the secret detention centers where prisoners were tortured and murdered. Father von Wernich, who was well known for his cooperation with the repression, was "something of a paradigm of a fascist priest." He was chaplain to the police in the province of Buenos Aires and a personal friend of General

Camps. Testimonies from camp survivors and from a former police agent in the province of Buenos Aires described von Wernich's involvement in several kidnappings and in torture sessions.[78]

A controversial figure within the church hierarchy was Archbishop Pio Laghi, Argentina's papal nuncio. In 1976 Pio Laghi received an invitation from the governor of Tucumán, General Antonio Domingo Bussi, whose repressive activities were notorious; he visited the province's zone of operations and gave the papal blessing to the troops. He saw the church as being part of the "process of national reorganization," cooperating with the armed forces "not only with words but with actions." When his name appeared on a 1984 list of 1,351 persons involved in repressive activities, a heated debate ensued.[79] Although a camp survivor claimed that he had met the archbishop on a helicopter pad when he was illegally imprisoned by the army, his testimony could not be confirmed. Prominent members of the new democratic government from President Alfonsín to Interior Minister Antonio Tróccoli, progressive members of the church, and well-known intellectuals defended the archbishop.[80]

While the church hierarchy justified and spoke approvingly of the junta's actions, the junta persecuted those members of the church who identified with the progressive ideas of Vatican II and the 1968 Medellín conference—those who envisioned the church as a community of equals. Priests, nuns, and seminary students cast their lot with the oppressed: working in the slums, creating peasant organizations and agricultural cooperatives, holding literacy classes, and challenging the traditional alliance between the Argentine oligarchy and the church. They brought hope and a sense of empowerment to the poorest of the poor. Consequently, the junta treated them as subversives. While imprisoned at the ESMA, one of them was told by the officer interrogating him: "You aren't a guerrilla, you're not involved in violence, but you don't realize that when you go to live there [a shantytown] you are bringing people together, you are uniting the poor, and uniting the poor is subversion."[81]

Many of these clergy paid with their lives for their commitment to social justice. Between 1974 and 1983, nineteen ordained Catholic priests (including two bishops) were murdered or disappeared, and about one hundred members of religious orders suffered torture, went into exile, or were detained. The most prominent was Enrique Angel Angelelli, bishop of La Rioja, a northern province where racism and economic exploitation, with the church's blessing, kept the indigenous population practically enslaved. Angelelli allied himself uncompromisingly with the poor, challenging the wealthy landowners and the local government. A charismatic and inspirational figure, he was killed in August 1976 in a "car accident." In 1986, as the investigation of the case finally moved ahead, the appointed judge formally declared that his death "was not due to a traffic accident, but rather to a coldly premeditated homicide, which the victim was expecting": the label of the file was changed from "accident" to "undeniable murder."[82]

JEWS AND STATE TERRORISM

In Argentina, anti-Semitism runs deep in the fabric of national consciousness. From the colonial times, when *Conversos* and Jews were a favorite target of the Inquisition, to the 1919 pogrom of the *Semana Trágica* (Tragic Week), Jews have been seen by the dominant culture as "unassimilable aliens," as foreigners whose loyalty to society was always questioned.[83] The extreme right in Argentina is notoriously anti-Semitic and has consistently fostered the image of a "hebraic and communistic infiltration" of the country.[84] Xenophobia, racism, and rabid attacks from members of the Catholic Church have helped keep this image alive.

At the beginning of World War II, the Argentine Nazi Party had 60,000 members. Only in 1944, and at the last moment, did Argentina reluctantly declare war against Germany. Argentina soon became a well-known haven for Nazi criminals, who fitted easily into the large and prosperous German community. Joseph Mengele, Adolf Eichmann, and many others found refuge in Argentina.[85]

During the Onganía regime the Jewish community had been assailed mainly by a notorious anti-Semite, Enrique Horacio Green, chief of police and brother-in-law of the president.[86] Under the Peróns' presidencies and the junta, the anti-Jewish campaign continued to grow unopposed. Attacks on the predominantly Jewish quarter in Buenos Aires and bombs in synagogues, cultural centers, schools, and banks became commonplace. In June 1976 the body of a physician, Dr. Salvador Ackerman, was found gunned down on the street, as vengeance for his alleged role in the kidnapping of Adolf Eichmann.[87] Thoughout this time anti-Semitic literature circulated freely, appearing in virtually all newsstands and bookstores. One publisher, Editorial Milicia, proudly announced that it had produced ten Nazi books, all of which were selling in "impressive numbers."[88] In 1977, after twenty-nine years in Argentina, the American Jewish Committee was forced to close its doors because of repeated threats and acts of intimidation. Its representative returned to the United States, stating: "It is apparent to us that the Argentine government has not cleansed itself of subversive and anti-democratic forces within its own structure."[89]

Having a religious and cultural background different from the majority of the population put the Jews in a "high risk" category; they became likely scapegoats. The accusations against the Jews were varied and contradictory: they were part of a Jewish-Bolshevik conspiracy, or capitalists exploiting the workers, or members of an international Zionist plot. The common thread running through these scenarios was a view of Jews as outsiders, a menace to the economic, social, and political life of the country.

Under the junta's rule anti-Semitism reached new heights. When Jews were kidnapped they were often interrogated about the "Andinia Plan," which supposedly was guiding an attempt by Jews to take over a part of Patagonia in order to colonize it with Jewish immigrants.[90] Jewish prisoners received special treatments: the guards painted swastikas on their bodies, made them raise their hands and shout "I love Hitler!" and threatened that they would "become soap." One form of torture was particularly aimed toward Jews: the "rectoscope," which consisted of a tube with a rat inside it inserted into the anus of the victim or the vagina of the women. As the animal looked for an exit, it would try to get away by gnawing the victims' internal organs.[91] The camps' atmosphere is vividly conveyed by a survivor who describes the case of a Jewish man nicknamed "Chango," whom the guard would take out of his cell and force into the yard:

> He would make him wag his tail, bark like a dog, lick his boots. It was impressive how well he did it, he imitated a dog as if he really were one, because if he didn't satisfy the guard, he would carry on beating him. . . . Later he would change and make him be a cat.[92]

In 1985 Jewish survivors of the camps described their experiences to the National Commission on the Disappeared (CONADEP). Nora Strejilevich was kidnapped as she finished packing for a trip to Israel:

> They threatened me for having uttered Jewish words in the street (my surname) and for being a bloody Yid, whom they would make soap out of. . . .

They took me straight away to the torture room where I was subjected to the electric prod. . . .

They kept asking me for the names of the people traveling with me to Israel . . . they centered the interrogation around Jewish matters. One of them could speak Hebrew. . . . He tried to find out if there was any military training in the kibbutzim. They asked for a physical description of the organizers of the study tours, like the one I was on (Sherut Laam), a description of the building of the Jewish Agency (which I knew very well), etc.[93]

Another Jewish survivor, Miriam Lewin de García, remembers:

The general attitude was of deep-rooted anti-Semitism. On one occasion they asked me if I understood Yiddish. I replied that I did not, that I only knew a few words. They nevertheless made me listen to a cassette they had obtained by tapping telephones. The speakers were apparently Argentine businessmen of Jewish origin, talking in Yiddish. My captors were most interested in finding out what the conversation was about. . . . The only good Jew is a dead Jew, the guards would say.[94]

Though it is difficult to obtain reliable quantitative data, there is general agreement that the percentage of Jews who disappeared during the repression—5 to 10 percent—far exceeds their representation in the general population—about 1 percent. The Israel-based Committee of Relatives of the Victims of the Repression estimates the number of disappeared Jews at 1,500.[95]

Argentine writer and philosopher Marcos Aguinis states: "When the security forces arrest a Jew, be he innocent or guilty, they make him suffer more insult and torture not only because anti-Semitism excites them, but because this anti-Semitism has the noble justification to be at the service of the Western and Christian victory."[96] In the mind of the regime, Jews were "outsiders," foreigners, who would not fully identify with Argentine society: as such, they were seen as suspects, dangerously close to the "subversives" whom the junta also considered non-Argentine and whom it was determined to annihilate.

TWO

THE FALL OF THE REGIME

Your Honours, I shall renounce any pretensions to originality, by using an expression which is not mine, but which belongs to the Argentine people. Your Honours: Never Again.
Julio Strassera, prosecutor in the trial of the juntas (1985)

During the 1976–83 dictatorship, Argentine society was largely paralyzed by fear. The leaders of the political parties and the civic, cultural, labor, and religious organizations kept silent, in spite of the massive human rights violations directed against many of their members. But at the grassroots level, there were attempts at resistance. Trade union workers in particular opposed the systematic dismantling of the rights they had gained through long years of struggle.

The repression of workers was crucial to enforcing the economic policies of the juntas. As real wages for workers dropped by 50 percent, weakening the power of unions was a government priority. The Statute for the Process of National Reorganization suspended all union activities. It prohibited strikes, annulled collective bargaining, authorized the firing of workers without giving a reason, and revoked occupational health legislation. Production in factories was placed under the control of the military.[1]

Six months after the coup, workers in several automotive factories went on strike, protesting the reduction of the workweek and the freezing of salaries. Electrical workers from the powerful union Luz y Fuerza (Light and Power), who were leading proponents of workers' self-management practices and of the nationalization of power companies, challenged the massive firings and the plans of the military to privatize the industry. The supply of electricity to the capital fell sharply. One of the disappeared, held at the Navy Mechanics School, recalls the torture sessions being interrupted because there was no power for the electric prod.[2] Around the same time, longshoremen in Buenos Aires and

Rosario paralyzed both ports to protest new work regulations. Telephone workers organized slowdowns and acts of sabotage, resulting in 75,000 phone lines going dead. Railroad workers mobilized to oppose the announced firing of 15,000 workers and the elimination of thousands of kilometers of railway lines, both actions demanded by the World Bank as a condition for its financial "help" to Argentina.[3]

Defiant workers took their protest to the international workers' organizations. In Geneva, the governing body of the International Labor Organization (ILO), which oversees the right to form independent unions, took up the case of Argentina. Moreover, six months after the coup it published a list of disappeared trade unionists and accused the junta of violating the right to freedom of association. In May 1978 it asked the junta to explain the large number of disappeared and detained trade unionists.[4]

Most important to ensuring the reign of terror was control of the media; the population had to be kept ignorant of the real course of events, so that no public protests could develop. Even before the coup, the mainstream press had been brought into line: newspapers and magazines presented only a positive image of the junta and exaggerated the guerrilla threat. But Videla and his allies were not taking any chances. As soon as they took power, they announced prison terms of up to ten years for anyone who used the press to "publish, divulge or propagate news, communiqués or images with the purpose of perturbing, damaging, or impairing the reputation of the activities of the armed forces, security forces or the police." The retaliation against journalists who dared express views opposing the government was ferocious. Foreign journalists critical of the official version of events were threatened and forced to leave the country.[5]

Only the *Buenos Aires Herald,* a daily English-language newspaper, and occasionally *La Opinión* mentioned the petitions for habeas corpus and other appeals made by relatives of the disappeared. In the midst of this depressing situation, Rodolfo Walsh, a highly respected investigative journalist, started an underground communications network to inform people of the daily abuses taking place. A member of the Montoneros, Walsh used his journalistic skills to organize the Agencia de Noticias Clandestinas (ANCLA) and to disseminate its reports to local and international newspapers and other media outlets. In October 1976 he wrote and distributed a document providing detailed information about the Navy Mechanics School (ESMA) and analyzing the events leading to the coup and the repressive actions of the junta.[6]

Walsh also started an underground newsletter, *Cadena Informativa* (Information Network). Its first issue ended with a strong call to action:

> *CADENA INFORMATIVA (CI)* is one of the instruments that the Argentine people are creating to break the blockage of information. *CI* can be yourself, an instrument to liberate yourself from the terror and to liberate others. You can reproduce this information with the resources within your reach: by hand, by typewriter, with a mimeo machine. Send copies to your friends: nine out of ten will be waiting for them. Millions are waiting to be informed. Terror is based in the lack of communication. Break the isolation. Feel again the moral satisfaction of an act of freedom. DEFEAT TERROR. CIRCULATE THIS INFORMATION.[7]

One year after the coup and one day after he sent an open letter to the junta denouncing its multiple abuses, a Task Force of the ESMA machine-gunned Walsh down in the streets of Buenos Aires. He was taken to the ESMA where a prisoner saw his corpse, riddled with bullets.[8]

The relatives of the disappeared became the regime's most outspoken and visible critics. In their endless searches for their loved ones—visiting police stations, hospitals, ministries, military barracks, morgues, and churches—they started to recognize each other. The same faces appeared in the endless lines in the Ministry of the Interior where, incredibly, the government had opened an office to register the denunciations of the disappearances. On the few occasions when authorities received them, the relatives were dismissed peremptorily or reprimanded for raising "subversives." One of the few places where the relatives received a measure of support was the Liga Argentina por los Derechos del Hombre (Argentine League for the Rights of Man). Founded in 1937, the Liga was the oldest human rights organization in Argentina and was traditionally linked to the Communist Party; it familiarized the relatives with the habeas corpus process and suggested sources for information and help.

By August 1977 the relatives had their own organization, the Comisión de Familiares de Desaparecidos y Detenidos por Motivos Políticos (Commission of Relatives of Disappeared and Detained for Political Reasons). By October the group had drafted a petition listing the names of hundreds of disappeared and detained individuals; it organized its first demonstration, where hundreds of people were beaten and arrested.[9]

THE MOTHERS OF THE PLAZA DE MAYO

Among the relatives of the disappeared a group of mothers emerged, galvanized by a woman in her fifties, Azucena Villaflor de DeVincenti, whose son and daughter-in-law had been abducted.[10] Azucena had worked in a factory as a young woman, but after her marriage she devoted herself completely to her family. Her energy and charisma became sources of inspiration for the other mothers. They started meeting in her home to draft petitions, gather information, and plant the seeds of their future organization. It was Azucena's idea to go to the Plaza de Mayo and to ask for an audience with President Videla to find answers to their questions about the disappearances.

On April 30, 1977, fourteen mothers gathered at the Plaza de Mayo, traditionally the heart of Argentine civic life.[11] By meeting there, the Mothers placed themselves in the public eye in a desperate attempt to bring attention to their families' plight. Labeled *Las Locas de Plaza de Mayo* (the crazies of the Plaza de Mayo), they broke the conspiracy of silence that had permeated the country and found a way to channel their despair and frustration into action. After that day, they and Argentina would never be the same.[12]

The Mothers' marches became a weekly event, taking place every Thursday at 3:30 P.M. Forced to walk because of the regime's orders prohibiting public gatherings, they would walk slowly for half an hour. When the police tried to intimidate them and make them leave, they resisted and affirmed their right to demonstrate on behalf of their disappeared children. Slowly their numbers started to grow, and they began wearing white handkerchiefs and carrying pictures of their missing children. The women asked their husbands not to join them in their weekly gatherings, afraid that the presence of the men would make the situation worse. María Adela Antokoletz remembers: "We endured pushing, insults, attacks by the army, our clothes were ripped, detentions. . . . But the men, they would not have been able to stand such things without reacting, there would have been incidents; they would have been arrested for disrupting the public order and, most likely, we would not have seen them ever again."[13] The minister of the interior, General Albano Harguindeguy, finally agreed to meet with three of the mothers. He tried to convince them that their children had left the country of their own free will, and warned them to stop their demonstrations. It was the first time that a high-ranking official had received the relatives. But the Mothers responded that they would continue their marches until they knew with certainty of their children's fate.[14]

Placing advertisements in newspapers to publicize the names of the disappeared was one of the Mothers' main outreach activities. The newspapers requested hefty fees for these ads and demanded the certified addresses of ten of the signers, addresses that they subsequently gave to the police.[15] On December 8, 1977, at a meeting held in the Church of Santa Cruz to raise money for an ad, an ESMA Task Force broke in and kidnapped nine people. Among them was Sister Alice Domon, a French nun who had worked with peasants in some of the poorest regions of Argentina and who was a supporter of the Mothers. In Buenos Aires, Sister Domon had taught catechism to children with Down's syndrome, the son of General Videla among them.[16] Another supporter of the group was kidnapped from his home. And two days later—on December 10, Human Rights Day—Azucena Villaflor de DeVincenti and Léonie Duquet (another French nun) were abducted and joined the ranks of the disappeared. Survivors from the ESMA testified to having seen these twelve people at the camp, where they were brutally tortured.[17]

The kidnapping of the two French nuns would eventually become a rallying point of international protest, which continues to this day. The government, which tried to blame the Montoneros for the kidnapping, showed pictures of the nuns under a fake Montonero sign. Sister Domon was forced to write a letter stating that she was in the "hands of an armed group" opposed to the government.[18] In fact, Lieutenant Alfredo Astiz, a twenty-six-year-old sailor, had infiltrated the Mothers group, claiming to be the brother of a disappeared. Blue-eyed, young, and innocent looking, he had gained the trust of Azucena and Sister Domon. Showing up at the gathering at the Santa Cruz church, Astiz alerted the ESMA Task Force as the meeting was drawing to an end. Azucena's disappearance failed to deter the group. "It was a hard time for us, but we weren't broken. They thought there was only one Azucena, but there wasn't just one. There were hundreds of us," said Aída de Suárez, one of the Mothers. Azucena herself, in a premonitory mood a few days before her abduction, had said: "If something happens to me, you continue. Do not forget it."[19]

Thanks to their determination, courage, and intelligence, the Mothers began to attract international recognition and to receive support from governments and organizations concerned about human rights. Foreign journalists often covered their weekly marches; and on the occasion of the World Cup soccer championship in Buenos Aires in 1978, they focused on the Mothers, providing them with instant international exposure. The Mothers became the moral conscience of the country and gained a space in the political arena, challenging the notion of women as powerless and subservient to family and state.

Among the Mothers' weekly gatherings at the Plaza de Mayo were also women whose grandchildren were missing. In October 1977 twelve Mothers established the Association of the Grandmothers of the Plaza de Mayo and organized around one specific demand: that the children who had been kidnapped as a method of political repression be returned to their legitimate families. The Association grew quickly as dozens of grandmothers joined the group.[20]

During the dictatorship, nine human rights organizations were active throughout Argentina. Some of the groups—such as the Mothers of the Plaza de Mayo, the Grandmothers of the Plaza de Mayo, and the Relatives of the Detained and Disappeared for Political Reasons—were started by relatives of the disappeared who were pressing the government for information about their family members. Others—like the League for the Rights of Man, the Permanent Assembly for Human Rights (APDH), and the Center for Legal and Social Studies (CELS)—collected and reported evidence of human rights violations and did a considerable amount of legal work. Religious human rights groups also arose, such as the Peace and Justice Service (SERPAJ), the Ecumenical Movement for Human Rights (MEDH), and the Jewish Movement for Human Rights (Movimiento Judío por los Derechos Humanos). These last groups, respectively, incorporated members of the Catholic clergy who were critical of the church hierarchy, Protestant ministers, and Jews. All of the organizations were committed to a broad vision of social justice, and each responded to different pressures and particular histories of the community from which it emerged. They often helped each other and formed various alliances in response to the regime's multiple abuses.[21]

INTERNATIONAL SUPPORT FOR HUMAN RIGHTS ACTIVISTS

As news of the disappearances continued to spread abroad, foreign governments and international organizations began paying closer attention to the situation in Argentina. In 1978 the Organization of American States (OAS), through its Inter American Commission on Human Rights (IACHR), asked to visit Argentina to investigate the reports of the disappearances flooding their Washington office. The Argentine government turned down the request. U.S. Vice President Walter Mondale, at a meeting in Rome for the papal coronation of John Paul II, pressured General Videla to accept the IACHR fact-finding mission. As a trade-off, Mondale offered to approve loans that the United States had been blocking because of the human rights violations in Argentina. Videla accepted the deal, tolerating the visit in exchange for the loans.[22]

In September 1979 the IACHR went to Argentina. People stood in a line five blocks long to present their testimonies.[23] The IACHR interviewed government officials; church leaders; representatives of human rights organizations, political parties, professional associations, labor unions, industry and commerce, university associations, and the Jewish community; and individuals prominent in various fields. The commission received a total of 5,580 denunciations.[24]

During the IACHR visit, the junta tried to "sanitize" its image. Prisoners at the ESMA were hidden in other centers or killed. The generals launched a campaign with the slogan *Los argentinos somos derechos y humanos* (We Argentines are upright and humane), as the ubiquitous motto appeared in shops, on bumper stickers, and on billboards. In spite of these efforts, the commission produced a devastating book-length document confirming the reported human rights violations and asserting unambiguously that the rights to life, liberty, security, personal integrity, justice, due process, and freedom of expression had been violated. It further stated that the "security" forces had killed thousands of people, noted the high number of NN graves in Argentine cemeteries, and urged the investigation, trial, and punishment of those responsible.[25]

However, the IACHR had to submit its final draft to the Argentine government for its consideration. As a result, the published version did not contain important information, including some testimonies of the victims and the list of names of the security agents involved in the repression.[26] In spite of these changes the junta banned the report from Argentina. Emilio Mignone, who was in the United States when it was released, managed to bring five hundred copies into the country.[27] The OAS report, which was a severe blow to the credibility of the junta, helped boost the morale of the families of the disappeared.

The United Nations also received thousands of complaints from the victims' relatives. When Theo van Boven, director of the UN Center for Human Rights, repeatedly inquired about the fate of the disappeared, the Argentine government simply ignored his requests.[28] Foreign governments, too, began to ask about what happened to their citizens who had disappeared in Argentina. France wanted to know the fate of Alice Domon and Léonie Duquet, the two French nuns abducted in December 1977. In a 1978 meeting between Admiral Massera and French President Valéry Giscard d'Estaing, Massera admitted that the two nuns were dead but claimed that they had been killed by the First Army Corps.[29] The Swedish government kept inquiring about Dagmar Hagelin, a seventeen-year-old Argentine-Swedish woman who had been kidnapped and shot by Alfredo Astiz and his henchmen in what looked like a case of mistaken identity.[30]

In 1977 Patricia Derian, President Carter's assistant secretary of state for human rights, made several official visits to Argentina to inquire about the disappeared. Argentines living in exile, some of whom were survivors from the camps, provided the international organizations and foreign governments with firsthand information about the regime's atrocities. A 1979 *New York Times Magazine* article coauthored by an Argentine scientist living in the United States and a U.S. journalist first broke the silence about Argentina in the international press. Then, in Paris in October of that same year, three women who had been in the ESMA for two years held a press conference in the building of the French senate detailing the tortures they had suffered and the brutal acts they had witnessed.[31] The Amnesty International report on secret detention camps in 1980 alerted the human rights community to the existence of the concentration camps. As the international pressure continued to mount, and realizing how badly Argentina's international reputation had been damaged, the junta hired a Madison Avenue public relations firm, Burston Marsteller, to clean up its image.[32]

Foreign support for the human rights organizations kept growing. In 1980, socialist members of the European Parliament nominated the Mothers of the Plaza de Mayo for the Nobel Peace Prize. The prize was eventually awarded to Adolfo Pérez Esquivel, an architect who was the Latin American coordinator of the SERPAJ, one of the human rights organizations active in Argentina. This was another blow to the international image of the junta. Pérez Esquivel had been imprisoned for fourteen months, and for eighteen months after his release he was under police surveillance. When the junta accused him of being involved in terrorist activities, such as the kidnappings and murders of business leaders and the military, there was an international outcry. Norwegian Chancellor Knut Frydenlund proclaimed the award "an inspiration to all those that fight to protect human rights"; the vice president of the Norwegian Labor Party, Gro Harlem Brundtland, stated that Pérez Esquivel occupied a key role in the contemporary nonviolent movement; and Patricia Derian characterized the award as a "warning to all the nations that still practice repression."[33] Pérez Esquivel, a friend of the Mothers, announced that he would donate 10 percent of his $212,000 Nobel Prize money to them, highlighting both the importance of the Mothers' work and the respect with which they were regarded by other prominent human rights activists.[34]

THE REGIME STARTS TO CRUMBLE

In the fall of 1979, in an attempt to erase the results of its terrorist activities, the junta passed Law No. 22.068, the law of "presumption of death." Its intent was to redefine the disappeared as officially dead despite the absence of any explanation about the circumstances surrounding their demise. Another law providing economic reparations to the families of the "dead" was also passed. These laws were designed to end discussion on the issue of the disappearances and to silence the victims' relatives, but the families of the disappeared and human rights groups swiftly rejected them.[35]

It became increasingly difficult for the regime to ignore the demands of the human rights organizations and the pressures from abroad. A sign of the changing times was an ad that appeared in *Clarín,* one of the main Buenos Aires daily newspapers, in August 1980. Demanding information on the disappeared, it was signed by 175 prominent personalities; they included Jorge Luis Borges, who had previously expressed support for the coup, and César Luis Menotti, head coach of the national soccer team and a hero in the eyes of millions of Argentines. Just a few months before, this action would have been unthinkable.[36]

But it was the economic crisis and the defeat in the Malvinas/Falklands war that finally spelled doom for the junta regime. Government spending, particularly for the military, had caused foreign debt to balloon from $19 billion at the beginning of 1980 to $39 billion in 1982. Unemployment was rampant and real wages fell dramatically.[37] State companies borrowed money from foreign banks, and speculation on international markets caused huge sums of money to leave the country. The military itself, through Fabricaciones Militares, was the nation's largest single employer, producing $2.2 billion in goods (about 2.5 percent of the gross national product). It directly and fully participated in the financial manipulations that were ruining the country.[38]

Old divisions and rivalries between the various branches of the military intensified. In 1979 General Luciano Benjamín Menéndez, commander of the powerful Third Army Corps, had staged a revolt in Córdoba to protest the government's decision to free Jacobo Timerman, as ordered by the Supreme Court.[39] Although the revolt was squelched, it was a sign that factions within the military were once again fighting for control. A rift had developed between Admiral Massera and General Videla, and the government was losing its grip on the country. As Massera secretly plotted to launch his own political party and become a "second Perón," he developed a plan by which Montoneros detained in the ESMA worked on his behalf, while he established contacts with guerrilla leaders in exile.[40] The second junta that came to power in March 1981 lasted only eight months; its president, General Roberto Viola, was continually undermined by General Leopoldo Galtieri, who became the next president.

In July 1981, five political parties (Peronists, Radicals, Intransigents, Christian Democrats, and members of the Movement for Integration and Development) joined forces and created the *Multipartidaria* to negotiate the return to civilian power. The group met with a delegation from the Mothers and other human rights organizations and listened sympathetically to their demands that the issue of the disappeared not be overlooked in the transition to democracy.[41]

On March 30, 1982, the CGT Brazil (one of the two factions of the General Confederation of Labor, the country's umbrella labor association), headed by Saúl Ubaldini, organized a strike and a demonstration attended by thousands of people. For several hours, the demonstrators battled the police to protest the harsh economic situation and to demand that the authorities reveal the fate of the disappeared.[42] Earlier, the CGT had been conspicuously silent, even though workers had been one of the prime targets of the repression. Only a year before, Ubaldini had refused to sign a document that the Mothers were circulating. Nora de Cortiñas recalls:

In 1981, I went to ask Saúl Ubaldini to sign a petition. They were all together, the leadership of the CGT Brazil, and he told me: "Yes, I understand, but I cannot sign in behalf of the CGT." So I asked him: "Mr. Ubaldini, why don't you sign as an individual?" And he said, no, I can't do that. Then I asked all the other union leaders to sign the petition, but nobody did.[43]

The final blow to the regime was the Malvinas/Falkland Islands war fiasco. For over 150 years the British had ruled over the islands, while Argentine children at school drew maps with the islands as part of the national territory and learned that *Las Malvinas son Argentinas*.[44] On April 2, 1982, in a move designed to gain popular support and distract attention from the economic crisis, Argentina invaded the islands. In thinking that the British would not bother to send troops from across the world and that his cozy relationship with the Reagan administration would guarantee U.S. support, General Galtieri had gravely miscalculated. Although Galtieri had been instrumental in arranging for the Argentine military to train the Nicaraguan contras in Honduras, President Reagan stood by his friend Margaret Thatcher, imposed economic sanctions against Argentina, and provided the British with the technology necessary to detect the movement of Argentine troops on the islands and ensure Thatcher's victory.[45]

On June 14, two and a half months after the invasion—the first "real" war that the Argentine military had fought in a century—Argentina surrendered. One thousand Argentine and 250 British lives were lost in this last adventure of the generals. Shortly afterward, General Galtieri resigned, a fourth junta took over, and General Reynaldo Benito Bignone became provisional president. The pressures for the return to a civilian government started to bear fruit. In July the ban on political activity was lifted and parties were allowed to hold public gatherings. In October 1982 the human rights organizations organized a national march with strong participation from political, labor, and religious leaders. In spite of the government's prohibition, "The March for Life" attracted more than 10,000 people; the government soon announced that elections would take place in October 1983.[46]

In April 1983 the military, realizing that the end was in sight, released the "Final Document of the Military Junta on the War against Subversion and Terrorism," defending its genocidal acts and distorting the history of the previous seven years. The document caused national and international outrage. Italian President Sandro Pertini, a longtime friend of the Mothers, sent a telegram to the government condemning the report's "chilling cynicism . . . beyond human civility." Pope John Paul II criticized the document, expressing solidarity with the families of the disappeared. Practically the only group that defended it was the executive committee of the CEA—the Bishop's Conference—which praised it as a step toward "reconciliation." In June human rights organizations called for a march to protest the "Final Document," and

50,000 demonstrators participated. In September the government passed the Law of National Pacification to provide amnesty for the past nine years' worth of crimes committed by the armed forces.[47]

As elections approached, the political parties included in their platforms an explicit rejection of the Doctrine of National Security. Raul Alfonsín, the candidate of the Radical Party, declared that if elected, he would not compromise on the topic of human rights and he would annul the Law of National Pacification.[48]

THE NATIONAL COMMISSION ON THE DISAPPEARED AND THE TRIAL OF THE JUNTAS

Running on a strong human rights platform, Alfonsín won comfortably with 52 percent of the vote. His government was inaugurated on December 10, 1983, the anniversary of the signing of the Universal Declaration of Human Rights. Shortly after being elected, President Alfonsín sent Congress a bill declaring null and void the Law of National Pacification; at the same time, he created the Argentine National Commission on the Disappeared (CONADEP). CONADEP's charge was to investigate the disappearances and provide the information necessary to prosecute those responsible. Human rights groups had lobbied for a parliamentary commission that would have the power to subpoena witnesses; CONADEP lacked such authority to force people to testify. The armed forces, and even some judges, refused to cooperate with it. The Mothers, and especially Hebe Bonafini, strongly criticized CONADEP and its chair, well-known writer Ernesto Sábato, whose opinion of General Videla had once been positive. Other human rights activists, such as Adolfo Pérez Esquivel and Emilio Mignone, who had been asked to become members of CONADEP refused.

After nine months of research and interviews with thousands of witnesses, CONADEP presented President Alfonsín with 50,000 pages of testimony. A 500-page book, *Nunca Más* (*Never Again*), documented the methods used to terrorize the population; both it and a companion volume, listing the names of 8,961 disappeared, were published in 1984. According to the report, 70 percent of the disappeared were male and 30 percent were female; 3 percent were pregnant women. The great majority (81 percent) were young, between the ages of sixteen and thirty-five; students and blue- and white-collar workers made up 70 percent of the disappeared. CONADEP acknowledged that the number of disappeared far exceeded the number of cases investigated. Graciela

Fernández Meijide, the CONADEP secretary, reported that the commission processed only 30 percent of the material received during its nine-month tenure.[49]

The total figure was highly contested. The APDH estimated it as 12,261, a count that combined "definitive disappearances," acknowledged deaths, and survivors or official prisoners who were later freed.[50] Emilio Mignone, from CELS, investigated cases in which it was possible to know the identity of the disappeared and found that only half had been reported, because of fear, ignorance, isolation, lack of resources, or hopelessness. His own estimate was 20,000, and he believed that the 30,000 figure, frequently put forward by some human rights groups, could be explained by including people who disappeared and later reappeared.[51] A new list of 290 disappeared who had not been reported to CONADEP was released by the government in 1995, and another list with 300 names is in the process of verification.[52]

More than 200,000 copies of *Nunca Más* were sold in the first weeks after its publication. Regrettably, *Nunca Más* did not include the names of the repressors, but a list with 1,351 names was given to President Alfonsín and subsequently published by the magazine *El Periodista de Buenos Aires* in November 1984.[53] In spite of its limitations, *Nunca Más* was a powerful public indictment of the military and the doctrine of national security. The members of CONADEP became the targets of attacks, and some had their homes or offices bombed.

On the topic of the disappeared children, *Nunca Más* stated:

> When a child is forcibly removed from its legitimate family to be put in another, according to some ideological precept of what's "best for the child's welfare," then this constitutes a perfidious usurpation of duty. The repressors who took the disappeared children from their homes, or who seized mothers on the point of giving birth, were making decisions about people's lives in the same cold-blooded way that booty is distributed in war. Deprived of their identity and taken away from their parents, the disappeared children constitute, and will continue to constitute, a deep blemish on our society. In their case, the blows were aimed at the defenseless, the vulnerable and the innocent, and a new type of torment was conceived.[54]

A few days after becoming president, Alfonsín announced that the nine members of the first three juntas, whom he considered the most responsible for the repression, would be tried by the military courts. The human rights organizations were dismayed. They did not trust the military to judge their peers; more important, they wanted the military tried by the civilian justice system in order to assert the principle of equality under the law. At the same time, President Alfonsín sent to trial seven members of two guerrilla groups, ERP and Montoneros, who were accused of "terrorist activities."

Alfonsín was putting forward a theme that he would continue to harp on for the next few years: the theory of the "two devils." On this account, the *guerrilleros* and the military were equally responsible for criminal acts, and both deserved to be punished. Human rights activists pointed out that the theory of the two devils opened the door to justifying all kinds of abuses by the state. They argued that the state should act only within the limits of law and moral principles; moreover, they emphasized that when the state commits crimes, the victims find themselves totally defenseless, with no recourse.[55]

The trial of the military by their peers, as the human rights group had foreseen, quickly turned into a farce. After months of procrastination, the Supreme Council of the Armed Forces refused to judge the juntas and even tried to justify their actions. Alfonsín and his advisers admitted that they had committed a "historical error" in expecting that the military cadres would be willing to punish their own colleagues. The trial was then assigned to a civilian court.[56]

The civil trial of the members of the three juntas officially started in April 1985. For five months, the proceedings of what in Argentina came to be known as "the trial of the century" electrified the country. During this time bombings, threats, and hostile statements by the military created an atmosphere of tension and political uncertainty. The public prosecutor, Dr. Julio César Strassera, and his assistant, Dr. Luis Moreno Ocampo, brought 711 charges against the generals for murder, illegal detention, torture, rape, and robbery. The court heard the testimony of over 800 individuals, including survivors of the detention camps, relatives of the disappeared, former members of the Peronista government, union leaders, military officers, human rights activists, members of international organizations, scientific experts, and representatives of foreign governments.[57]

Strassera characterized the actions against the guerrilla organizations as "ferocious, clandestine, and cowardly." He pointed out that by renouncing ethical principles, the state had created its own brand of terrorism, reproducing in itself the evils that it was trying to combat: "What did the state do to combat the guerrillas? Kidnap, torture, and kill on an infinitely bigger scale." And he asked, "How many victims of the repression were guilty of illegal activities? How many were innocent? We will never know, and it is not the victims' fault."[58] In one of the most dramatic moments of the trial, the lawyer of one of the generals asked Magdalena Ruiz Guiñazú, a well-known radio journalist and a member of CONADEP, if she knew of any innocent people who had been persecuted. In her two and a half hours on the witness stand, she brought to the court's attention the disappearances of children; a profound silence followed her testimony.[59]

Moreno Ocampo brought out the contradictions that had pervaded the junta's defense. The ex-commanders denied the actions of which they were accused, while at the same time trying to justify them as acts of war: "So, they deny that torture and murder have taken place, but at the same time they speak of the horrors of war and the need for that war." He concluded that either there had been no war, in which case the generals were common criminals, or there had been a war, in which case they were war criminals.[60]

Strassera closed with the phrase, now famous in Argentina: "Your Honours, I shall renounce any pretensions to originality, by using an expression which is not mine, but which belongs to the Argentine people. Your Honours: Never Again." His words elicited such applause and cheering that the courtroom was emptied and public access to the hearings was barred. Five generals were condemned to sentences ranging from four and a half years to life imprisonment, and four generals were found innocent. All nine were absolved of the charges of theft of children and substitution of identity, thus freeing them of any responsibility for the disappearance of hundreds of children.[61]

The trial's result did not satisfy the human rights organizations, which considered the punishment insufficient and indeed dangerous, for it could help lay the foundation for a culture of impunity. The military, in contrast, demanded the exoneration of all the accused, depicting them as martyrs and participants in a "holy war." However, the trial clearly established the responsibility of the military for the countless human rights violations that had taken place, and it signaled a new political climate: it was the first time in Argentina that members of the military had been brought to trial and condemned.

THE AMNESTY LAWS

After the trial of the junta members, hundreds of armed forces members charged with "following orders" were due to be brought to trial.

Threats to the government continued. President Alfonsín, in an effort to pacify the military, sent Congress a law setting a sixty-day deadline for initiating new prosecutions. The law, passed on December 24, 1986, became known as the *Punto Final* or Full Stop Law. The only cases excluded from this law, in what looked like a concession to the Grandmothers of the Plaza de Mayo's demands, were those concerning rape, theft, and the abduction and concealment of minors. The Grandmothers reacted by pointing out the absurdity of separating the kidnapping of the parents from the disappearance of the children:

> But what about the children; did they appear spontaneously in the police stations, in the secret detention camps? How can the change of identity of the children be separated from the kidnapping of the parents? . . . We cannot fight for the recovery of those children and forget the suffering of their mothers, our daughters. We cannot close the book on the tortures that they suffered, on all that we know about giving birth, handcuffed and blindfolded, lonely and terrorized. . . . We want to recover the kidnapped children. But we will continue demanding, as on the first day, truth and justice for them and for their parents.[62]

The Grandmothers' swift response was typical: they consistently refused to be singled out and separated from the other human rights organizations. They called the law an "abomination" and issued a call for "collective memory," stressing that they were searching for two generations.[63]

The *Punto Final* caused a flurry of activity among victims and human rights groups, who tried to file new charges during the sixty days allotted. By the end of the deadline, it appeared that more than a hundred officers would be brought to trial.[64] One of the officers accused of crimes in Córdoba province, Major Ernesto Barreiro, refused to appear in court, and his regiment backed him. This ignited the military in Buenos Aires, and, led by Lieutenant Colonel Aldo Rico, it rose in arms against the government, demanding an amnesty law. The rebels, who became known as the *carapintadas* (because they painted their faces black), quickly emerged as an unrelenting source of hostility toward President Alfonsín. The government called for support from the citizenship. Hundreds of thousands of people demonstrated for the democratically elected government, and nearly 50,000 showed up at the military barracks where the rebels had established their headquarters. On Easter Sunday, April 19, 1987, President Alfonsín announced that he had met with the rebels and that they had agreed to put down their arms.[65]

Soon thereafter, President Alfonsín sent Congress another law, which granted immunity to a large number of potential defendants; it covered almost all the crimes committed during the dirty war. The new law, the *Obediencia Debida* or Law of Due Obedience, exempted from amnesty only three types of crimes: rape, theft, and falsification of civil status.[66] But even Alfonsín's two amnesty laws were not enough for the military. Two more uprisings by the *carapintadas* took place in 1988, resulting in more negotiations and compromises. In January, Aldo Rico again rebelled, but the majority of the military remained faithful to the government, and the insurgency fizzled out. In December, Rico and another officer, Colonel Mohamed Alí Seineldín (who had just been passed up for promotion to general), once again defied the government. They demanded increased pay for the military and recognition that the acts of the juntas in the "fight against subversion" were legitimate. This last uprising was put down through the combined efforts of civilians, the police, and loyalist forces. However, President Alfonsín did increase funding for the army and give a pay raise to the military.[67]

In January 1989 fifty members of a small left-wing group, Movimiento Todos por la Patria (MTP, All for the Country), attacked army barracks at La Tablada in Buenos Aires. It was a bloody confrontation on both sides: nine soldiers and two members of the provincial police as well as twenty-eight of the attackers were killed. Eighteen of the assailants were taken prisoner. Some were killed after surrendering, while others disappeared, raising anew the specter of human rights violations by the military. There was wide speculation that the MTP had been infiltrated by the military's intelligence services that, under the guise of preventing another *carapintada* uprising, led the group into a suicide attack. The episode resulted in President Alfonsín increasing the armed forces' power in matters of internal security and drafting a law limiting freedom of expression.[68]

THE PRESIDENTIAL PARDONS

Hyperinflation, food riots, and a general sense of hopelessness about the country's economy forced President Alfonsín to relinquish the presidency five months ahead of schedule. For the first time in sixty years, two constitutionally elected governments followed each other. The new president, Carlos Saúl Menem, was a member of the Peronista Party; he went even further than Alfonsín in his attempts to appease the military. In October 1989 he pardoned high-ranking officers who had not been covered by the previous laws, preempting any further investigations or convictions. He also pardoned the *carapintada* officers who had masterminded the uprisings against Alfonsín. And in December 1990 he issued a pardon for all the members of the juntas tried in 1985 and still serving their sentences. To make his actions toward the military more palatable, Mario Firmenich, a Montonero leader who had been sentenced to thirty years in prison, was pardoned as well.[69]

President Menem's rationale was that it was time to unify the country and move toward reconciliation. But 80 percent of the population was against the pardons. Human rights groups, political leaders, and trade union organizations all protested the president's action, with the human rights organizations calling for peaceful demonstrations. On December 30, at the worst possible time of the year and with practically no time to organize, 80,000 people attended a rally in Buenos Aires protesting President Menem's decision.[70] The pardoned military officers not only expressed no regret about their actions but saw the pardons as a step toward full vindication. Barely twenty-four hours after leaving prison, General Videla demanded an apology and full recognition from society for his work on behalf of "democracy."[71]

The amnesty laws and the presidential pardons made moot the legal redress of most human rights violations. But because the *Punto Final* and the *Obediencia Debida* laws do not cover the crimes of abduction and concealment of children, the Grandmothers of the Plaza de Mayo can still achieve some measure of justice. Their work to find the missing children forces the country to continue to face the consequences of the state terrorism that had dominated Argentina. Defying the stereotypes of sex and age, the Grandmothers show the world that persistence, love, and commitment to truth and justice are an unbeatable combination in the struggle for human rights.

THREE

THE GRANDMOTHERS ORGANIZE

On this long road, we Grandmothers got together and organized a group to look for the disappeared children, at first thinking that there were just a few of us, and then realizing to our horror that there were hundreds of us.

María Isabel Chorobik de Mariani (1986)

The majority of the children who disappeared in Argentina were kidnapped together with their parents or were born in captivity in the detention camps. Some were murdered. As of 1997, the Grandmothers of the Plaza de Mayo had documented the disappearance of 88 children and 136 pregnant women, but they estimate that the true number of missing children is around 500.[1] The exact number may never be known, because fear is still keeping some abductions unreported. Moreover, when entire families disappeared, no one was left behind to tell what happened to them; and some families probably did not know that their daughters were pregnant at the time of their disappearance.

In 1984 General Ramón Juan Camps, former police chief of the province of Buenos Aires (eventually sentenced to twenty-five years in prison for his role in hundreds of homicides), stated: "Personally, I did not eliminate any child. What I did was to take some of them to charitable organizations so that they could find new parents. Subversive parents teach their children subversion. This has to be stopped."[2] Human rights activist Emilio Mignone was told by Army General José Antonio Vaquero that "one of the problems we have to face is that of the children of the disappeared, who will grow up hating the military institutions." In the same vein, a well-known diplomat and politician, Mario Amadeo, reported that the secretary of the presidency called the separation of the children from their families a doctrine established by the high commanders to forestall hatred of the military in the children of the disappeared.[3]

General Camps's plan of finding "new parents" for the children meant, in practice, that many of them were given—like pieces of property or war booty—to highly placed government officials, to members of the military, or to police officers. Others were abandoned in the street or left at orphanages with no information about their origins.[4] In targeting children as part of its repressive policies, the military devised an especially cruel way to discipline those the regime considered "subversives": it robbed them of a future by destroying the identity of their children. The military well understood the importance of families, particularly mothers, in transmitting values and identity from generation to generation, and it punished the women for raising those who would dare challenge the regime. A metaphor commonly employed during the dictatorship was "La Nación Argentina es una gran familia." The military, as "father," saw itself as "saving" the young from becoming the next generation of subversives. Separating the children from their legitimate families was necessary in order to incorporate them in the "big Argentine family."[5]

The case of Argentina was not unique in Latin America. We know that thirteen Uruguayan children disappeared in the 1970s. They were all kidnapped or born in captivity in Argentina, offering further evidence that the security forces of the two countries undertook joint operations.[6] Recently, evidence has emerged that in the early 1980s, during the civil war in El Salvador, children of guerrilla sympathizers and political activists were taken away and either given in adoption to foreigners from Europe and the United States or kept by the military.[7]

The Grandmothers have coined the term *desaparecidos con vida* (the living disappeared) to describe the condition of these children. As an integral part of the Argentine human rights movement, the Grandmothers' Association seeks truth and justice on many fronts, but its primary purpose is the identification and reunion of these children with their families. The Grandmothers feel great urgency, for they know that every day that goes by is one more day in which their grandchildren are being socialized in a world with a set of values dramatically different from those their parents envisioned for them.

THE EARLY DAYS OF THE GRANDMOTHERS

On November 25, 1976, the day after the armed attack on, and destruction of, her son's house, María Isabel Chorobik de Mariani (known to her friends as "Chicha") learned of the death of her daughter-in-law and the disappearance of her three-month-old granddaughter. She had gone to visit her ailing father. When she came back to her home, she found that she also had become a target:

> When I got to my house I saw my neighbors in front of the house. They were crying. They thought I was dead inside. As I tried to go in, a neighbor warned me. There was an electric cable connected to the door, so that if I walked in I would be electrocuted. The house was totally ransacked. It was a wreck. There was nothing intact. And they had stolen everything.[8]

Because her son had been away when his house was destroyed, he was still alive. She managed to see him before he went underground and they met a few more times during the following months, always in total secrecy. However, nine months later, Chicha Mariani received two more blows: an anonymous phone call informed her that her son had been killed, and some of her close relatives, who had managed to contact sources close to General Camps, were told that her granddaughter was also dead. In spite of this devastating information, Chicha Mariani started, against all odds, to look for her missing grandchild.

During one of her innumerable visits to police stations, army barracks, and courthouses, Chicha Mariani met Dr. Lidia Pegenaute, one of the few public officials who showed concern for her story. Pegenaute, a juvenile court judge, repeatedly told her of two other women also looking for their grandchildren. Chicha Mariani remembers:

> I did not fully realize what she was telling me. I was crying all the time. Then, one day I finally understood. She had been trying to tell me that I was too alone and that maybe it would be better if I got together with the other women. When I realized what she was saying I asked her how I could reach those women. She jumped up and gave me the address of Alicia de de La Cuadra, and I immediately went to her house. Alicia herself, a tall, elegant woman with blue eyes, opened the door. I told her who I was, why I was looking for her, and who had sent me.

Alicia de de la Cuadra's daughter had been five months pregnant when she disappeared. From survivors of the secret detention camp where her daughter had been taken, Alicia had learned that she had given birth to a baby girl that she had named Ana. She also learned that the baby weighed 3.75 kilos and that four days after the birth the baby had been taken away from her mother. The meeting between the two grandmothers lasted hours. They exchanged stories and ideas, thus beginning what would become a long and devoted friendship. Alicia told Chicha Mariani that she had been attending the weekly gatherings of the Mothers at the Plaza de Mayo, and Chicha Mariani decided to join her.

In the spring of 1977, U.S. Secretary of State Cyrus Vance visited Argentina. The Mothers organized a demonstration and approached him with petitions regarding the situation of their missing children. It was Chicha Mariani's first demonstration. She froze and could not deliver her message:

A woman came next to me and said: "What? You did not give him your petition?" She took the piece of paper from my hands, went back through the barrier of soldiers protecting Vance, and gave him the message. It was Azucena Villaflor de DeVincenti. That day, Azucena showed me that we were capable of doing things that we could never have imagined. We all knew that we were risking our lives. But there was no other way.

That same day, at the demonstration, Alicia introduced Chicha Mariani to other women whose pregnant daughters had also disappeared. They decided to meet again to discuss their common plight, thinking that together they would not be so easily dismissed by the authorities.

Haydée Vallino de Lemos was another of the original members of the group. Both her son and her daughter, who was eight months pregnant, disappeared. Haydée's family went broke looking for her children. She recalls the early days:

I was a member of the Mothers of Plaza de Mayo. Yes, those that go around in the Plaza. At first when my children disappeared I just laid down in bed, looking at the ceiling, blank. That was all I could do. My weight went down to forty kilos. One day my husband brought the newspaper and said: "Look, people are getting together." I jumped up saying, "Then it is not me alone, there are others." I started to go to the Ministry of the Interior. There I met a woman who said to me: "Why don't you come on Thursday to the Plaza de Mayo? Take a little nail; that is how they will recognize you." So I went, and I sat on a bench and my husband sat a little away from me. I had this little nail in my hand, and I saw that the others also had a little nail, and that is how I knew it was them.[9]

At a demonstration, a woman began to tell me her story and, when she learned that I had a pregnant daughter disappeared, she took out a little notebook and put me on her list. She also had a disappeared pregnant daughter. . . .

In the Plaza we secretly passed notes about where our meetings would be. We met in churches . . . we met in my house, in my sister's house. . . . My sister lived on the twelfth floor, and we did not want to take the elevator and make noise. We were quite a few, and the meeting was at an hour when the janitor was sleeping. So we went tiptoeing to the twelfth floor. And then, what a moment! When we got together, we discussed about whom to send letters, we collected signatures, we brainstormed. Each meeting was bigger than the one before. We were simply housewives. Most of us had never done anything outside the home. I did not even know how to take a bus alone. I was not used to going out without my husband. Even now I do not think I could do the things I did then.[10]

Raquel Radío de Marizcurrena, also one of the founding Grandmothers, lost her son, kidnapped on his twenty-fourth birthday, along with his wife, who was four months pregnant. She remembers her arrest after one of the marches at the Plaza de Mayo:

I joined a small group of women who had started to meet at the Plaza de Mayo. One day, while at the Plaza, the police stopped three buses. They got all the passengers out and they herded us in. They took us to the police station. As soon as we got out of the buses we ripped every piece of paper we had in our purses, anything that could be used to incriminate us. The street turned completely white!

I was arrested with Azucena Villaflor de DeVincenti. Azucena was a fantastic woman. She would call you, organize you in the churches, in the public squares, anywhere and everywhere. One day we would go to the botanical garden, the next day to the zoo. We would spread out on the benches, and we would sign petitions. And every single Thursday we went to the Plaza.[11]

Soon, however, Raquel remembers, some of the Mothers started to raise the issue of their missing grandchildren:

One day Chicha said, "Let's celebrate the day of the child; let's take the pictures of the children to the Plaza." So, we did a big poster with all the pictures of the children and the pregnant women. That marked our separation from the Mothers. Two Mothers did not want us to be in the Plaza. They said that if we wanted a plaza we could go to another plaza, the Plaza del Congreso, that the Plaza de Mayo was the plaza of the Mothers. But it was only two of them, and it happened only once. So, we kept going to the Plaza de Mayo. I think what happened is that they thought that we wanted to divide things. That because we were looking for our grandchildren we were abandoning our children. But that was not the case, we never forgot our children.

Delia Giovanola de Califano, a founding Grandmother whose adopted son and daughter-in-law, eight months pregnant, disappeared, remembers her initial skepticism about meeting with other Mothers:

At first, I thought it was a waste of time to talk to other mothers who were in my situation. I wanted to find my son and I did not see the connection. What was the use of speaking to others who were going through the same? But another mother kept insisting and one day I finally agreed and went to the Plaza with her. We were very few, just two or three mothers; it was right at the beginning. She introduced me to Azucena Villaflor. Azucena took out pencil and paper and wrote down some notes. The group kept growing. The police ordered us to keep moving and we walked around the pyramid. One day somebody stood outside the circle and, as we passed by, she asked if anybody had a pregnant daughter or daughter-in-law disappeared. So I approached her and we started meeting on our own.[12]

The Grandmothers started to meet in La Plata and in Buenos Aires and began compiling a list of names with the pictures of each child and pregnant woman kidnapped. They distributed the list to individuals and organizations in Argentina and abroad. The original group was composed of twelve women.[13] They carried on their work in public places—coffee shops, restaurants, and bus stops—trying to look like conventional older women having tea and pastries, pretending to celebrate birthday parties or other family events. They developed a code to use on the phone without being understood: "The White Man" was the pope; the "pups," "the notebooks," or "the flowers" were the children; the "girls" or "the young ones" were the Mothers; and the "oldies," or "the old aunts," were themselves.[14]

Rosa Tarlovsky de Roisinblit, the current vice president of the group, whose pregnant daughter disappeared in 1978, describes how she tried to get information about her daughter and how she learned about the other Grandmothers:

I presented a writ of habeas corpus, I went to the Ministry of the Interior. And I went to the Jewish organizations that, unfortunately, did not help at all. I want to say that clearly—although finally, after so many years, I almost can justify their failure to respond because the terror was so great. They probably did not want to get involved for fear that it would hurt other people in the Jewish community. I went to see Rabbi Marshall Meyer; he was very understanding. I was not the first one from the Jewish community to go see him. He gave me the address of the Permanent Assembly for Human Rights. There, a lawyer received me, Dr. Galletti. He recorded my story and told me that a few grandmothers were going to his house to prepare a report for the Organization of American States. He invited me to join them.

I was terrified because I did not know who Dr. Galletti was and whether he could be trusted. I didn't know at the time that he also had a daughter disappeared. I was going blindly. But I mustered the courage and went, and that is how I started to work with the Grandmothers, who were not yet called Grandmothers of the Plaza de Mayo. And that gave me a sort of internal peace, though I was still very worried, but at least I knew that I was working for my daughter and my grandchild.[15]

The first name of the group, and the one they used to sign their petitions and advertisements, was Abuelas Argentinas con Nietitos Desaparecidos (Argentine Grandmothers of Disappeared Small Grandchildren). In 1980 they changed their name to the Grandmothers of the Plaza de Mayo, the name that people were beginning to call them, as they continued to gather every week at the Plaza. On their own they started preparing writs of habeas corpus, which they presented to the judges. Written on an old typewriter, one of the few items salvaged from Chicha Mariani's home, these documents represented the first visible results of the Grandmothers' organizing.[16]

Much of the early work of the Grandmothers was centered on the juvenile courts, because they suspected that most of the children had passed through them on their way to being adopted, placed in custody, or transferred to children's institutions. The Grandmothers visited the courthouses and the juvenile judges of the province of Buenos Aires and wrote to the judges throughout the rest of the country. The judges were either disinterested or overtly hostile. It was eventually ascertained that many of the judges had given the children away for adoption without investigating their origins or family histories. In 1984 one of these same judges was the lawyer defending a policeman who had kept one of the children for himself.[17] Dr. Delia Pons, a judge from a juvenile court in Buenos Aires, was particularly strident in her hostility toward the Grandmothers:

> I am convinced that your children were terrorists, and "terrorist" is synonymous with "murderer." I do not intend to return children to murderers because it would not be fair. They do not have the right to have them. So, I will rule not to return any children to you. It does not make sense to disturb those children that are in the hands of decent families that will be able to educate them right, not like you educated your children. Only over my dead body will you obtain custody of them.[18]

The Grandmothers began to accumulate convincing evidence that their grandchildren were still alive and had been given in adoption to families connected with the regime, or had been entered as NN into children's institutions. For example, in December 1976 Chicha Mariani had received a phone call from an acquaintance who wanted to meet with her in utmost secrecy:

> The call was from a man I trusted, and he said that he had important news to tell me. Almost paralyzed by fear, he told me that my granddaughter was alive, and that he knew that for a fact since he had been like a father to the policeman who had been the chief of the operation. I went to see this policeman, and he confirmed that the child was alive. But he also said that he would never publicly acknowledge it, and that he would always deny that he had spoken with me.

Similarly, Alicia de de la Cuadra's husband was told by an auxiliary bishop in La Plata, Monsignor Picchi, that their daughter had given birth in captivity, that the child had been given to a very influential family, and that nothing further could be done.[19]

Pressed by the Grandmothers, the politician Mario Amadeo reported that a meeting had been held between those we might call the "current parents" of the disappeared children and important members of the military to test their reactions to the idea of restituting the children. But the current parents, denying the origin of their children, were unanimous in asserting that they would never give them up.[20]

In July 1978 the Grandmothers wrote to the Argentine Supreme Court in an attempt to reclaim their disappeared grandchildren. Anticipating the issues that would arise if the children were "legally" adopted, they asked the Court to prohibit the adoption of children who were registered as NN and to require thorough investigations into the origins of children three years old and younger who had been given in adoption since March 1976. The Court refused to take up their case, declaring itself incompetent to deal with the issue and claiming that the "separation of the different branches of government" justified its inaction.[21]

On August 5, 1978, Children's Day, one of Buenos Aires' major daily newspapers risked publishing an open letter from the Grandmothers addressed to whoever had their grandchildren. Titled "Appeal to the Conscience and the Hearts," it reminded the readers of *La Prensa* that the children had a fundamental right to be reunited with their grandmothers, who, in any case, would be looking for them for the rest of their lives.[22] This document put the Grandmothers squarely in the public eye. There could be no further denial of their existence or their intentions. Their individual searches had converged and had created a movement. The open letter, reproduced thousands of times, shocked the world. In Europe—particularly in Italy and Spain, where many Argentines have family members—the strong reactions to the letter ranged from incredulity to outrage. It marked the beginning of what would become a wave of international attention and support for the Grandmothers' work.

In August 1978 Estela Barnes de Carlotto, the current president of the Grandmothers, joined the group. Her twenty-two-year-old daughter Laura, a member of the Montoneros, was two months pregnant when she had been kidnapped. She was held in a secret detention camp until she was killed. From the testimony of released prisoners, Estela de Carlotto knew that her daughter had delivered a child while in captivity. She recalls the day she found out about her daughter's death:

On August 25, 1978, the police in Matanza requested that we go to the police station. They informed us that Laura had been killed. They said that she had been in a car and had disobeyed the order to stop. It was all a lie. We were not able to have an autopsy done. I could not get a physician that would certify the cause of death. When I asked about the child, the officer said he knew nothing about that.[23]

Estela de Carlotto and Chicha Mariani shared a fateful history: Estela's daughter and Chicha's son, also a Montonero, had been close friends. He had been assassinated after helping her move, and she was the anonymous caller who phoned Chicha Mariani to inform her of her son's death. Each one had information that helped fill the gaps in the story of the other's child. With their strong and charismatic personalities, they would become an unstoppable team for the cause of the Grandmothers in the years to come.

The Grandmothers' work style was collaborative and informal. They worked in teams, and when visiting judges they went in threes. Chicha Mariani would often write the letters and public announcements. Since they lived far from each other, when it became too cumbersome to gather their signatures, Chicha Mariani would bring blank pages that all would sign; the text of the letter would be added later.

As their work started to be known and respected, it became necessary to create some type of structure to allow them to deal efficiently with their network of supporters. They formed a board of directors, with officers elected annually. The first president, in 1978, was Alicia de de la Cuadra; when she went to Italy for an extended period of time, Chicha Mariani took her place, with Estela de Carlotto as the vice president. In 1989 Estela was elected the Grandmothers' third president. Rosa Roisinblit recalls how she came to be the treasurer, a position she held for seven years:

We received a donation from Canada, the first country to help us, from an organization named Desarrollo y Paz (Development and Peace). They sent us $10,000, which for us was a huge sum. Three of us went to the bank to get the money and we had to decide where to put the money. A bit nervous, I said: "Look, I have a safety box in the bank. We can put the money in the safety box and as we need it I'll take it out." And they agreed. As we started receiving money from other organizations, we also put it in my safety box and when we formed the board of directors, I became the treasurer because I was the one who had access to the money.

Grandmothers from various parts of the country joined the organization. Soon they had contacts and branches in other cities, including

Mar del Plata and Rosario, and in the provinces of Córdoba, Tucumán, and La Rioja. Otilia Lescano de Argañaraz, a grandmother from Córdoba, joined the organization in 1977, after the disappearance of her daughter:

My daughter was six months pregnant. We know from survivors from the camp where she was taken that she was well treated because they had their eyes on the baby. They gave her vitamins, a real mattress, and made her believe that they would set her free. Our work in Córdoba was and is very hard, because of the lack of resources. The office of the Grandmothers is in my house because we do not have enough money to pay for rent. A group of grandmothers from Córdoba, in Spain, gave us a typewriter. That was a big help.[24]

As the Grandmothers started to organize and became increasingly visible, they began to receive threats. A masked man in a car followed Chicha Mariani. Alicia de de la Cuadra was almost hit by a car. Emma Spione de Baamonde, who was looking for her three-year-old grandson, found the walls of her apartment complex covered with huge red graffiti saying "Mother of a subversive, Mother of a communist," and received death threats over the phone. When a policeman appeared at her house to inquire about her participation in the Grandmothers' activities, she answered with aplomb: "Yes, I am part of the Grandmothers' organization. And so? I have every right to do whatever I choose with my life. I do not disturb or harass anyone, I am simply looking for my son. Do you understand what it means to look for a son?"[25] A military officer warned one woman looking for her grandchild, Julia de Grandi, to keep away from the Grandmothers of the Plaza de Mayo if she wanted to find the child. She responded:

Look, colonel, I want you to know that this is the last time that I come to see you. I have joined the Grandmothers and from now on I, too, am going to the Plaza de Mayo. And you know why? Because when I go alone the judges do not even receive me. But when the Grandmothers go, yes, they do receive them.[26]

Antonia Acuña de Segarra, a grandmother from Mar del Plata, recalls:

We received many threats over the phone. Once they called and said that I should go to the cemetery, that there they would tell me what had happened with my three children. On another occasion, they threatened several Mothers in Mar del Plata and I received a letter saying that I too would disappear any moment. But after what had happened to us, after they took away the best that we had, our children, I had to disregard those threats.[27]

None of the Grandmothers disappeared. They credit the recognition and support they received from international organizations and foreign governments with preventing their own disappearances and enabling them to pursue their work.

APPEALS TO THE CATHOLIC CHURCH

The Grandmothers, many of whom were observant Catholics, looked for support and solidarity from influential members of the Catholic Church. With few exceptions, the church ignored their concerns. They wrote to the president of the Argentine Bishop's Conference (CEA), Cardinal Raúl Primatesta; to the archbishop of Buenos Aires, Cardinal Juan Carlos Aramburu; and to the representative of the pope, Archbishop Pio Laghi.

In one of their visits to Archbishop Pio Laghi, they obtained further confirmation of their suspicions. Trying to reassure them, the archbishop's secretary told them, "I do not think you should worry about the future and the fate of your children. Those who have them have paid a lot for them. It clearly shows, by their attitude, that they are people with great resources. That means that the little ones will never suffer the deprivations that derive from poverty. Even more, I would say that their future is assured."[28]

The Grandmothers sought help from those priests they knew personally. Chicha Mariani went to see Monsignor Montes, an auxiliary bishop to the archbishop of La Plata, who had been present at the marriage of her son. At first, he received her cordially, but the politeness was short-lived; eventually he screamed at her, accusing her of not having enough faith and insisting that the solution was in prayer. She also visited Monsignor Emilio T. Grasselli, a military chaplain who had built a reputation as an ally to the thousands of families looking for their missing relatives. Monsignor Grasselli acknowledged that her granddaughter was in the hands of "powerful people," but told her that nothing could be done.[29] Grasselli is now suspected of having played a dual role. While appearing to be sincerely interested in helping the relatives, he collected information, verified familial relationships, created confusion, and tried to placate the families of the disappeared. Emilio Mignone, himself a Catholic who has analyzed the role of the hierarchy of the Catholic Church during the repression, has no doubts: "Given the knowledge of the facts that Grasselli came to have, thanks to his daily contact with hundreds of witnesses, one can only assume that, under the direction of the vicar, his function was that of an accomplice within the sinister machinery of genocidal repression."[30]

When Grandmother Mirta Baravalle asked a priest to celebrate a mass for her disappeared daughter, he refused, not wanting to mention disappearances in public. Mirta recalls:

> I asked him if he didn't know what was going on in the streets. "I know nothing," he told me, "I don't know what you are talking about; I work with the souls, which is the mission of the church."
>
> I could not control myself. I grabbed one of his arms, violently. I pushed him toward the door, and I screamed that if he didn't know what was going on he should go out and find out. Surprised and agitated, he said, "Madam, Madam, calm down, don't scream, or something may happen to you too."[31]

The Grandmothers finally realized that even though highly placed members of the church hierarchy knew the fate of some of the disappeared children, they would not openly denounce the crimes. They decided to pressure the Argentine Bishops' Conference, the most powerful body of the Argentine church. From April 1978 on, Mothers and Grandmothers regularly gathered at the location on the outskirts of Buenos Aires where the CEA met for their deliberations. Heavily armed police protected the bishops while the women tried, unsuccessfully, to deliver their petitions. One grandmother bitterly commented, "What can these men know of our pain; they will never know what it means to have a child."[32]

In January 1978 the Grandmothers attempted to reach Pope Paul VI. The letter they mailed him still remains unanswered:

> We are addressing ourselves to your Holiness to implore you, in the name of God, to intercede before whomever you consider appropriate, so that our small grandchildren, disappeared in the Argentine Republic, will be returned

to us. We are some of the Argentine women who have suffered the disappearance or death of our children within the last two years. And to this wrenching pain of the loss of our children has been added the pain of being deprived of our grandchildren, newly born or a few months old. We do not understand this. Our minds do not comprehend why we are subject to this torture. We are Christian mothers. We do not know if our children are alive, dead, buried, or unburied. We do not have the consolation of seeing them, if they are in prison, or praying at their tombs, if they are dead. But our small grandchildren have also disappeared: Herod has not come back to the earth; consequently somebody is hiding them, we do not know for what. Are they in orphanages? Were they given as gifts or sold? Why do they have to grow up without love, when their grandmothers have so much love to offer them? In some cases, the child who we are searching for is our only descendant: there is no future for us, only abysses of pain renewed daily in the incessant search for these innocents, lasting thus far months and even in some cases more than a year. We have knocked on all the doors but we have not had a reply. So, we beg Your Holiness to intercede to end this Calvary that we are living.[33]

Every time the Grandmothers traveled to Italy they asked to be received by the pope. Chicha Mariani recalls:

On one of our trips Alicia de de la Cuadra and I went to the Vatican and we requested an audience. They told us to place ourselves in the first row so that the pope would see us. We prepared a poster with the name of our group and we placed ourselves in the first row. When the pope appeared, the men dressed in black that followed him told him something and he skipped us. He saluted those before us and shook the hands of those after us. It was a terrible blow. Every time we went to Rome we requested an audience and every time we left our folder with the pictures and all the information about the children. But he never did anything, he never spoke up in behalf of the children. It was a big disappointment.

Nélida Gómez de Navajas, herself a practicing Catholic, comments:

I have been very saddened and disappointed with the Catholic Church, my religion. The church has not been coherent with its beliefs. They have killed so many priests and the church said nothing. I believe that the young priests that work in the slums, laying bricks, helping people, are the ones that represent the true Christian religion, a religion of solidarity, of stretching hands. Not those that operate under pomp and riches and fancy appearances.[34]

INTERNATIONAL OUTREACH AND SOLIDARITY

The Grandmothers had declared that their organization was "dedicated specifically to demanding the return, investigating the events in the disappearance of, and searching for our disappeared children." Demonstrations, appeals to the courts and to the church, and paid advertisements in the major newspapers were the beginnings of their public efforts in Argentina.[35] Soon though, they started reaching out to the rest of the world. Realizing that the image of the Argentine government was rapidly deteriorating abroad, the Grandmothers looked to international pressure to help their cause. They became great communicators, writing extensively to international human rights groups, international organizations, foreign embassies, newspapers, and prominent politicians. The Vatican, the United Nations, the World Council of Churches, the Organization of American States (OAS)—all heard from the Grandmothers. During the first two years of their work they contacted more than 150 international groups and politicians from other countries.[36]

The pressure they put on the OAS is a good example of the impact of their international outreach campaign. In April 1978 the Grandmothers wrote to the agency in Washington, D.C. When no reply appeared, they wrote again four months later. This time they did get an answer: the OAS registered their complaint as "case #3459, the case of the disappeared children."[37] After the organization's visit to Argentina in 1979, after which the OAS issued its report, the case of Chicha's granddaughter was highlighted: for the first time, the agency brought the subject of the disappearance of children to the attention of the international human rights community. The Grandmothers often testified at OAS assemblies and held extensive discussions with the executive committee and its secretary, Dr. Edmundo Vargas Carreno. Almost ten years after the Grandmothers had initially contacted the organization, the General Assembly of the OAS resolved in 1987, by consensus, to officially consider children in their next convention on disappearances.[38] The Grandmothers' long and relentless work had finally borne fruit.

Most important, with practically no resources, they began to travel and tell their stories to a wide variety of audiences, from college students to women's groups to premiers and presidents of foreign states. Chicha Mariani describes one of the Grandmothers' trips to Rome:

Hebe Bonafini [the president of the Mothers of the Plaza de Mayo] called me and said that she and two other Mothers were coming to Rome. She wanted me to arrange an interview with the president of Italy, Sandro Pertini, and with the pope. We all ended up sleeping on the floor. We used the Rome telephone books as pillows. We went to see President Pertini, who received us very well. But first we had to buy food, because we were cooking in the apartment. So, we went to the presidential palace carrying the groceries in a plastic bag.

In 1979 they managed to establish a very important connection with the Committee for the Defense of Human Rights in the Southern Cone (CLAMOR), a Brazilian human rights organization created under the sponsorship of Archbishop Evaristo Arns in São Paulo. Jaime Wright, a Presbyterian minister and one of its founders, became one of their most loyal allies and supporters.[39] CLAMOR connected the Grandmothers with Argentine exiles living in Brazil and opened its archives to them. That gave them access to the testimonies of dozens of survivors from the secret detention camps, which the Grandmothers copied and smuggled into Argentina. The survivors testified about the presence of children in the camps, and about the children being used as hostages. They described the torture of pregnant women, their anguish about giving birth in captivity, and their anxiety about the fate of their babies.[40] Estela de Carlotto learned from a couple who had been in La Cacha that there her daughter Laura, handcuffed, had delivered a baby boy and named him Guido, after her father. She also learned that Laura had been led to believe that she would soon be liberated and that her mother had refused to accept the child.[41]

In August 1979, an event electrified the Grandmothers. Two disappeared children—Victoria and Anatole Julien Grisonas, ages four and six—were found in Valparaíso, Chile, where they had been living for two years with a couple who had adopted them, unaware of their origins.[42] Chicha Mariani had sent a picture of the children—members of an Uruguayan family that had taken refuge in Argentina and had been kidnapped in 1976—to CLAMOR, which had published it in a bulletin. A Chilean woman from Valparaíso who saw the picture recognized the children.[43] The oldest child remembered his real name, the name of his little sister, and their address in Argentina. He remembered that men with "big guns" had taken them and that after a "long trip in a big car, Aunt Mónica" had left them in a public square. He said that his mother was not "feeling well"; in fact she was feeling so badly that she had fallen to the floor and there were red patches all over her. . . . He also remembered that they had crossed high snow-covered mountains (the Andes Mountains that separate Argentina from Chile), before arriving in Valparaíso.[44]

CLAMOR arranged for a Uruguayan exile who had known the family to go to Valparaíso and identify the children. The two grandmothers were informed and one of them went to Valparaíso, accompanied by a lawyer from CLAMOR, to meet them. Cardinal Arns's strong support for the work of the Grandmothers contrasted sharply with the silence and complicity of his Argentine brethren. The grandmothers decided that the children should continue living with their adoptive parents, and an extended visitation regime was established.

In consultation with the Grandmothers, CLAMOR developed other projects. For three consecutive years, the organization published and widely distributed a calendar with colored photographs and information in four languages about all the known missing children; it also published a book with the most complete list of disappeared persons in Argentina. This list was to be instrumental in helping the work of the National Commission on the Disappeared (CONADEP) in 1983.

The case of the Julien Grisonas children confirmed the Grandmothers' hunches. Yes, there was a network coordinating the repressive forces in Argentina, Uruguay, and Chile that had made such kidnapping possible. But since these two children had been found alive, there was hope: other children would have been similarly treated, and they would find them.

In 1982 the Grandmothers were in Geneva, seeking an institution that would help them make a presentation at the UN Commission of Human Rights. When they learned about the International Movement for Fraternal Union among Races and Peoples (UFER), a nongovernmental organization holding consultative status with the Economic and Social Council of the United Nations, they applied for membership.[45] By 1984 they had gone abroad more than forty times, mostly to Brazil and to Geneva to attend the UN sessions on human rights. They had particularly fruitful visits to Germany and Austria, where the wide publicity for their search resulted in an outpouring of emotional and economic support.

The ongoing interest of international groups, religious communities, municipal organizations, and intellectuals all over the world created a network that enabled the Grandmothers to amass resources and compile information, both greatly aiding their work. Their travels abroad galvanized international attention and helped them develop useful contacts. The trips also gave them access to Argentine exiles and survivors of the secret detention camps who, as in the case of Estela de Carlotto's daughter, had critical information about the fate of their children and grandchildren.

THE GRANDMOTHERS TURN DETECTIVES

Bolstered by the success of CLAMOR in finding the Julien Grisonas children, the Grandmothers continued the process of transforming themselves into detectives, following every trace and investigating every possible lead. Gradually, they started to receive tips; somebody would hand them a piece of paper with an address on a Thursday at the Plaza de Mayo; a Grandmother would get an anonymous phone call at her home; the answering machine at their office would record a message about a child who looked like one they were looking for. Emma Baamonde recalls how she began to search for the children:

When we received a tip, we would go and survey the street in question. We watched endlessly. If the alleged kidnapper had a beauty shop we would go and have our hair done. Once I went to see a pedicurist with another Grandmother. While he was working on our feet we tried to get information. We worked like ants, we worked like spies. Nobody trained us. We learned everything by ourselves.

Chicha Mariani summarizes their work style:

There is nothing we are not able to try in order to learn something about the children. When we have some clues that a family is suspected of having unlawfully adopted a child, we start following the family very closely. There have been cases in which one of us has offered her service as a home helper in order to get into a house. In another case one of the grandfathers has posed as a plumber looking for a job.

But the biggest help is from the people. We periodically publish information in the newspapers accompanied by pictures of the missing children and people come forward with information about them. When we cannot get close to the children, we even use a telephoto lens to follow them from a distance.[46]

The Grandmothers' investigations helped create what we might call a "methodology of hope." Determined to find the children, they became experts on how to search the area where a child had disappeared and how to check every lead. They also had to learn how to protect themselves, which minimal security measures to take, how to connect with people who knew the family where a child might be and who could provide information, how to get through resistant neighbors, and how to get close to the child or family involved without raising suspicion.[47]

As the work of the Grandmothers grew in volume and complexity, they formed teams (legal, medico-psychological, and investigative) to deal with the myriad of details that emerged from every case. Rosa Roisinblit explains:

> In the beginning, we did all the research ourselves. But the moment arrived when we became too well known; people knew our faces and we could no longer go ourselves to do the investigating, so we formed an investigation team. As time went on, different teams were needed. After we started to receive tips about our grandchildren, we needed judicial expertise to present our claims to the courts, so we formed a legal team. Both our families and ourselves were in pretty bad shape from an emotional point of view. We needed psychological help, for us, for the children, and for the families that would receive their found grandchildren. So a team of psychologists joined us.

In March 1980 the Grandmothers were rewarded with their first success at home: two sisters, Tatiana Ruarte Britos and Laura Malena Jotar Britos, who had disappeared in 1977, were found living with a family who had adopted them in good faith. The same judge who three years earlier had presided over their adoption now contacted their paternal grandmother and asked her to identify the children. In the Grandmothers' long experience, this was the only instance of a judge able to change his mind and recognize the legitimacy of their demands. However, he was extremely cautious and wanted incontrovertible evidence of the origin of the sisters. The Grandmothers faced a crucial problem, as they realized that locating the missing was only the first step. They now had to prove to the judges that these children were indeed their relatives. Old photographs and hair samples were not considered sufficient evidence. And what about the babies who had been born in captivity, who had left behind nothing tangible? How could they be identified? Chicha Mariani explains:

The quandary we faced had been born in the uncertainty of how we would identify the first two little girls we located in 1980. We had photos and other evidence, but that wasn't enough. The judge wanted more. It had been three years since their kidnapping and they were taller and of course they had aged. And so we asked ourselves, "What are we going to do with children who were born in detention?" In some cases, we didn't know their sex, or even to whom they belonged. Well, we thought of everything possible. For instance, I had cut locks of hair from my granddaughter before she was kidnapped. I sent them to Amnesty International to see if they could be used to identify her. I received a reply saying it would be difficult, particularly because the hair had been cut many years before and because it didn't contain follicles. Other grandmothers asked, "I have a baby's tooth which I've kept of my grandchild, could it be used in identifying him or her?" Then one day in 1981 I read an article in *El Diario del Día,* a newspaper in La Plata, that said scientists had found a way of identifying a person through analysis of the blood. Well, I did not understand all the scientific terms but the gist of it was that there was an element in the blood that repeated itself only within the same family. I cut it out. And when I traveled abroad I'd take it with me. I asked scientists and doctors and scientific institutes if this new discovery would help us identify our missing grandchildren.[48]

SCIENTIFIC HELP: A TEST

After Chicha Mariani learned that blood testing made it possible to establish the biological link between a child and her or his parents, the Grandmothers, during their travels abroad, started to ask scientists about the feasibility of developing a test that would show biological affiliation even when the parents were dead. Argentines in exile proved helpful once again. Dr. Victor B. Penchaszadeh, currently professor of pediatrics at Albert Einstein College of Medicine in New York City, had left Argentina in 1975 after the Argentine Anticommunist Alliance (Triple A) attempted to kidnap him in the middle of the day in downtown Buenos Aires. In November 1982 a group of Grandmothers who were visiting the United States contacted him. Penchaszadeh recalls:

The Grandmothers came to New York for one of their presentations at the United Nations and they called me. They had my name as a member of AISC [Argentine Information Service Center] and they knew I was a geneticist and a supporter of human rights. We met one afternoon in a coffee shop. I knew about their work and had heard about the disappeared children but I did not know the details nor the magnitude of the problem. They had a lot of information. It was still during the dictatorship and they were working under threats. The key question they had was how could they check, when they found a child, if that was one of the children they were looking for. I told them about paternity testing and that for their situation, what was required was a statistical modification of the information used in standard paternity testing to account for the fact that the parents of a given child had disappeared. I started to search to see who would be the geneticists who knew about genetic markers in the blood and I put them in touch with Dr. Fred Allen from the New York Blood Center.[49]

Dr. Allen agreed that with the appropriate mathematical formulation, a "grandparentage" test could be developed. The meeting with Allen confirmed the soundness of the Grandmothers' idea and greatly strengthened their determination to find scientific support for their work. With characteristic persistence, they began an international search for scientists who would help them. By following every lead, they eventually made it possible for their idea to become a reality.

During one of their trips to Washington, in October 1983, the Grandmothers met with Eric Stover, director of the science and human rights program of the American Association for the Advancement of Science (AAAS). Another Argentine living in the United States, Isabel Mignone (Emilio Mignone's daughter), had arranged the meeting. Stover himself had been briefly "detained" during a trip to Argentina in 1976. He was immediately supportive and attentive as the Grandmothers posed one question: How could genetic testing be applied to determine grandparenthood? Stover remembers, "The Grandmothers came to my office and we started talking. I will never forget it. They had already seen Penchaszadeh. I discussed the issue with Cristian Orrego, a Chilean scientist working at NIH [the National Institutes of Health], and he contacted researchers at Stanford who referred him to Mary-Claire King, a geneticist from Berkeley, California, as a person who could help develop the statistical treatment that was needed."[50]

Orrego, in turn, was struck by the Grandmothers' creativity: "The idea that the Grandmothers had, and it was their idea, was to use genetics to confirm circumstantial evidence."[51] Mary-Claire King, too, believed that genetic markers could be used to determine grandparenthood with a high degree of certainty.

In 1983, after Raúl Alfonsín became president, CONADEP ordered the excavation of hundreds of mass graves. The exhumations were callous and primitive, as hundreds of bones were piled next to the open graves, making any identification impossible. In February 1984 the Grandmothers met with CONADEP and urged the commission to contact Eric Stover at the AAAS and to request his advice about the proper procedures to be used.[52]

In June 1984 the AAAS sent a delegation of forensic scientists to assist in the exhumations and to make recommendations regarding the identification of the disappeared. The Grandmothers insisted that Mary-Claire King be added to their number to work on the genetic testing. CONADEP, which was starting to take an interest in such testing, had previously arranged a meeting between the Grandmothers and two Argentine scientists who were experts in the field. The Grandmothers rejected them: one of them worked in a military hospital, which created a potential conflict of interest that might endanger the integrity of the work. The Grandmothers had shared with Allen and his colleagues their reluctance to work with the Argentine scientists suggested by CONADEP and their concerns about the lack of genetic experts in Argentina. Dr. Pablo Rubinstein (a Chilean) had then informed them that Dr. Ana María Di Lonardo, head of the immunology unit at the Durand Hospital in Buenos Aires, had a laboratory fully equipped to carry out the identification work that was needed.[53] When Mary-Claire King arrived in Argentina the Grandmothers introduced her to Di Lonardo, and the two collaborated in developing the mathematical formula for the tests.[54] King was impressed with the facilities, the cooperative spirit of the lab, and the sophistication of the Argentine scientists.[55]

As King joined them, the Di Lonardo team had just completed the biological work on the case of an eight-year-old girl, Paula Logares, who was living with a policeman and whom the Grandmothers had identified as the granddaughter of one of them. Through genetic testing and by applying the new mathematical formulation, it was established with 99.9 percent certainty that Paula was indeed the granddaughter of Elsa Pavón de Aguilar. She was the first kidnapped child identified through genetic testing. On the basis of the test and circumstantial evidence, she was returned to her family of origin.

It was immediately clear that genetic testing would be a crucial procedure that could be ordered by the judges in future cases of found children. The Grandmothers had accomplished their goal. Scientific expertise had validated Chicha Mariani's hunch, and their investigative work could henceforth proceed on firmer footing. Empirical, objective evidence could now be used to convince previously skeptical judges. Faced with this new information, the government's Commission on Human Rights and the Department of Public Health of the city of Buenos Aires set up a technical commission to oversee the implementation of the genetic testing. And ironically, Dr. Penchaszadeh, who had once fled Argentina to save his life, became an adviser to the commission.

THE NATIONAL GENETIC DATA BANK

The Grandmothers lobbied actively for the creation of a genetic database to permanently store the genetic information of the families looking for the disappeared children, because there was no way of knowing when the last missing child would be found. The Grandmothers fought for the testing to be done in a public institution, both as a matter of principle and to ensure its accessibility to anybody who requested it. They thought that such a service was the minimal reparation that the state should make to the citizenry, given its culpability in the children's disappearance.

In February 1986, two years after first seeking it, the Grandmothers were finally granted a meeting with President Alfonsín. They presented him with four demands: that he publicly order all government officials to work toward the restitution of the disappeared children, that he call on the Argentine population to actively help find the children, that an official link be created between the president's office and the Grandmothers to facilitate communication, and that the proposal to create a National Genetic Data Bank be speedily sent to Congress.[56] The accumulation of evidence about the children and the effectiveness of the test made a strong case, and President Alfonsín agreed to their request.

The Grandmothers, together with a host of governmental bodies and the Immunology Service of the Durand Hospital, drafted a law that was unanimously approved by Congress in May 1987.[57] The data bank was created to solve *any type of conflict that involved issues of affiliation,* including cases of disappeared children. The law specified that the services of the bank would be free to the relatives of the disappeared; moreover, it mandated that every court in the nation perform the studies of genetic markers on any child with doubtful affiliation and established the procedures to be followed by relatives living abroad who wanted to make use of the bank. It also established that failure to submit to the genetic testing would be regarded as a sign of complicity in the kidnappings.[58] Given the average life expectancy in Argentina, it is estimated that the bank will be used by the kidnapped children at least until the year 2050; at any moment in their lives, they will be able to be tested.

In 1987 for the first time a child born in captivity was returned to her family of origin after genetic analysis carried out at the National Genetic Data Bank gave proof of her identity.[59] By 1996, 2,100 individuals had deposited their blood in the bank, representing about 175 family groups; and over thirty children have had their identity established by the work of the bank. That work benefits not only the disappeared children but also children whose parents disappeared (or were abandoned) and were left with no information regarding their identity.[60]

Although all studies done at the data bank are carried out under court rulings and the bank reports to the judges, its work and very existence have constantly been threatened. The regulations establishing it in 1989 required the city of Buenos Aires to pay for the scientific equipment and personnel, while the Ministry of Health and Social Action would pay for the chemical reactives and other substances needed to conduct the testing. The reality, however, has been different. Dr. Di Lonardo explains:

> The ministry never lived up to its obligation. Never. The municipality, halfheartedly, paid for part of the personnel budget. I had to make an appeal to the international scientific community. And they responded. Scientists from various parts of the world have helped. The French government and the French scientists have been especially helpful. The Foundation France Liberté, one of Danielle Mitterrand's projects, has been a great supporter of the bank, with chemicals and equipment. And in 1989 I was invited by professor Jean Dausset, [who won a] Nobel Prize for medicine, to work in his lab in Paris, to learn the new techniques of molecular biology with DNA that I could then apply to our work.

To maintain and update the bank has been—and remains—an uphill battle; it has become one of the main concerns of the Grandmothers. In

September 1988 the Grandmothers met with government officials to pressure them to enforce the laws supporting the bank. Because of the lack of resources needed to perform the tests, the work had practically stopped.[61] In November the Grandmothers met again with President Alfonsín and requested that he ensure the financial support needed for the bank to function. They also asked that he nominate a special prosecutor to follow up on the cases of the disappeared children in order to expedite the investigations. After listening to them, Alfonsín appointed a commission to speed both the investigations into these cases and the initiation of the legal proceedings necessary to resolve them.[62]

Incessant rumors about the stability of the bank created a climate of deep insecurity.[63] In March 1991 a judge responded to the complaints of a policeman who had abducted a child born in a secret detention camp by ordering members of the federal police to raid the bank. The police removed biological samples, and the work of the bank was interrupted. This episode clearly indicates that even under democracy, the Argentine judicial system has tended to ally itself with the perpetrators instead of with the victims.[64]

But the bank, which offers a model of scientists working on behalf of human rights and justice, has an even broader mission. Di Lonardo gives an idea of what its future work may be:

> The Grandmothers have done a great job spreading the news about the bank. Though its historical motivation was because of the disappearances, the law broadened the work of the bank to all cases where affiliation is an issue. Ten to 12 percent of what we do regards the disappeared children. The rest are requests, from all over the country, regarding paternity testing, cases of incest, rape, etc. Very serious cases. Of course, it is an ideal tool against the traffic of children, which is a significant problem in our country. Many times young people have come to the bank to ask for help to find out their roots. I see the future of the bank in the direction of assisting anybody who has doubts and wants to know about their origins. The bank will be able to help them.

FORENSIC SCIENCE AND THE GRANDMOTHERS' WORK

In 1985 a group of forensic scientists assembled by the AAAS went to Argentina to train local scientists in the archaeological techniques used to open graves, remove skeletons, and determine the cause of death. Dr.

Clyde Snow—a well-known forensic anthropologist from Oklahoma, who had participated in the work that led to the identification of Nazi scientist Mengele's remains in Paraguay—headed the team. Jorgelina de Pereyra, the mother of a disappeared young woman, had learned that her twenty-one-year-old daughter, Liliana, had been five months pregnant when she was abducted. The police had reported that Liliana had been killed in a shoot-out in July 1978 and that she had been buried in a particular cemetery. After the fall of the regime, Liliana's mother began to check the cemetery records for the physical characteristics of the NN buried in July 1978. Through the Grandmothers' connections she found out about the visiting forensic scientists and asked for Clyde Snow's help in identifying the remains of her daughter. The grave presumed to be that of Liliana was opened and the skeleton was examined.

Premortem records confirmed that the grave *was* Liliana's. But contrary to the assertions of the police, the postmortem studies revealed that Liliana had died from a close-range gunshot wound to the head. Her death, said Snow, had "all the markings of an execution." It was also determined, from a study of the pelvic bones, that she had given birth to a term or near-term infant, confirming reports already received from her fellow detainees in the ESMA camp. This was a breakthrough for the Grandmothers. It was now possible, if remains of pregnant women were found, to obtain scientific proof regarding the birth of their grandchildren and continue their search certain that their daughters had delivered in captivity.[65] Clyde Snow was hopeful as he presented the case of Liliana Pereyra at the trial of the juntas in 1985: "All this seems grim, but here at least, we have looked for death and found life. We were able to tell her mother that although her daughter is dead out there somewhere she has a grandchild. That opens the way for the Grandmothers of Plaza de Mayo to begin a search and possibly track down the child."[66]

Clyde Snow's work also provided evidence of the military's careful cover-up techniques for concealing the kidnapping of children. In September 1976 the Lanuscou family, two parents and three children, disappeared. When democracy returned, the Grandmothers were informed of a set of five NN graves that matched the date of disappearance of the family. Snow remembers:

I was giving a presentation in La Plata and at the end of it, this group of older women asked a question: Would it be possible, could we expect the bones of a fetus to disintegrate in a grave? I said no, fetal bones can last for centuries.

I could not figure out what that question was all about. But later on at the break, they explained. They talked about the Lanuscou case. The bones of the family had been exhumed but they did not find the bones of the youngest child, Matilde, six months old. They were told that the bones had disintegrated. I took the case and went through all the bones; we found the two older children, the mother and the father, but not a single bone of the child. We took a couple of bushels of sand and gravel that had been collected at the same time that the bodies had been exhumed and we sifted; we got some strainers and washed it. It took hours and hours. Every little speck of gravel and there was absolutely no evidence that there had been a child there.[67]

All that was found was a teddy bear, a pacifier, and a few other objects. "Matilde was never in that coffin. It's as simple as that," Snow told the judge in charge of the case. Later on, circumstantial evidence indicated that she had been given for adoption by the military, whose cover-up had been exposed.[68] Amelia Herrera de Miranda, the grandmother of the child, joined the Grandmothers of the Plaza de Mayo in their search for her granddaughter, strengthened by the hope that the girl was alive.

THE GRANDMOTHERS' GIFT TO SCIENCE

The support that the Grandmothers elicited from the international scientific community is unusual. A group of women with no scientific background, they used common sense and prodded scientists to develop the scientific tools that would put their work on a firmer footing. They offer an outstanding example of lay citizens enlisting scientists to work for human rights. It has become increasingly clear in our times that while presenting itself as "a neutral activity" based on rationality and objectivity, science in practice has traditionally been allied with the powerful and has represented the interests of an affluent white male elite. In our century the image of science has been tarnished by Hiroshima and by the obvious complicity of the scientific establishment in the nuclear arms race. Threats to the survival of the planet by technologies running amok—as well as the exploitation of genetics to modify life and control the future of our species—have made science appear to be an alienated and somewhat dangerous enterprise. In the midst of this dismal picture the use of science to support a worthy cause is indeed refreshing.

The scientists who assisted the Grandmothers have expressed their appreciation at being able to contribute to a cause that furthers justice and provides them the opportunity to fully engage, as whole human beings, in their work. Eric Stover muses:

What was so interesting was that it wasn't like this was just a scientific question. It was a humanitarian question in which people who felt strongly about retrieving their children wanted science to help them. In the cases of Coque Pereyra and of Estela's daughter, we were dealing at a level of intimacy that you don't normally deal if you are a lawyer or if you are there simply to make a technical report. You have to be present to absorb the emotion, either when the identification was made or to share the joy when a child was returned. It is very powerful. I used to say that the only time I got really depressed was when I would come back from a trip to Argentina after working with the Grandmothers for weeks, and somebody called me and invited me to play tennis.

Theirs was really the first case in which science was used to further human rights: scientists as detectives. Since then we have had forensic science exhuming graves and determining the cause of death of people in at least fourteen countries: Bolivia, Brazil, Chile, Venezuela, Peru, Colombia, Guatemala, El Salvador, Honduras, Mexico, Iraq-Kurdistan, Ethiopia, the Philippines, and the former Yugoslavia. So what started with the Grandmothers has turned into this whole idea of using the forensic sciences for humanitarian questions. Their contribution has clearly transcended the Argentine situation.

Victor Penchaszadeh, at the 1992 International Seminar on Affiliation, Identity, and Restitution—organized by the Grandmothers to celebrate their fifteen years of struggle—further commented:

We are here to analyze the role of science in the defense and promotion of human rights and specifically, on the genetic identification of the children kidnapped by the last military dictatorship. . . . Science is not "neutral" but it is influenced by the political and economic relationships in society, and in its turn it influences them through its applications. . . . In the United States, at the beginning of this century, racist and elitist ideas helped promulgate laws that allowed the involuntary sterilization of tens of thousands of people labeled as "asocials," "retarded," or "defective." . . . Nazi Germany raised the flag of "racial purity" based on the ignorance and distortion of the principles of genetics. . . . The most famous German scientists pressured and convinced politicians of the justness of their views and contributed to giving a "scientific" facade to genocide. . . . When Grandmothers Chicha Mariani and Estela Barnes de Carlotto asked me in New York in 1982 if it was possible to prove the identity of the children, having only grandparents and other relatives alive, they were making a social claim to the science of genetics. . . . The challenge inherent in that claim resulted, a few months later, in the first identification and restitution of one of the victims: Paula Logares. And this made it possible for human genetics, which for so long served death and backward interests, to serve life.[69]

Clyde Snow also credits the Grandmothers with the idea of using forensic science as a tool in human rights investigations:

Forensic science had not been used in human rights work. It really all started in Argentina. And the Grandmothers were instrumental in developing the idea. Personally, I had the privilege of recruiting young people in Argentina, of creating a team and having the satisfaction of doing something worthwhile. It brought me into a new area of work, and it opened a new world for me. Had the Grandmothers not come to my talk in La Plata and asked their question, I would have returned home and that would have been the end of it.

Snow's work in Argentina resulted in the creation of the Argentine Forensic Anthropology Team (EAAF), a group of young professionals who were mentored by Snow and have learned the techniques to be used for the exhumation and identification of remains. The only such organization in the world, the EAAF continues to work in Argentina; it has also worked in several other countries where human rights violations have made its expertise necessary.[70]

The Grandmothers have provided a model for laypeople and scientists working together, challenging the alienation of the scientific establishment and making it possible to imagine a different relationship between science and society. They have helped redeem science by offering a new type of partnership. The gift that the Grandmothers have given to science is really a gift to the world—to all those who desire a science that incorporates human values and is a positive and life-affirming force.

Grandmothers at work, looking at pictures of disappeared children and grandchildren (photo by Estelle Disch).

María Isabel Chorobik de Mariani (photo by Estelle Disch).

Elsa Pavón de Aguilar.

Otilia Lescano de Argañaraz.

Emma Spione de Baamonde.

Delia Giovanola de Califano with the pictures of her disappeared son and daughter-in-law.

Estela Barnes de Carlotto with picture of her kidnapped and murdered daughter.

Raquel Radío de Marizcurrena.

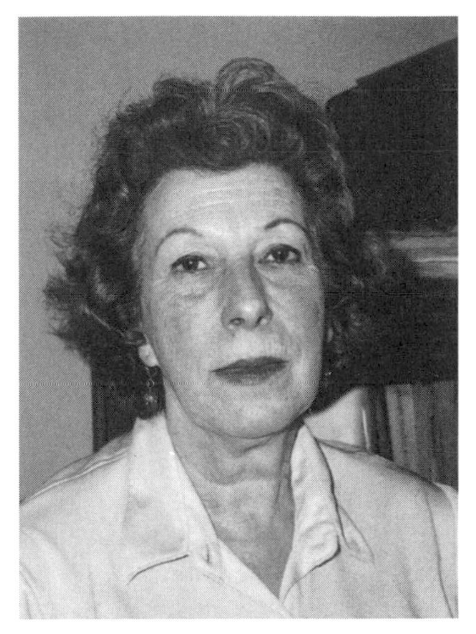

Amelia Herrera de Miranda.

Nélida Gómez de Navajas.

Elsa Sánchez de Oesterheld.

Argentina Rojo de Pérez with Mariana Pérez (sibling of child born in captivity).

Rosa Tarlovsky de Roisinblit.

Antonia Acuña de Segarra.

Reina Esses de Waisberg.

Alba Lanzillotto.

Nya Quesada.

Elena Santander (her found granddaughter is shown at right).

María Victoria Moyano (born in captivity, found when she was ten).

Berta Schubaroff.

Sonia Torres.

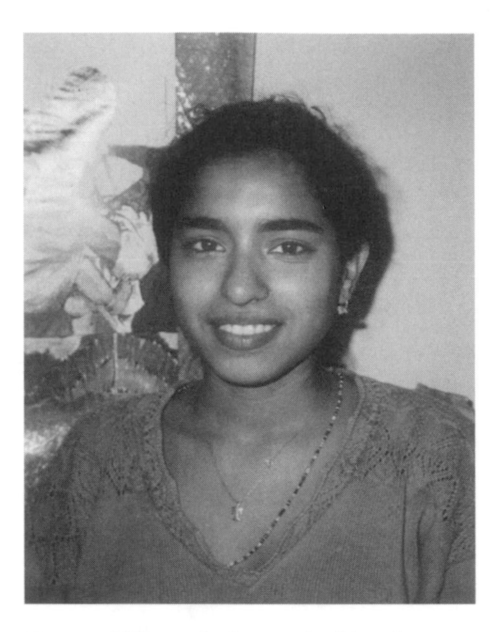

Tatiana Sfiligoy (kidnapped when she was four years old, found when she was eight).

Tania Waisberg (sibling of child born in captivity).

"Buscamos Dos Generaciones" (We Are Searching for Two Generations), poster (from the Grandmothers' collection).

"Niños Desaparecidos—Busquemoslos" (Disappeared Children—Let's Search for Them), award-winning poster by Jorge Proz (from the Grandmothers' collection). The daisy represents the family, with a missing petal.

"Pregnant Woman," poster in a Buenos Aires street (from the Grandmothers' collection).

"Restitución es regreso a la vida—Mi abuela me sigue buscando . . . díganle donde estoy" (Restitution is a return to life—My grandmother is looking for me . . . tell her where I am), poster (from the Grandmothers' collection).

Demonstration: "¿Donde están los centenares de bebes nacidos en cautiverio?" (Where are the hundreds of children born in captivity?) (from the Grandmothers' collection).

Demonstration: "Niños Desaparecidos" (Disappeared Children) (from the Grandmothers' collection).

Demonstration with policeman in front and poster of kidnapped child (from the Grandmothers' collection).

Bulletin board at Grandmothers' office: "Niños Localizados" (Found Children).

Grandmothers' handkerchief, with the logo of the Association: "Identidad—Familia—Libertad" (Identity—Family—Freedom) (photo by Estelle Disch).

FOUR

FROM TERROR TO RESISTANCE

I think those of us who decided to work with the Grandmothers have an easier time coping with what happened than those who stayed at home. Many people ended in mental hospitals or alcoholic or committed suicide. Silvina disappeared at 6:30 in the afternoon; by 7 P.M. I was already at the police station. Every day I would do at least one thing to find my daughter. One learns by doing. We did not know what to do until we started doing it.
Sonia Torres

During the 1970s, as political instability mounted, Argentine women were reminded more strongly than ever that their primary role was in the home and that as wives and mothers their function was to ensure conformity and obedience to the state. Isabel Perón's government had instituted a series of measures that reinforced the subordinate position of women in the family. The president herself had vetoed the "patria potestad," a law that would have given both parents the same legal rights over their children.[1]

Once the dictatorship was established, popular women's magazines launched what amounted to a psychological campaign designed to discredit human rights organizations and to rally women's support for the regime's economic and social policies. Articles denouncing "Marxist" infiltration in schools called on women to become the watchdogs against "foreign" ideologies. For example, one author, as she extolled Generals Videla and Viola and Minister of the Economy Martínez de Hoz, exhorted women to support the regime. She proclaimed: "The destiny of the country depends mostly on women. In our hands lies nothing more and nothing less than the education of our children. It is our struggle, our example, our interest in the affairs of the country that will help them to grow and mature. . . . Our duty is to participate."[2] In another well-known case, a leading women's magazine (*Para Tí*) published an interview with Thelma Dorothy Jara de Cabezas, mother of a disappeared young man, in which she denounced the human rights organizations for "using" her. She warned other mothers to be vigilant about their children so that they would not become dupes of the "subversives." It was later revealed that the "interview" had taken place while she was detained and tortured at the ESMA; she had never made the declarations attributed to her. The editors of the women's magazine clearly were directly connected to and complicitous with the repressive forces.[3]

Eventually, the disappearance of their loved ones galvanized many women into political action, leading some to question the traditional patterns of domination and submission in Argentine society. The Mothers of the Plaza de Mayo challenged the dictatorship and transformed their personal grief into political activism. The efforts of the regime to ensure docile compliance backfired as individual women joined together and transferred their concern and love for their own children to all the oppressed and persecuted. In so doing the Mothers were creating a new form of political participation, outside the traditional party structures and based on the values of love and caring. Motherhood allowed them to build a bond and shape a movement without men.[4]

Similarly the Grandmothers, many of whom first became active as members of the Mothers, stepped outside their traditional roles, refusing to be silent victims. With ingenuity and perseverance they searched for their missing grandchildren, whom they hoped the dictatorship had spared. Their protest had a clear, pragmatic focus: they wanted to find the children, return them to their legitimate families, and punish those responsible for the crimes committed. Though the Grandmothers always stated that their work was "for two generations"—both their children and grandchildren—their creative energy found its main outlet in the search for, the identification of, and the return of their grandchildren. They were mostly housewives and mothers, and their backgrounds and experiences varied widely. A few worked at typically female occupations, like teaching or social work. Grandmother Elena Santander describes them as a group of "common women who would otherwise never have met." Not interested in challenging the gender system and the sexual division of labor, the Grandmothers were committed to the preservation of life; and they demanded the right as "traditional" women to secure the survival of their families.[5]

Dealing with the feelings of helplessness that naturally followed the horrors they had endured presented an enormous challenge. As middle-aged and older women, a group usually devalued in Argentine society, they elicited little support and even less interest from the general public. But instead of becoming overwhelmed and paralyzed by the tragic events that struck their families, and instead of retreating into their private pain, the Grandmothers reached out to each other. Against the odds, they organized and succeeded in restoring a sense of meaning and justice to their lives and to the larger community. The Grandmothers drew on the memory of their children and sustained each other to overcome fear as they challenged the official story. Their success in finding some of the grandchildren gave them hope, and support from other groups reinforced their sense of empowerment. The Grandmothers' courage, the clarity of their thinking, and their insights about their own processes of transformation helped them resist the dictatorship and inspired many others to follow their example. By 1983 the general public's perception of the Grandmothers had changed dramatically; now highly respected, the group was often celebrated and cheered when appearing at public events.

FACING TERROR

Grandmother Nya Quesada remembers:

> People were totally frightened. It was horrible. That is why people did not protest, because they were paralyzed by fear. If everybody had protested, things might have gone differently. Let me give you an example. There was an episode called "La Noche de los Lápices" (the Night of the Pencils) in La Plata in September 1976. A group of high school students—fourteen to sixteen years old—were seized from their homes by the security forces. Their crime? They had taken part in a campaign for student bus subsidies. They were treated like terrorists, tortured, and killed. Fear spread like wildfire in La Plata. Everybody felt incredibly hopeless. If that could happen to adolescents, what could happen to the rest?[6]

The terror that the disappearances created was unmatched by anything the population had ever before experienced. Equating dissent with subversion had been extraordinarily effective in silencing even the mildest critics of the regime. *Por algo será* (there must be a reason) was a common expression used when people learned of disappearances.

Many coped with the stress by retreating into private worlds and turning inward. As they became separated from each other, their lives were controlled by the terror that influenced every thought, action, and feeling.

One sociologist, Guillermo O'Donnell, has called the tension of living with the continual experience of human rights abuses "the culture of fear."[7] The Grandmothers dealt with that fear permeating everyday life in many different ways. Elsa Sánchez de Oesterheld, whose whole family was destroyed by the dictatorship, was worried only about her surviving grandson, Miguel:

I never felt any fear for myself. The reason is a simple one. For me it was the same to live or to die. I thought that I was condemned, that I would be abducted or that I would be shot. The fear that I have not been able to overcome is the fear that something would happen to Miguel. To this day, when he is late or I don't know where he is I am afraid that something may have happened to him. That is the remnant of fear resulting from the terror that I lived through.[8]

When the military came to Berta Schubaroff's home looking for her son, and demanded at gunpoint to know where he was, she realized that her fear of death was gone:

I answered a question that I had asked myself all my life and about which I felt a lot of shame. The question was: Would I be willing to give my life for my children? I did not want to face that question. I have always been afraid of dying. But that day I was able to answer it. I realized that nothing was going to force me to tell where my son was. I felt a great happiness. I realized that they would get nothing from me. Let them kill me.[9]

Elena Santander describes how the fear came and went:

My lowest point was the day when I came into the office and I tore up the notebook with all the names and addresses of the Grandmothers. I was so petrified I said, "I do not want to have anything else to do with this group, do not bother me anymore." After two or three days I recovered my senses and I came back.

Among those who paid a heavy price was Raquel Marizcurrena, as her relatives gave in completely to fear:

After my son and his wife disappeared, I never again heard from any of my seven sisters or my brother. They all avoided us. It has been seventeen years since I last saw them. They were terrified that the same thing would happen to them.[10]

Haydée Lemos recalls a generalized sense of fear. Burning her daughter's books helped her relieve some of the anxiety:

Like many others, I burned books. They told us they were "subversive" books. I did not want to do it; when I looked at them I felt I should be reading them. But I had to burn them, since the police could come into the house at any moment. When democracy returned, I bought some of the books back. One was Eduardo Galeano's book *The Open Veins of Latin America.* It was one of the books that really helped me open my eyes.[11]

Otilia Argañaraz, a Grandmother active in Córdoba province, notes that an important way to move through the fear was to face it:

I cannot say that I have not felt fear. Fear is human. Luckily we did not hide under the bed crying. We went out to face the situation and fight and that has helped to counter the fear. In Córdoba we have the church against us; the archbishop is extremely reactionary. He closed the doors of the church on us while they were taking away our children. Now we are already well known, so hiding would not make any sense, even if one is afraid.[12]

But facing fear does not mean ending it. Rosa Roisinblit acknowledges that it is still a presence in her life:

I was very frightened. When I joined the Grandmothers and we met in coffeehouses to do our work we had to hide who we were. When they called the office and said they were going to bomb us, of course we were afraid. When I went abroad on behalf of the group I did not know if they would let me back into the country or if they would arrest me. Sometimes I think that even now something could happen. I don't think that I have totally overcome the fear. One gets used to it, though. The love for one's children and grandchildren, the need to do something, to work and get some results, is stronger than the fear.[13]

CHALLENGING THE OFFICIAL STORY

When the Grandmothers asked the authorities about the fate of their children and grandchildren, they were met with denial, evasion, and outright lies. The knowledge they had of their children, their own sources of information, and their personal experiences all told them that there was something amiss.

Ignacio Martín-Baró, a radical psychologist and Jesuit who was assassinated in El Salvador in 1989 for his commitment to the poor, described the "official story" that authoritarian regimes produce:

> Above all, the object is to create an official version of the facts, an "official story," which ignores crucial aspects of reality, distorts others, and even falsifies or invents still others. This official story is imposed by means of an intense and extremely aggressive display of propaganda, which is backed up even by all the weight of the highest official positions. . . . When, for whatever reasons, facts come to light that directly contradict the "official story," they are "cordoned off." . . . Public statements about the national reality, the reporting of violations of human rights, and, above all, the unmasking of the official story, of the institutionalized lie, are considered "subversive" activities—in fact, they are, since they subvert the order of the established lie.[14]

When the military took power in 1976 there was at first a general sense of relief in Argentina. The media, the political parties, and business interests all painted a rosy picture, and many believed that political stability and economic well-being were around the corner. But Estela de Carlotto rejected the takeover and the fantasies of progress and order that it promised. When one of her friends called her to celebrate the coup she bluntly told her, "You are totally wrong. This is an illegal occupation. There is nothing to celebrate. They are getting rid of a constitutional government. It is a terrible event and we will cry a lot about this. Very hard times are in store for us."[15] After her daughter Laura disappeared in 1977, Estela looked for her in vain for several months. When she was called in by the police to identify her daughter's body and was told that she had been killed in an armed confrontation, she did not believe their story: she accused them of killing Laura in cold blood. She was proved right. In 1985 the Argentine Forensic Anthropology Team determined that Laura had been killed execution-style after having been held in captivity for several months.[16]

Antonia Acuña de Segarra's three children disappeared in 1978. After her initial shock she contacted a lawyer about obtaining a writ of habeas corpus. He suggested that she wait before taking action, in case her children had simply moved without alerting her:

> But I could not be still. I felt I had only two options, to kill myself or to get out and search for my children. I presented several writs of habeas corpus, which were totally ignored. This was during the World Soccer championship and Argentina was trying to create a good image for the rest of the world—an image of a peaceful country where nothing strange was going on and where we were all happy. But many people disappeared in 1978, including my three children, their two spouses, and my two daughters' babies about to be born.[17]

When Elsa Pavón de Aguilar was repeatedly told by her brother-in-law, a policeman, that she would not be able to find her granddaughter, she steadfastly refused to believe him:

> He said, "You will not get her back. She is probably in the hands of the chief of the kidnapping operation. It is useless. Give it up." I told him no, that I would continue looking for her and that after I found her I would bring her to him so that he could see for himself.[18]

And she did find her granddaughter (see chapter 5).

Raquel Marizcurrena remembers her immediate reaction when her son and his pregnant wife were taken away:

> They had come to dinner at my house to celebrate his birthday. After the cake and everything, we started to play lotto. The bell rang; it was the police. Six men came in and said that they were searching for certain books. My son showed them the books that one of their friends had left. And the men said they had to go with them, that they would be back in an hour. I started to scream and cry. My husband and the others said, "Why are you crying? They will be back soon." I told them that they did not know what was going on, that they should read the papers, that they would not be back.

They also directly challenged the official story publicly. Berta Schubaroff describes one episode:

For five years every Sunday I had a booth in a park, in an artisan's fair. I had pictures of the disappeared, the pregnant women, the children. I distributed the materials of the Grandmothers. A woman tried to provoke me. She had her little girl with her and I said: "What if somebody comes and takes away your daughter, what would you have done?" She said that could not happen to her. I told her that those things did happen. She started to insult me and said we should leave the children with the families that raised them. It got really rough. The artisans from another booth had to come to defend me.

In *Powers of the Weak,* Elizabeth Janeway suggests that certain resources are available to the "powerless" if they have the courage to use them. A crucial power she names is *disbelief,* a refusal to accept the dominant, official versions of reality:

> Let us doubt, let us not take for granted, what the powerful say about events, their causality, their meaning and their importance. . . . Disbelief, then, signals something that the powerful fear, and slight as it may appear, we should not underestimate its force. It is, in fact, the first sign of the withdrawal of consent by the governed to the sanctioned authority of their governors, the first challenge to legitimacy.[19]

The Grandmothers had the courage and strength to believe in and define their own reality, at moments when confusion and fear were paramount. They thus kept alive the hope needed to pursue their work. Fueled by their anger at the crimes committed against them and using the power of disbelief, they were able to hold their ground and join with others to engage in their search. And as the stories about the regime began to be confirmed and the disappeared children located, their insight, suspicions, and mistrust of the "official story" were vindicated.

COMING TOGETHER

Mistrust of those in power, as Janeway points out, is a necessary first step; but it must be acted on and validated by others who share one's doubts. Once this begins, when links start to form between disbelievers, then the ground becomes fertile for the growth of a movement. As the Grandmothers started connecting and began building a new framework of belief, trust in themselves and each other increased. This helped make it possible for activism to emerge. Though some of the Grandmothers came from families actively interested in politics, they themselves, with few exceptions, had never taken part in public action of any sort. Speaking up, demanding accountability from government officials, and joining with others in protests and marches were new behaviors that came to seem routine as they gathered strength and inspiration from each other.

Berta Schubaroff remembers the rush of positive emotion when she first found the Grandmothers:

I first joined the Mothers; the Grandmothers did not exist yet. Then in 1979 I went to live in Spain and stayed there for five years. After I came back, I was rather depressed, feeling lonely, crying a lot, and one particular day it was raining and I was despondent. I found the Grandmothers' address in my address book. I went immediately to the office. When they opened the door I saw all this light coming into the dark hall and I heard the strong voices of strong women. I felt like the sun was rising. They received me well, they gave me tea and cookies, they asked me all sorts of questions. From that moment on I joined the Grandmothers. When I found the remains of my son after fourteen years, I was accompanied and surrounded by the Grandmothers. I felt as if the hand of a mother was around me. I felt protected. I was not alone.

The story of another grandmother inspired Nélida Gómez de Navajas to have hope and to begin to search for her grandchild:

I went to the Grandmothers' office to deliver a letter from a relative. They asked me if I had a family member disappeared. I told them about my daughter, who was two and a half months pregnant when she disappeared, and that I thought that she had probably had a miscarriage in the camp. Estela told me that her daughter had also been pregnant when she disappeared and that she knew that she had given birth to a child, in spite of the fact that she had lost two pregnancies under normal conditions. They explained to me that they knew there were children born in captivity and that they were looking for them. I immediately filed my case with them and have been a member for more than ten years.[20]

Amelia Herrera de Miranda, too, describes the importance of discovering that she was no longer alone:

I saw that others had gone through even worse things. I realized I was not the only one who was suffering. I said to myself: "The best thing here is to struggle together. All these other women are also suffering, there are many of us." And that gave me strength. I learned how to keep fighting. We are united here by our problems, our pain, and our hope. When I was alone, I was lost. I did not really understand what was going on.[21]

They actively tried to support and respect each other's pain. Antonia Segarra explains:

When we make public appearances and present our work it is our practice to speak in the name of all the Grandmothers. Not all the Grandmothers can travel and attend meetings, so it is our duty to represent them. Only if asked and after I have spoken about the work of the organization, will I give my personal testimony.

Rosa Roisinblit gives another example of this commitment to mutuality:

Our commitment here is for life, till the last day of our existence. We have several grandmothers here who have found their grandchildren and they continue working with the group. And I plan to do the same, after I find my grandchild.

OTHER SOURCES OF INTERNAL STRENGTH AND EMPOWERMENT

By mistrusting the official story and coming together as a group, the Grandmothers created a safe environment where they could vent painful feelings and, at the same time, challenge hopelessness and despair. Truth-telling, collaborative action, and linkages with other human rights groups all helped increase their sense of empowerment and hope. Feminist thinker Dorothy Dinnerstein distinguishes "open-eyed hope, which by definition embodies uncertainty and counsels action," from "blind hope, which is passive and shuns available fact."[22] "Open-eyed hope" describes well the Grandmothers' positive energy and clarity of spirit. A major source of that hope was the deep connection that many of the women had with their disappeared children. Because they cared for and trusted those children, the Grandmothers felt that their memory needed to be kept alive, their values upheld, and their idealism honored.

That motive is clear in Sonia Torres's account:

In the beginning what kept me going was the absence of my daughter and the need to find her. Afterward, when I realized I would not find her, it was the need to do something for her, to find her child and tell him or her who his or her parents were. They were not just regular parents, they were people who were willing to die for their ideas. After the first time my daughter was detained, I wanted to send her abroad. She said: "No, I am staying here. I have done nothing wrong. Why should I leave? If everybody that dissents leaves the country, what is going to happen here?"[23]

Berta Schubaroff recalls her relationship to her son and how the insults her daughter-in-law suffered in the camp for having a Jewish husband strengthened her determination to fight:

I was extremely attached to my son. He was very sweet, intelligent, an excellent student. Always concerned about social justice. In elementary school they wanted to reward him with special responsibilities because of his competence. He refused, he said he would not accept a leadership role, that he believed in collaborative efforts. And he wrote a letter to the teacher, explaining his point of view. I still have that letter.

The guards at the camp asked my daughter-in-law if it did not turn her stomach to be married to a Jew and they told her they were going to kill all those "shitty Jews." When I heard that I felt like a wall started to grow inside me. I felt strong and hard like a brick wall and decided that they would never be able to demolish this wall. That I was ready to fight these savages until the day I die.

After the death of her daughter, Estela de Carlotto committed herself to activism for the rest of her life:

After I buried my daughter, a new level of struggle started. People sometimes think that because one recovers the body one will say, "All right, enough, this is the end of the story." Quite the contrary. My work was just beginning. I started to search for the murderers of my daughter and to search for my grandson. I found out that my daughter in the camp said to her friends, "As long as my mother lives she is never going to forgive the military." And she was right. She knew me better than I did. If somebody had told me then that I would dedicate my life to searching for the truth and struggling against historical amnesia, I would not have believed it.

Nya Quesada attributes her persistence to the hope she still carries of seeing her daughter alive:

I have the feeling that I owe it to her, to keep going on. And a part of me still keeps hoping, having the hope of seeing her again. It is a hope with no basis. Reality is different and sometimes one does not want to see reality. I know that many years have gone by and I understand it is a stupid hope. Other Mothers have a different perspective. I respect them. But each person has to find how to best cope and go on living.

Chicha Mariani, who had a close relationship to her son, felt that he was instrumental in helping her understand the wider social reality:

My son awakened my social conscience. It was through his example and the conversations we had that I understood about social issues, poverty, exploitation. Once I tried to warn him about his activism and he told me that yes, I had given birth to him, but his life belonged to him now. I fought with him; we had long discussions, me trying to stop him. When he was being chased and we wanted him to go abroad, he refused and stuck to his ideals.[24]

For Amelia Herrera de Miranda, finding the remains of her daughter and grandchildren was extremely important. It confirmed that her daughter was dead and allowed her to focus on finding her surviving granddaughter:

It was not a happy moment but it put an end to the uncertainty of not knowing what had happened. She was dead, there it is, here are the remains. Now, I had to ask "Where is my granddaughter?" and I started to fight for her. I will search for her until the last day of my life. I will work so that this does not happen to anybody else. The disappearance of people is the cruelest thing that can happen to anybody. So one has to speak up; otherwise one becomes an accomplice.

Argentina Rojo de Pérez gathered strength in a number of ways:

I never had any psychological help. I made myself strong because I knew I had to take care and fight for my remaining granddaughter. I survived because of her. Also, after the disappearance of my son, writing, putting my thoughts down, helped. It was like a form of therapy.[25]

Delia Califano, too, reflects on the source of her resiliency:

What gives me strength? The memory of my son and my daughter-in-law. They were both wonderful. I cannot leave a child of theirs alone in the world. Some times I don't feel like fighting anymore. I am seventy years old, I get tired. I only want to stay home. But when I think of them I gather strength. It is the least I can do.[26]

Alba Lanzillotto talks about the respect she felt for her disappeared younger sisters to whom she acted as a mother, and describes their ongoing presence in her life:

I respect their militancy because they chose it in full conscience as thinking adults. I did not agree with them in every point but I respect them because these two young women had everything, came from a comfortable background, and became political activists. They went through a big change and they devoted themselves to a cause in which they deeply believed. They abandoned an easy and leisurely life. They were not in need for themselves but they had a sense of responsibility and obligation towards others. After all that has happened, I learned to understand and value my sisters even more. They would have been forty-six years old now. They had a lot to give to the world. They are always present in my family, they are still with us, never absent. My daughter loved them and she always remembers them. They are a part of our lives and we are very close to their children.[27]

Those occasions when their efforts succeeded were consistently mentioned by the Grandmothers as among the most exhilarating and empowering experiences of their lives. Having their hunches confirmed, actually seeing and touching children who had been disappeared for years, provided an incredible boost to their morale. Bringing the children back to their original families gave them a sense that some measure of justice could, after all, be achieved and that their extraordinarily demanding work was worth the toll it had taken on their lives.

Raquel Marizcurrena worked on the case of Pablito Moyano, a child found years after his disappearance at the age of one:

One of the most beautiful moments of our work is when we find one of the children. We had published the pictures of the disappeared children in a magazine. An acquaintance called me, having recognized Pablito. He had disappeared as a baby and now he was six years old. He had the same face, the same big eyes, the bushy eyebrows, the long lashes. It was him. When we took his grandmother to meet him, he recognized her, he threw himself in her arms. It was a fantastic moment. It almost did not seem possible.

More generally, Antonia Segarra reflects on their years of hard work and the satisfaction they derive when finding the children:

The fifty-four children that we have found are the result of much sacrifice. But it is such a joy to see the children with their true families. Even when we do not know a child personally, it is beautiful. It gives us so much happiness, I can barely describe how it feels. It is as if each child carries a little piece of us.

Like the other Grandmothers, Reina Esses de Waisberg's belief in the importance of the children knowing that they were not abandoned by their parents gives her strength:

Every time we find a child it is as if I found mine. We fight so hard because the disappeared children have to know that they were not thrown away, that their mothers did not abandon them, that they were conceived with love. That they were wanted. I know this because of my son and his companion. They were very happy when they told me that they expected their second child.[28]

EXTERNAL SUPPORT

The expressions of solidarity that the Grandmothers received from their families and from other groups working for social justice, both in Argentina and abroad, also empowered and vitalized them. Elena Santander says:

I was lucky to have supportive family and friends. They understood what was going on and they were very happy when we found the child. My daughter and my son came from Brazil to help me. Having my family at my side made all the difference. We have had support from many different quarters: not only the other human rights groups but gays, people with AIDS, prostitutes. During the trial of the military while I was in line waiting for the doors to open, I met a woman who said she knew who I was (I was wearing the handkerchief [characteristic of the Grandmothers] on my head) and that she fully supported us. She said she was the president of the prostitutes' organization. She told me: "The only thing I want to ask you is that you do not call the military 'sons of bitches,' because we bitches do not give birth to such monsters." I thought that was fabulous. I never forgot what she said. She still goes to all the marches.

Nélida de Navajas describes a similar experience:

One of the most beautiful things that came out of my work with the Grandmothers was learning that there was so much interest and solidarity from people in other parts of the world. It was an extraordinarily positive experience. We have had support from the women's movement, from the CHA [Comité Homosexual Argentino], even the transsexual groups. We need to support each other. I hope that the younger generation will carry that vision and that we will be able to pass on what we have learned. A legacy of solidarity.

Their successful searches, the founding of the National Genetic Data Bank, their ability to influence legislation dealing with children's rights, and the support they received helped give the Grandmothers the determination to continue their work without wavering. Taking responsibility for their situation and dealing with it to the best of their abilities contributed to their strength.

The dynamic at work here has been articulated by Judith Lewis Herman, a psychiatrist who directs training at the Victims of Violence Program at the Cambridge Hospital, in Cambridge, Massachusetts. Drawing on her twenty years of practice with women who have suffered sexual abuse, she notes that while survivors of rape, war, and other trauma are not responsible for the injury that was done to them, they are responsible for their recovery: "Paradoxically, acceptance of this apparent injustice is the beginning of empowerment. The only way that the survivor can take full control of her recovery is to take responsibility for it. The only way she can discover her undestroyed strengths is to use them to their fullest."[29]

The Grandmothers became precisely such survivors. In 1986 they stated:

Our work has not been easy. We started from scratch in October of 1977 in the midst of generalized terror. We were hurting like an open wound. If today we had to describe the predominant feeling of that time in one word, apart from pain, we could call it IMPOTENCE. . . . We discovered that we had to walk alone, that we had to invent our paths, to look for unknown methods, as unknown as the horror in which we were living. . . . In spite of the silence of some, the vacillations of others, the indifference of many, with the help of the people we will keep searching tirelessly for the hundreds of disappeared children to return them to their true homes, because only then will they return to life. It is a duty toward them, toward their martyred parents, toward the Argentine children that have lost their sense of safety, and toward the 30,000 disappeared who demand justice.[30]

The Grandmothers engaged in truth-telling despite the terror that dominated life in their country, and they refused to believe the lies that the regime foisted on the population. They created a place in which mutual cooperation and shared purpose enabled them to nourish their spirits and move toward empowerment instead of despair. Love for their children and the exhilaration of finding some of their grandchildren sustained them through their struggle. And solidarity from other groups made them believe that other people cared and that their message would eventually be heard.

THE ROLE OF MEN IN THE WORK OF THE GRANDMOTHERS

As the Grandmothers came together to build their organization, their husbands, sons, and other male members of their families generally played a supportive role, without directly participating in the work of the group. The traditional gender arrangement (women in the background and men actively involved in the political arena) was reversed as the Grandmothers put themselves in the foreground. It was not, however, their intent to exclude men. The Grandmothers expressed various views on the role of men in their movement. For some it was the greater vulnerability of men that kept them in the background; others thought that men had less ability to cope with pain; still others saw the need for men to earn a living as the reason for their keeping a low profile. Often the Grandmothers mentioned the specialness of the mother-child relationship in explaining the women's greater involvement:

Berta Schubaroff remembers:

> When our country was taken over by the military and they started to torture, maim, and kill, women started to scream our pain, because they had taken away the most precious thing in our lives. We decided to get out into the streets, precisely because as women we were the most despised group. We did not want our husbands and sons to join us because they would have been endangered.

Sonia Torres concurs:

> We thought that men would be more vulnerable, that the security forces would not dare attack or torture women. We were wrong, they kidnapped the first Mother and others too. But also, I think motherhood gives women a special quality; fatherhood is more of a secondary quality. A mother would take the food out of her mouth for her child. I do not think that men are prepared to do as much.

Raquel Marizcurrena, one of whose sons disappeared, expresses similar views about the greater vulnerability of men:

> We women went alone to the Plaza, because it would have been too dangerous for the men. We feared that they would arrest them immediately. But the men were behind us, supporting us and keeping an eye on us. I was afraid that something would happen to my other son because he has always been supportive of my work. I remember that Azucena Villaflor's husband and son

were often there; her son would come to the Plaza and would say to his mother, please don't always stand in front, be a little less obvious.

But Nya Quesada thinks that men's greater difficulty coping with pain played a role in their relative passivity:

I think that men do not have as much resiliency as women. Many people ask us, where were the men? I believe this has something to do with the ability to stand pain. Men do not have the strength that women have. They suffer tremendously, of course, and love their children as much, but mothers do not give up, they keep looking for them. They want the whole world to know what happened to their children. My husband died after two years because he could not take it anymore. I know many cases of men that died because of their enormous grief. If they ever bother to collect statistics, that is what they will find.

Amelia Miranda agrees though her husband, Juan, was one of the few men who became active in the Grandmothers' organization; he worked with the investigation team until he became seriously disabled:

He fought hard for our children, until he got sick. For many men, the pain of the disappearance of their children was too much, they could not take it. I think that women are more persistent. We women went out to the streets to scream and protest. Men also suffered a lot but they kept their pain inside. Our work is like the ant's work, like housework, very slow, every day, little things that pile up. You do not see it while it is happening but after many years the children are grown, the house is in order. Men are more impatient, they want to fight, to get results right away. Women are more resilient, are in it for the long run.

The thoughts of Otilia Argañaraz run along the same vein:

I think men wear the pants but it is women who run the show. Giving birth is so painful and at the same time it is such an exhilarating experience that from the moment children are born one turns into a lioness to defend them. The happiness to have a child after so much physical suffering makes you ready for anything. Fathers seemed more broken by what happened.

Even my brothers tell me to this day: "I envy you for being so involved. I could not do it."

There were practical considerations as well. For Antonia Segarra, living in Mar del Plata and commuting frequently to work with the Grandmothers in Buenos Aires, her husband's earning a living made it possible for her to become an activist:

My husband is the one who stayed home. We needed money to be able to travel and do all the things that had to be done. He had to keep working. I think that is the hardest role.

However, Alba Lanzillotto believes that women's greater capacity for activism was responsible for the Grandmothers' leading role:

In this country when things get done it is because of the women. In the teachers' union, it is women. In the church, who does all the work? The women. Here, the grandmothers, not the grandfathers. They say that the men had to work and that they were afraid they would be abducted, but I think it is because women take the initiative. They are the ones who are more torn apart when something happens to their children. Women are stronger and more likely to act. There are many women in all the human rights groups here. Sometimes it is men who initiate projects but the women have the staying power.

Whatever the reasons that kept men in the background, the Grandmothers stepped into the public arena and participated fully in the blossoming of the human rights movement. In the process, they transformed themselves from "traditional" women defined by their relationships with men (mothers, wives, daughters) into public protesters working on behalf of the whole society.

THE PERSONAL IS POLITICAL

Transforming powerlessness into social action, combining a practical outlook with the larger vision of a society in need of thorough change, and striving for justice, these "common women" irreversibly widened the field of politics and helped break down the boundaries between private and public. As mothers and grandmothers, they reacted to the attacks on their families by appropriating public space, challenging the notion that mothering is restricted to the private world.

Feminist theorist Sara Ruddick has written about the "demands" that are required by the practice of mothering: preserving life, nurturing offspring, and shaping children's growth in ways that are acceptable to the mother's social group. As a corollary to the distinction between birthing and mothering, Ruddick makes the point that all mothers are "adoptive": "To adopt is to commit oneself to protecting, nurturing, and training particular children. Even the most passionately loving birthgiver engages in a social, adoptive act when she commits herself to sustain an infant in the world."[31] As "adoptive" mothers of their grandchildren, the Grandmothers wanted to continue the mothering work that had been brutally interrupted by the military regime. Their commitment to protect, nurture, and train their children's children was a statement about the continuity and promise that each new life represents.

Because the Grandmothers' Association is a women-led organization, the question inevitably arises: Are the Grandmothers feminists? For that matter, what does "feminism" *mean* in Latin America? In their important article analyzing the regionwide feminist *Encuentros* convened biannually since 1981, Nancy Saporta Sternbach, Marysa Navarro-Aranguren, Patricia Chuchryk, and Sonia E. Alvarez write of "feminism*s*" because it is difficult "to generalize across countries in a region as diverse as Latin America when discussing any sociopolitical phenomenon." They argue that Latin American feminisms, forced to deal with state repression and extreme economic exploitation, have developed a solid political base that sets them apart from feminist movements in more affluent parts of the world. Feminists in Latin America, who have had to confront militarism, understand that "the dictatorship, which institutionalizes social inequality, is founded on inequality in the family."[32]

Latin American feminisms call for a revolution in everyday life, one that will challenge class and race privileges as well as the patriarchal sex-gender system. A key theme for Latin American feminists has been their relationship to the overall struggle for social justice—particularly to the *movimientos de mujeres*, women's grassroots groups, which organize to provide for the basic necessities of life and usually do not make gender oppression central to their analysis. The dialogue with women active in these *movimientos* is a rich source of ideas and challenges that keep the definition of Latin American feminisms fluid and constantly under revision.[33]

None of the Grandmothers called herself a feminist, though some, like Elsa Oesterheld, express enthusiasm for the struggle for women's equality:

I was totally disillusioned about humanity until I met the women's movement. It has given me an injection of hope; I have faith again. That is something incredibly new and people have not yet realized what it means. I believe that this will bring unforeseeable possibilities for the future. I am sorry I will not live another fifty years to see how the participation of women will change the world. The next century is going to be the century of women.

Elena Santander also was clear about the positive energy of the women's movement, but she saw the dangers of becoming an activist:

I like it when women defend their rights. The rights of women and of all human beings. The right to a home, to a fair salary, education for their children. Here we have the Argentine Women's Union, and I go to their celebration for Women's Day. They organize trips to Cuba, they fight for the rights of all women. But I am afraid that if women become part of political movements, they will lose the most important thing they have, which is their families. They may lose their own world. I have seen this. Many of us with husbands could not give them much attention because we were always working with the Grandmothers. It happened to me. I lost the companion I had because I abandoned everything for this work.

Amelia Miranda reflects on her marriage and on the roles of men and women:

I believe that a woman who works should have the same rights as a man. Equal pay for equal work. And if she has children, she has to have maternity benefits and a leave of absence. Women deserve opportunities. I do not think that all women should be at home washing dishes and having babies. If one has other interests, one should be encouraged to cultivate them. In fact I believe that if we had more women in leadership roles we would have a better society. I don't call this "feminism," I call it "justice." Regarding marriage, I am one of whose who got married forever. I do want to be listened to and respected, I do like freedom, but I do not want to get rid of men as some feminists do. We are not perfect, and neither are they. We all have our limitations and God made us male and female. I think that is how it has to be.

Bertha Schubaroff concurs with Amelia:

The struggles that women are carrying out in all fields are truly important. We are as good as men, but not better than them. Without men, we would miss something very important—love, sexuality, companionship. I could never separate women from men. However, I have a sister who never married, has a great profession, has done research, has a life full of friends, earns good money. It is not necessary to have children and a traditional home. She chose other things. That is the point, that one should be able to choose what one wants.

Reina Waisberg expresses her appreciation for the work of women activists:

I like the women's movement in Argentina. I believe that women must have the same rights as men. I support liberalizing abortion. It makes me very angry that the Catholic Church is against it. When I was eighteen years old my mother died of an illegal abortion and I had to take care of my siblings. She would not have died if abortion had been legal.

The Grandmothers have taken their message to national and international women's conferences where they have sought (and received) support for their work and demanded a condemnation of the amnesty laws and the presidential pardons that were given to the members of the juntas. At the VIII Encuentro Nacional de Mujeres held in Tucumán in 1993, Grandmothers Amelia Miranda and Otilia Argañaraz spoke about their experiences as women and mothers whose children and grandchildren were victims of the dictatorships. They reminded the audience—over 6,000 women from all over the country—of the "thousands of women, our daughters, who fought heroically for a better country" and who gave birth and nourished life in the regime's secret detention camps.[34]

In Latin America, at the end of the twentieth century, new social movements have emerged—movements that go beyond traditional political structures and institutions. In particular, the growing participation of women has clearly changed the established models of political mobilization.[35] People speak of a "new form of politics," of a new conception of what is political, of a transformation of the public arena. In Argentina, the image of the Grandmothers as the guardians of the cycle of life has entered this shared understanding with unprecedented force and has become a fixture of the new political landscape.

FIVE

FINDING THE CHILDREN

I want to touch you and kiss you. You are my mother's sister and only one year older; you must have something of my mother in you.
A found child after being returned to her family

The Grandmothers used a simple approach to gain information about the disappeared grandchildren: they appealed to the conscience and ethical sense of the general public to help them in their work. In April 1982, for the first time in Argentina, a list with the names of the children published by CLAMOR appeared in one of the main Buenos Aires newspapers. The publication of the list, whose signatories called for information to be provided about the children, had a secondary purpose: to show the Argentine military that the Grandmothers had the support of one of the most respected institutions on the continent, the Archdiocese of São Paulo.[1] Hundreds of people called the Grandmothers' office, offering information and suggestions.

The "established doctrine" of separating the children from their families (see chapter 3) was, in some cases, too much even for the repressors. A survivor from the camps reported that a member of the military, after abducting a young couple, disobeyed orders and left their small child with the janitor of the building where they lived.[2] Elsa Oesterheld, a Grandmother of the Plaza de Mayo whose husband was a well-known writer, confirmed that "exceptions" occurred:

The police went to my oldest daughter's house. She was not at home and they took her son, Martín, three and a half years old. The orders had been to disappear the child also, to turn him into a NN, but the man in charge of the operation admired my husband and did not follow the orders. He took the child to my husband who was then in prison. My husband gave him my parent's address and asked him to bring the child to them. That is how I recovered Martín.[3]

In 1983, with the return of democracy, the Grandmothers launched a campaign designed to recruit the support of the Argentine people. The Grandmothers plastered the city with posters and distributed thousands of leaflets with the children's pictures. Radio and TV spots highlighted the search for the missing children, while newspaper and magazines ran story after story. By 1997 the Grandmothers' Association had received over 8,000 anonymous tips and pieces of information: fifty-eight children had been identified, thirty-one were reunited with their biological families, thirteen stayed with their adoptive parents, eight children were found murdered, and six cases were in the courts.

RESTITUTION

Identifying the children is the first step in the laborious process of reuniting the children with their families. The Grandmothers see this reunion as an act of truth, a *vuelta a la vida* (return to life) that will restore to them their proper identity, allowing them to grow up without secrets or lies. The Grandmothers often equate the condition of the children living under false identities with slavery. Although Argentina abolished slavery in 1813, the women point out that there are hundreds of Argentine children currently living with people who separated them from their legitimate families and who hide from them their origins and their history.

The Grandmothers use the term "restitution" to describe the process of reunifying the children with their families of origin. Restitution is not simply an act by which a child meets with her or his family. It is a complex process requiring attention at all levels: individual, familial, and social. Estela de Carlotto remembers crying when the first restitution, that of Paola Logares, took place. During her childhood Estela had been temporarily separated from her mother, and she recalled the anguish she had felt. She sympathized with Paola's initial negative reaction. But then

I realized that my situation had been different. My mother was truly my mother, while in the case of Paola, she was being separated from those who had stolen her and hidden her history from her. My initial reaction was the conventional one, to say "poor little ones," we may be hurting them; but as we later learned, the separation of the found children from the perpetrators does not create a second trauma.[4]

Very little was known in the early 1980s about the dynamics of restitution and its possible effects on the children. To their credit, the Grandmothers always insisted that extreme caution be used in making decisions that affected the living arrangements of the found children. Accordingly, the Grandmothers worked with psychologists, physicians, and lawyers to create an interdisciplinary team that would enable them to deal with the multifaceted, complex process. Working with these professionals has helped them establish the best possible conditions for the healthy psychosocial development of the found children.[5]

The Grandmothers point out that these children have not been abandoned: they have been illegally appropriated, and they carry in their psyches the traumas of their kidnapping and of their mothers' torture. The Grandmothers believe that to heal from this trauma, the children need to return to their "ecological nests," so that they can grow up with the love and security that their legitimate families offer them. However, they also believe that when the children were adopted in good faith by families not involved in the repression, it is possible to fashion an extended family that will benefit all involved. Grandmother Reina Esses de Waisberg explains her views on the restitution process:

If I find my grandson or my granddaughter and he has been with a decent couple who adopted him without knowing that he was the child of disappeared, I will let the child stay with them. I would want us to visit and the child has to know that he has a sister, that he has a biological family and that his parents did not throw him away. But if he is with a couple who participated in the repression, I will fight until my last breath to have my grandchild come and live with us.[6]

Her granddaughter, Tania, was fifteen months old when her parents were abducted; her mother was two months pregnant. She was left in the streets with Reina's name and telephone number attached to her. Tania, now twenty years old, believes that

Restitution is obviously a very difficult process, but is necessary. The truth about one's origins is essential. If one is lied to about that, how can one believe anything else one is told? I asked my grandmother to join the Grandmothers because what they are doing is so important and I wanted somebody from my family to work with them. If my sister or brother ever appears, I know that it will not be easy. I will probably start by telling him or her about everyday things, simple things, and about the other grandparents who have already died.[7]

Many misconceptions have arisen about what the process means. Chicha Mariani explains:

Many people believe that we have been searching for the children to bring them to our homes, as if we had "won" something. In contrast, I have always thought of restitution as a return to the children of what is rightfully theirs. Not restitution of the children to us but an offering to the children of what is theirs. Each case is different because each child is in a different situation. In our early days, we had several children who were reunited with their families without the intervention of the judicial system. And it worked fine. We spoke with the families, we encouraged them to work things out between themselves, keeping in mind the best interests of the child. Other times the judges intervened, but it was a very low-key and simple procedure. If the family was not involved in the repression, the simplest and safest approach was to get together and talk things over.[8]

The case of Tamara Arze provides an example of "talking things over." In 1975, two-year-old Tamara was left with neighbors after her mother, Rosa Mery Riveros, was kidnapped by the police. Although Rosa Mery repeatedly asked about the fate of her daughter, she was denied any information. In 1981 she was freed and she went into exile in Switzerland. From there, she contacted the Grandmothers and asked them to search for her daughter. As a result of their investigation the Grandmothers found the child in 1983. The family that had taken care of Tamara had told the child, when she was six years old, that she was not their daughter. When the Grandmothers approached them, the family agreed, with sadness and after extensive discussion, that if the child's mother was alive, Tamara should be with her. Rosa Mery sent a cassette to Tamara telling her what had happened and explaining that she had not abandoned her, that they had been forcefully separated, and that she had tried to find her. After a lengthy telephone conversation,

Tamara, then nine years old, declared that she wanted to live with her mother. The Grandmothers took Tamara to Lima, Peru, where she met Rosa Mery. Chicha Mariani recalls:

> I witnessed the meeting between Tamara and her mother and the first few days of Tamara in that new situation. . . . From that moment we started to realize that the restitution of the children was not merely an act of justice. The most important thing was what we could give back to Tamara. . . . Tamara's mother told us that the first night, after playing with her and giving her a bath, she put her to bed. While Tamara was sleeping and while she caressed her hair, she smelled an odor that felt strangely familiar. It took her fifteen minutes to discover, surprised, that it was the smell that newborn babies have after being breast-fed by their mothers.[9]

The child understood the complexity of her situation clearly, commenting, "What happens is that I have two families, my own family and the family that raised me."[10] The family that raised her gave Tamara a big bouquet of flowers for Rosa Mery, as a sign of their desire to establish a meaningful connection with her. While living in Europe, Tamara still manages to visit and remain in touch with her family in Argentina.

In an effort to make Argentine society understand the process, the Grandmothers organized public education sessions. In a 1988 conference on the disappeared children and restitution, they addressed their opponents. With what seems to be only the best of intentions, some critics promote a "hands-off" policy of leaving the children where they are—"so that they don't suffer"—that in effect turns the victims into victimizers. They claim that if the children seem happy and well-adjusted, taking them away from their adoptive families amounts to a "second trauma."[11] This facile, reductive view greatly concerns the Grandmothers because it ignores the suffering that was inflicted by the kidnappings and assigns no blame to the appropriators. Most of all, such an approach errs in focusing on the children only in the present moment, as if history had not happened—as if their situation had not begun with a crime that has grave implications for their future and their rights.[12]

The concept of "psychosocial trauma" developed by Ignacio Martín-Baró can help us understand the restitution process. He believed that when an injury that affects people has been produced, nourished, and maintained through a certain set of social relations, then individual solutions are not effective. The social context responsible for the injury has to be taken into account. A new "social contract" to heal the trauma is needed, incorporating individual and sociopolitical factors into the equation.[13] In the case of the disappeared children, their loss of identity represents a trauma affecting not only their individual lives but also their relationship with society. For this relationship to be restored, the social distortions that took place need to be exposed. Restitution brings into focus the trauma's social dimension, as it provides the wider context for each individual story. Truth and justice must be part of the picture, if the children are to construct a meaningful future for themselves as individuals and as members of society.

OBSTACLES TO RESTITUTION

When a child has been found, the Grandmothers begin with negotiations between the two families; but if those discussions reach a dead end, then the judicial system becomes involved. Legal proof of the children's identity is needed to settle the disagreement and decide on their future. Many of Argentina's current judges were appointed during the repression, and in the Grandmothers' experience, they have seldom behaved fairly and professionally. With few exceptions, the procedures drag on and frequently bog down in minutiae, leading to long delays before any kind of resolution is achieved.

Often judges have disqualified themselves from the cases or adopted a passive attitude. The general attitude of the judiciary can be deduced from an internal memo leaked to the press in which Dr. Augusto César Belluscio, a member of the Argentine Supreme Court, criticized the restitution of a child to her family of origin, calling the process a "brainwashing operation worthy of the Muscovite psychiatric establishment." Belluscio also asserted that the child's relationship with the adoptive family was more important than her biological affiliation.[14]

In several cases, the judicial delays allowed the kidnappers to go underground or to escape to other countries with the children. Carla Rutila Artés and her mother, Graciela, were imprisoned in a clandestine detention camp in 1976. While the child's mother is still missing, in 1983 the Grandmothers were able to locate the child: she was living under a false identity with Eduardo Alfredo Ruffo, a member of the sinister SIDE and one of the most sadistic torturers at the detention camp where the two had been taken. When Ruffo realized that he had been found, he used his police connections to go underground with his wife and Carla. Hundreds of posters with their pictures, plastered in the streets of Buenos Aires, called for the citizens to help in the search. When Ruffo was finally arrested, he was carrying a false passport that would have enabled him to take Carla out of the country. Carla was eventually returned to her grandmother.[15]

In a February 1986 meeting with President Alfonsín, the Grandmothers delivered a set of demands that addressed the delays and obstacles they were encountering in their legal work and the consequences of these delays for the children's mental and physical well-being.[16] One particularly lengthy case that achieved international notoriety was that of Ximena Vicario. Under the headline "Adoption Dispute in Argentina," a calculatedly sensational photograph of Ximena Vicario crying in the arms of her adoptive mother, Susana Siciliano, appeared in a U.S. newspaper.[17] The text accompanying the photo grossly oversimplified the facts. Ximena, who had been abducted with her mother when she was nine months old, was subsequently left in an orphanage with a tag saying "My name is Ximena Vicario and I am the daughter of *guerrilleros*." The Grandmothers located her in 1983. She had been illegally adopted by Siciliano, who worked in the institution where she had been left. Ximena's grandmother proposed to Siciliano that they come to an agreement by which both would be involved in raising the child, but Siciliano refused. In 1987, four years after she was located, genetic testing established her origin and the judges ordered the child restituted to her family. Siciliano was charged with hiding the true identity of the child and providing false information in the adoption proceedings.

For the next nine months, Ximena lived with her maternal grandmother, reestablishing the connection with her family. However, the "adoptive" mother, with the support of influential members of the press, launched a media campaign to recover the child and appealed to the Supreme Court. In 1989 the Court issued a ruling based on an antiquated law by which grandparents or other relatives could not be parties in disputes regarding a child's custody. The lawyer appointed to represent the child—Dr. Carlos Tavares, who had been General Videla's defense lawyer in the trial of the ex-commanders—recommended that Ximena be returned to Siciliano, but the child's expressed desires and her family's model behavior led the judges to agree to let Ximena stay with her grandmother. Nevertheless, Siciliano was given weekly visitation rights under police surveillance; during those visits, she constantly denigrated Ximena's parents. Ximena, then fourteen years old, wrote to the judge in charge of her case, listing twelve reasons why she did not want to see Siciliano any more. Among them, she noted that Siciliano had lied to her about her origins and had attempted more than once to take her out of the country. The case reached an impasse. Left without other recourse, the Grandmothers brought the case to the UN Human Rights Commission to alert the international human rights community that the rights of the child and her family were being violated. Only in 1991, eight years after the Grandmothers had located the child, did a judge finally annul the adoption and make it possible for Ximena to recover her history, her identity, and her real name.[18]

THE CHILDREN

"I No Longer Hide What Happened to Me"

In October 1977, four-year-old Tatiana Ruarte Britos and her three-month-old sister, Laura Malena Jotar Britos, were kidnapped along with their parents. The police denied this, claiming they had found the children abandoned on the street. Even though Tatiana knew her full name and the name of her sister, the children were separated, sent to two different orphanages, and labeled NN. No efforts were made to find their family. After six months a judge gave provisional custody of the younger child to a married, childless couple, Inés and Carlos Sfiligoy. When the couple found out the child had a sister, they applied and obtained custody of her, too, thinking it inhumane that the children be separated.

But the Sfiligoy family soon began to suspect the true nature of the adoption. Tatiana had mentioned that her mother, sobbing and with her head covered by a hood, had been taken away by a group of "mean men." They contacted the judge to inquire about the origins of the children, but he dismissed their concerns. In 1980 the Grandmothers, who had been investigating the case, convinced the judge to arrange for a meeting between one of the grandmothers and the children. Tatiana Sfiligoy, now twenty years old, remembers the meeting:

I was seven years old. I recognized my grandmother, but I acted like I didn't. When I met my other grandmother, again, I acted like I did not recognize her. Naturally, she got very upset. As a small child I had spent lots of time with her. It must have been horrible for her. I did it because I did not want to be uprooted again. I was happy with my parents and all of a sudden this! So, I said: No, not again. That is why I denied knowing her.

When I was eleven years old I started to worry about what would happen if my real parents appeared. What if I ended up having four parents? Finally, I said to myself, I will live with the four of them![19]

The adoptive parents in this case were exceptionally caring. They had told the children that they were adopted and, concerned with their welfare, wanted them to learn their history. When the children's family was found, the Sfiligoys' open and friendly attitude defused a potentially explosive situation. They opened their home to the biological family. The children visited their grandmothers and met their cousins, aunts, and uncles. They learned about their kidnapping and about the disappearance of their parents. The two grandmothers agreed to let the children stay with the adoptive parents, and a warm extended family was established. The adoptive family displayed remarkable wisdom. When Tatiana was in the seventh grade and her teacher told Inés Sfiligoy that Tatiana should never tell in school what had happened to her, Inés's reaction was to immediately change schools. Living with a secret had been a burden for Tatiana:

I no longer hide what happened to me. When Estela de Carlotto came to my school to give a talk, they asked me if that was OK with me, and I said yes. At a certain point, Estela said: "Here is Tatiana, she will tell you about herself." I started to talk in front of everybody. Maybe it was a bit theatrical, but for me it was the best that could have ever happened. It helped me untie the knot that I was carrying. The longer you hide something, the worse it gets, and a lot of time had gone by and it was becoming really difficult for me.

I know I have made a hard choice, wanting to know the full truth. But I believe that is how it has to be. I cannot deny what happened to me. I have to say what I think, even when others react badly. We make choices in life. My choice was a difficult one, but I prefer a harsh truth to a lie.

Tatiana started to work with the Grandmothers, gathering data on the families of the disappeared children and registering them with the National Genetic Data Bank: "The Grandmothers need help and I want to work with them because what they are doing is so important and because it is part of my life." Sadly, Tatiana and Laura Malena's story is *not* typical. Their adoptive parents were not part of the repressive regime responsible for the disappearances: they were adopted in good faith, and their adoptive parents cared deeply for their psychic health. The Sfiligoys believed in the children's right to know their origins and even tried to instill in them respect for their disappeared parents, who had displayed such commitment to their beliefs. Unfortunately, most of the children identified since then have been in the hands of people who had taken an active role in the repression and who refused to let the children learn about their history and identity.

"She Had My Son's Hair and She Walked Just Like Him, As If on Clouds"

Elena Santander's son, Alfredo Moyano, and his Uruguayan wife, María Asunción Artigas, were abducted from their home in Buenos Aires in December 1977. María Asunción was two months pregnant. Elena recalls:

I had not heard from my son for the last two or three days and that was odd. I was unable to find any news about them for years. One day, the Grandmothers received information from Argentine exiles in Canada saying that they had seen my son and daughter-in-law in the camp and that she had delivered a baby girl. They sent me a cassette with all the details of the birth, how much she weighed, what name they had given her, the whole story. In 1987, ten years later, a woman approached the Grandmothers. She was a teacher in a school where my granddaughter was enrolled. She reported that there was something strange about one of her students, that she seemed different from the others, a troubled child. The investigative team went to work on the case. The blood tests showed that she was my granddaughter. She had been registered as the daughter of a couple related to the chief of the camp where my son had been imprisoned. The man had died but his wife, the "mother," had the child. At first, she kept insisting that María Victoria was her daughter, but she finally confessed.

The judge then asked me to go to the court, where the restitution would take place. They sent me to a floor above. I saw her from there when she came in. She had my son's hair, and she walked just like him, as if on clouds. It was December 31, ten years after the kidnapping. The judge introduced me and the other grandmother. I felt sorry for the girl, she did not know what to do. She gave us a kiss, I caressed her.

When I took her home, she cried, she kicked, she did not want to eat. She asked to see her "mother." I told her that she needed to bring that up to the judge. He was adamant about not letting her see the "adoptive" mother. Clearly, she felt affection for the woman, but afterward, when she found out the truth, she did not want to see her anymore. She had been told that her mother had died in childbirth and that her father had abandoned her.

María Victoria stayed with me for three months, and then her maternal grandmother said that she wanted the child to live with her. That was OK with me, if María Victoria agreed, which she did. So she is now living in Uruguay. I see her every three months. Whenever I can, I go to see her.

I hope that we keep finding the children who were taken from us. Some people have asked me, "Why do you keep at it, you already found your granddaughter?" I continue because I want to help others recover their family, their history. As the Grandmothers get older, some get sick, others die. It is more important than ever that we find the missing children. I will keep doing whatever I can, for me and for the others, until my last day.[20]

"The Child Is Too Beautiful. You Will Not Get Her Back"

That is what Elsa Pavón de Aguilar was told by her brother-in-law, a policeman, when she was looking for her granddaughter Paula Eva Logares Grinspon. Elsa's daughter, son-in-law, and twenty-three-month-old granddaughter were kidnapped in Uruguay in May 1978. According to Elsa,

A couple that was living with them called my son-in-law's father and told him what had happened. I knew nothing about disappearances. I thought people could be murdered or arrested, but disappeared? I did not have any idea that people could literally disappear, leaving no trace. I started looking for the three of them, until I realized that when I mentioned the adults even priests were hostile. When I mentioned the child, people paid attention.[21]

Elsa's strategy changed. Thinking that if she could find information about the child she might unravel the thread that might lead to the parents, she started to look for her granddaughter. During one of her visits to a juvenile court five months after the disappearance, she met four Grandmothers who were involved in a similar search. Soon afterward she joined the organization. Elsa left her job as a laboratory technician to dedicate herself full-time to the search for her granddaughter:

My brother-in-law said, "The child is too beautiful. You will not get her back. It is useless." My husband kept saying, "Enough, this is enough. You are destroying yourself." I did get quite sick and collapsed with a bad infection. At my lowest point, I said to myself, "I cannot let this happen. If I die, who will look for them? The three of them will be lost forever." The fever quickly disappeared.

In 1980 the Grandmothers received from CLAMOR pictures and information about the whereabouts of a child who looked like Paula. Chicha Mariani was immediately convinced that the child was Paula. As they started to follow the clues, they kept an eye on the child and the suspected family, until unexpectedly the family moved, leaving no trace. Three years later, thanks to the posters of the children that covered the streets of Buenos Aires, there was another tip. A man seeking revenge on the kidnapper revealed the identity of the family with whom Paula was living. The Grandmothers began their investigation anew. Again, Elsa speaks:

I would stand in the door of her school. I would go near her house and do my shopping there. I tried to become part of the scene so that the neighbors and the store owners would get to know me and think that I lived in the neighborhood. I did not dare talk to her or touch her. My sister-in-law accompanied me; she is very talkative and she established a good connection with her. I asked my husband to come and look at her. He agreed, yes, that was Paula. He established a nice rapport with her, and she would look at him with a longing expression.

The Grandmothers found that the alleged father, Rubén Lavallén, who had been the police chief of the unit where Paula and her parents had been imprisoned, had registered her shortly after the kidnapping as being born in October 1977. This made her almost one and a half years younger than her real age (Paula was born in June 1976). Another attempt to make Paula disappear for a second time was thwarted by lucky chance, as Elsa explains:

The lawyer working on Paula's case ran into a friend she had not seen in a long while and was invited to her apartment. This friend had a daughter who was very sad: the little girl who lived on the first floor had come to say good-bye because she was leaving the country. That little girl was Paula. The lawyer was able to stop Paula from being taken abroad.

The procedure used to convince the judicial system of Paula's identity was long and complicated. There was a considerable discrepancy between her age as judged from X rays of her bones and the age reported by her grandmother. The X-ray data indicated her age approximately as that of a six-year-old, but her grandmother claimed she was seven and a half years old. When genetic testing became available in 1984, it determined with 99.95 percent probability that Paula was Elsa's grandchild. However, the judge in charge of the case rejected the claim. Elsa appealed to a higher court. She went to the court accompanied by her husband and her son, whose presence made a crucial difference in a judicial system pervaded by sexism:

They looked at me differently because I was accompanied by my husband and my son. I was no longer a crazy woman from the Plaza de Mayo. I was with two men: my son, who is a big teddy bear, and my husband, who looks like a very serious and respectable man. That did it. Me alone, no. But with two men, yes.

In December 1984, Elsa finally met her granddaughter formally in court. Paula had a stormy reaction:

She made an incredible scene. She said that she had a mother and a father and that I was wrecking her family. I told her that her mother had been my daughter Mónica and that I had been searching for her for a long time. I showed her pictures of her as a small child with her parents. She threw them on the floor saying that they were false pictures, that they were too recent. I explained to her that they were new copies from old pictures. She finally looked at one picture and agreed that it did look like her, like one she had at home. I asked her if she remembered how she called her father. She used to call him "Calio" and as she started to repeat his name, her voice became like that of a two-year-old. She started to cry and fell asleep. When she woke up she seemed fine. She took my hand, and we went home, but only if I would promise to buy her favorite children's magazine every Monday.

At Elsa's house, Paula immediately went to the room where she used to stay as a small child and looked for her old toys. She knew where the bathroom was and seemed completely at ease with the surroundings. After eight months, X rays of her bones showed that her development was normal for her age. The physicians who had been monitoring her case noted that this was a common occurrence among small children who had been separated from their mothers. The trauma of the separation had stunted her growth but, as in other cases, the effect was reversible.

Paula's kidnappers, however, managed to obtain visitation rights, and she was ordered by the judge to continue to see them; finally, she flatly refused, announcing that she would not have any more contact with her parents' torturers. It took four more years until Paula was able to recover her real name and the legal documentation that established her identity. Eighteen years old, Paula comments on her experience:

There were some difficult moments, such as when we all had a meeting in the court. There was my grandmother, my uncles and aunts, a couple of psychologists, the kidnappers, and the judge. It was really ugly. The judge suspended the meeting right away. Another time, Lavallén appeared around my house. He screamed at me, so I stuck my tongue out at him. He then got into a car, and drove past me. When I went to see the judge, I told him what had happened, and the judge blamed me for sticking out my tongue, as if I had provoked him. I got really angry, because if he had not followed me, I would not have done anything. At the same time, I have to admit that this judge was the first one to have the courage to restitute a person. If the judge had been a complete disaster, I would not be living with my family now.

When I returned home, we went into family therapy. My grandmother, my uncles and aunts, we all did joint sessions, everybody went. My grandmother started therapy before I went back, to prepare herself to receive me, and I went to therapy afterward. I think it helped. I was a child, I played during the sessions, but I think it was important.

There were some happy moments too. It was nice to meet my uncles and aunts. They would come one at a time or in couples, trying not to overwhelm me. I started to get to know them individually, and they would play with me. I have three aunts and one uncle. Two of the aunts are married. I have four cousins who were born after me, so I am the oldest. I also met my paternal grandfather, his new wife, and their two children. They are younger than me though they are my uncle and aunt. I agree with the way I was told the truth. The judge told me about it in the court, and he brought my grandmother into the room. I knew nothing until that moment. It was hard, but there was no confusion. It is really important to give support to the person who is going through the restitution process. One has to also establish limits, though. For instance, when I returned home, I made a list of the things that I wanted from my other house, my favorite dolls, my skates, etc. They never gave them to me. I complained about it a couple of times, but their point was that now I had other things, another family. I believe I was testing them by saying "I want that," and I understand why they did not give it to me.

Going through the restitution process, one needs a lot of support, because it is a very big change. One is restructuring one's life, realizing what one is and what one is not. One has to be contained, emotionally and psychologically. The family that one is reentering into also needs support; it is a complex and difficult situation for everybody.[22]

The work of integrating Paula into her family has taken years. Elsa points out that it is only recently that she and Paula have been able to laugh, fight, and cry together freely. The reconstruction of Paula's identity is an ongoing process, which they both believe is essential so that she can create a life based on the truth.

"That Is My Aunt"

On May 12, 1978, at 2 A.M., a group of armed men burst into the home of Adriana Mirta Bai and Miguel Arellanos. Nya Quesada, Adriana's mother, remembers:

They broke the door while they were sleeping. They took them away in the middle of the night, the two of them and their son, Nicolás, two and a half years old. My daughter was an architecture student; neither she nor her husband were involved in politics. The following day I sensed something was wrong. We used to speak every day on the phone, and she had not called me. I sent her brother-in-law to their house to check what happened. Neighbors told him that they had heard Adriana crying and calling her next-door neighbor.

I went to talk to this neighbor. She had seen Adriana's husband being beaten. The next morning my husband and I went to present our first writ of habeas corpus. I cannot even count anymore how many writs of habeas corpus I have presented. The judges always said they did not know anything. I went to all the jails. I traveled all over. I did everything you can think of. I wrote to the pope. I wrote to all the human rights organizations. I testified when the Organization of the American States came. I testified at CONADEP. I wrote letters all over the world. What happened with Nicolás borders on the miraculous. It really is like a novel. Compared with other

Grandmothers I consider myself very fortunate. About twenty days after the disappearances, my sister Menchu [a well-known TV and theater actress] received a phone call from the San Martín juvenile court. They asked her if she had a nephew named Nicolás. She said yes, and they said he was at the court. They wanted to know how old he was. They could not believe it when she said he was two and a half years old. He was so articulate they thought he was four years old. He had appeared at the doorstep of the court with two suitcases full of clothes. For the last few days, the secretary of the court, who had gotten very fond of him, had taken him to her home. There, watching TV, when the announcer mentioned my sister's name, Nicolás started to scream: "That is my aunt, my aunt Menchu!"

The secretary told the judge what Nicolás was saying. The following morning the judge called the TV channel and asked for my sister's telephone number. He then asked her to go to the court. When the judge brought the two of them together, Menchu opened her arms and Nicolás immediately threw himself onto her. The judge allowed him to go home with my sister right away. TV has never served a better purpose. Were it not for the TV announcer, the judge would have never found us.

Upon his return, Nicolás sometimes would lie on the floor or hide under a table and say: "Grandma, I am going to sleep, cover me up. Come down with me." We think this is because probably, when he was kidnapped, he was taken to a police station and slept on the floor with his mother. Nicolás would also tell us that the "garbage men" had come to their apartment, because he saw men stuffing their bags and taking everything away. Of course, they were looting the house. They stole everything: the TV, the record player, the encyclopedia, my son-in-law's tools. This is what Nicolás saw and remembered at such a young age.[23]

Nya believes that she was incredibly lucky in that the judge in charge of the case was sensitive and fair. Most judges would have sent Nicolás to an orphanage or would have given him to a repressor for an illegal adoption. If that had happened, all traces of the child would have been lost. Nya thinks that her daughter must have pleaded for the child to be taken to the court to increase his chances of being reunited with his family.

Nicolás, now eighteen years old, is a talented and accomplished student at the National Conservatory Music School. He grew up with Nya and her husband and has been fortunate to be in a school where attention to children's emotional well-being was paramount. Nya commented with pleasure that at this school they observe Family Day, instead of Mother's Day, and thus he has been able to celebrate his family together with the other children.

"She Would Have That Baby Even If They Tortured Her"

Haydée Lemos is one of the founding members of the Grandmothers' organization and has been involved in many of the aspects of their work. In July 1977 her daughter Mónica, eight months pregnant, was kidnapped with her husband, Gustavo Lavalle, and their fourteen-month-old daughter, María. Five days later, María appeared on Haydée's doorstep in a pitiful condition. Haydée always felt confident that her daughter would deliver her child, even while imprisoned:

My daughter was very strong. When she had her first child, she practically delivered alone, though she was in the hospital. She was very resilient, would never complain. One would never know if she was in pain or suffering. I thought that she would have that baby even if they tortured her. At that point, her other grandmother and I still believed in the good faith of the military. Thinking that they were going to call us after the birth, we started preparing the clothes for the baby. We always thought they would set them free. But nothing happened.

Ten years later, Estela de Carlotto met a friend of her daughter's at a bus stop. This friend told Estela that she had been detained in the Banfield camp and Estela asked her if she remembered the names of other prisoners. It turned out that she had met my son-in-law in the camp and he had told her that my daughter had delivered a baby girl. I was convinced that my daughter was going to have a boy, so I assumed she was wrong and did not pay much attention to the story.[24]

Haydée worked as part of the investigation team, checking on the numerous anonymous tips they received continuously. She had already lost hope by the time one of the tips led to the identification of her granddaughter:

I was not expecting it to happen. It is like playing the lottery; one plays, but winning is another story. . . . I was simply helping in the work. I was classifying pictures. We were extremely careful. Everything had to be checked many times, to make sure that the judges would not dismiss our work. A certain child seemed to fit the picture and when the genetic testing was ordered, the child turned out to be my granddaughter María José.

As soon as she was born, María José was taken away from her mother; she spent her first ten years living with a policewoman and her husband who had registered her as their own. When the child was identified, Haydée had mixed feelings and wondered about the best course of action:

I asked myself if it was right what I was doing. I was worried. After all, in that home she had a mother and a father. I was trying to figure out what was best for her. When she came to live with me and started to cry, I was really afraid. But the morning after, while I was preparing breakfast, she came over and pointing to her arm said, "Look, I have a mole, just like the one María has, in the same place."

María José found herself with a large family: her sister María, uncles, aunts, her paternal grandparents, and her maternal grandmother. At Haydée's house she shared a room with María and slept in the same bed and on the same mattress where her mother had slept as a youngster. Haydée comments:

María José is now sixteen years old. She is in very good shape. I like people to see for themselves because otherwise they might think I am biased. She is an excellent student, finishing high school, studying English. She draws, she paints. She looks a lot like my daughter. Not only physically but in her way of being. She is very resilient. Those ten years with the police did not destroy her, they don't seem to have affected her. When she came to live with me I asked her what she wanted to be when she grew up and she said "a policewoman." Of course, that was what she knew. And she had been watching a TV show where the main character was a policewoman. I got worried, I thought they had brainwashed her. But after a while she never mentioned it again.

María José and her sister are activists. They have done volunteer work in a community center; they have taken care of poor children and worked in a home for low-income old people. I think they are following the footsteps of their parents. They love doing that, but they also love going to parties and having a good time with their friends from school. María José wants to be seen as a regular young woman, not as a "case."

María José herself, now finishing high school, reflects on some of the events in her life since the return to her family:

It is difficult to understand what happened. I don't mean my personal case or the restitution, because one goes on with life, one keeps on living. That is not hard to understand. What one cannot comprehend is what happened to a whole generation. Everybody thinks that the restitution is the difficult part, that it is traumatic. No. The hardest thing is what one cannot get back, not being able to recover one's parents. That is the hardest thing.

The best thing is that one can find oneself, and from then on, it is possible to think about the future. When one is at peace with oneself, inside, and knows what happened, one is with the truth, with reality, and it is easier to plan the rest of one's life.

I was lucky to learn the truth when I was small. It is different for those who are older. It is more difficult. It is one thing to be ten years old, and another to be eighteen. An older child is already formed. I was lucky.[25]

María José established a strong relationship with the judge in charge of her case—Juan Ramos Padilla, one of the few judges who understood the urgency and importance of the Grandmothers' work:

When I was small I did not like him. I was afraid of him. I think he was more worried than I was. Now I get along very well with him. I often visit him in his office. During the holidays, I always make sure that I go and greet him. He is a fine person. I think of him as a father.

During her summer vacations, she enjoys her extended family in the South of Argentina:

I like to go to the South for the holidays, because there we have a lot of family. My grandfather is from the South and all his brothers and sisters, nephews and nieces are there. For me, they are like cousins or uncles of third or fourth degree. The name Lavalle, my father's name, is very well known in the town. When you say our name, everybody knows who you are.

The town is full of relatives. I was there twice, two years and four years ago. I would love to go back.

María José has a wide range of interests and an impressive knowledge of the arts, both in Argentina and abroad. She is considering a career in fine arts or in "something related to the earth." She and her sister are part of a group of children whose parents have disappeared; they have been active participants in the yearly March of the Resistance, a twenty-four-hour event that the Mothers of the Plaza de Mayo and other human rights groups organize to honor the disappeared and to demand justice.

"Knowledge of the Truth Is the Best Therapy"

The Grandmothers' experience with the restitution process has led them to recognize a typical pattern when the children learn of their origins. Learning the truth hurts, and a strong emotional reaction usually follows the news. But following that first critical phase, lasting one to three days, the children bond with their found families, asking detailed questions and noting any signs of resemblance to their relatives. Members of the interdisciplinary team who have assisted the Grandmothers in restitution have commented on how the children identify with their legitimate families almost immediately. They have observed that a gesture, a voice, or a particular piece of information can become the specific agent that unleashes old memories, creating a moment of insight, the "click" that helps the child reconnect with the past.[26]

Grandmother Nélida de Navajas comments:

People ask us how it is possible that a child who has lived many years with a certain family can return and adapt so quickly to her or his new home. When the children, some illegally adopted, others registered under a false identity, meet their family of origin, they start looking at their eyes, their hair, their teeth, their manner, and checking for similarities. Our consulting psychologists have suggested that we let the children find their own rhythm. They go freely investigating and, as they ask questions, we satisfy their desire to know. The first thing they ask is, How did my mother look? How did my father look? So we show them their pictures, and from there they start reconstructing everything. From the pictures they move to objects that belonged to their parents. They start gathering them as their own. They claim them and they become their personal treasure. It looks as if the children had not found a real point of contact with the families that had them and now, very quickly, from the physical to the spiritual, they get easily connected to their true families. In short, it shows that it is not possible to build an identity based on lies.[27]

The Grandmothers have also noted that despite their pain on learning of their parents' disappearances, many children felt great relief in finding out that they had not been abandoned, that they were wanted children. In the case of Tatiana Sfiligoy, when her grandmothers appeared and she learned her story, the child became very anxious. The adoptive mother, however, reminded Tatiana, who was then seven years old, that she had not been abandoned, that her parents were kidnapped and had left her against their will. The reaction of the child was immediate: her anxiety diminished and she became calm and tranquil, in spite of the sad news regarding her parents' fate. Estela de Carlotto put it succinctly: "the knowledge of the truth is the best therapy."[28]

Some children openly expressed their satisfaction at being finally identified. On the day that a child was restituted to her family, when her grandmother told her, "I have searched for you for so long," the child answered, "And I was waiting for you, grandmother."[29] In the case of María José Lavalle Lemos, when the judge told her about her origins, she answered that she had always thought she had another home, another family, and a sibling.[30]

Truth becomes a cornerstone of the recovered identity of the found children. By changing their names, their ages, and their identities, the appropriators turned the children into objects, depriving them of their history. Some children resisted the efforts to erase any trace of their past by refusing to have their names changed. The significance of one's own name as a remnant of one's identity reflects the relationship with one's parents, who gave one that name.[31] Other children, obliged by judges to meet with their appropriators, refused to speak with them because of the lies that they had been told. Sometimes they openly challenged the judges. When Ximena Vicario was told by the judge, "I represent your father, and I decide your fate," the child responded that he was not her father, that her father had disappeared. When the judge invited her to see her "mother," Ximena answered that her mother was assassinated and that Siciliano was not her mother. When he addressed her as Romina, the name that Siciliano had given her, she claimed her true name, Ximena. And when the visit with Siciliano took place, Ximena confronted her about her lies.[32]

A child psychoanalyst who has worked with the Grandmothers through many restitutions has been deeply impressed by the found children:

All the children whom I met were extremely intelligent, one could say almost superendowed. I am not surprised about that, because those children know at a deep level, unconsciously, some important truths. They had to build up a defense system about lying, a very powerful system to be able to survive. They have a great capacity of adaptation, quite exceptional in most cases. They have had to tolerate lies and to know what questions to ask and which ones not to. They have had to steer themselves carefully. As a result, they have developed great sensitivity and intelligence.[33]

Psychologists had to recognize that in working with the Grandmothers, they entered uncharted territory. The situations they encountered, ranging from the disappearances of the parents to the restitution of the children, were new and forced them to reconsider many of their theories and clinical practices. Another psychologist, who worked with the Grandmothers for eight years, reflects:

The Grandmothers taught us about some fundamental aspects of the human condition. They forced us to rethink issues of identity. We had to revise our thinking. Many of us did not know what they meant when they spoke of "restitution." They had to explain it to us. We eventually realized that what they were saying was full of common sense and wisdom, and it helped us develop new perspectives. There is a *before*—and an *after*—the Grandmothers. Their contribution cannot be overestimated, and the personal and professional growth that those of us who worked with them experienced was phenomenal.[34]

The Grandmothers refused to accept that the trauma the children had suffered could be totally defined and dealt with in terms of individual relations between children and caretakers. They consistently saw the larger picture. They recognized that ignoring the social and political trauma at the center of the children's lives would prevent their healing, because individual identities develop as part of a larger social process.

They understood that for the children to become active agents and create their own lives, the cruel mechanism that had turned them into objects had to be exposed. Their vision was an ecological one, requiring the recognition of truth and justice as fundamental prerequisites for a healthy future—both for individuals and for society.

SIX

CAPTIVE MINDS, CAPTIVE LIVES

The most effective sphere of action . . . will be the affective. Emotions and feelings will prevail over the intellect; aimed toward the unconscious they will influence critical judgment, directing it toward certain predetermined effects.

Manual of the Argentine Armed Forces on "Psychological Operations"

As we saw in earlier chapters, separating the children from their legitimate families was one of the strategies of the military regime. Aimed at resocializing the children and at terrorizing their families, the technique was chillingly effective. After the fall of the regime the Grandmothers found out that some of the kidnappers had left the country and were living abroad with the children. The Grandmothers requested that the United Nations investigate these second disappearances, insisted on the difference between appropriation and adoption, and called attention to the risks that the appropriations posed for the children's physical and mental health.

The idea of separating children from their families for political reasons in order to erase their identity was not new. During World War II the Nazis kidnapped Polish, Czech, Yugoslav, and Russian children and gave them to German families. From Poland alone they took over 200,000 children. Survivors have described methods similar to the ones uncovered by the Grandmothers. "Psychological methods were used to make a child forget or even hate its parents[;] . . . the object was to give a child a sense of inferiority about its origins and of gratitude to the Germans who had rescued it from the degeneracy of its home environment."[1]

At the end of the war, the Allies failed to return those "adopted" children to their countries of origin, on the grounds that it was in the children's best interests to leave them where they were. Concerns about how the children might suffer if "new dramas" were created and if they were taken from comfortably off families and given to poor ones ensured that they remained in Germany. Only 15 percent of the Polish children taken from their families to be Germanized were repatriated. When some of the adoptions were challenged in court, many of the judges—ex-Nazis themselves—sided with the German families and ruled against restitution. The last Polish child to be repatriated, in 1953, subsequently reflected: "I had become a fanatical Nazi. I wept with rage when the men condemned at the Nuremberg trial were hanged. It took years before I stopped hating the Poles, as I had been taught, and then the French, who occupied our city of Koblenz."[2]

More recently, in the 1970s, East German authorities declared that parents who had tried to flee to the West or were convicted of espionage were unfit to raise their children; the children were given for adoption to officially approved families. "It is now clear that the state acted as a kidnapper," said Thomas Krueger, Berlin's minister for youth in 1991.[3]

The case of the Finaly children in France after World War II bears a striking resemblance to the situation of some of the children in Argentina. The Finalys were Austrian Jews who took refuge in France, where their two boys were born, in the late 1930s. In 1944 the Gestapo arrested the couple and deported them to Germany. The two children were placed in a Grenoble nursery, whose director took a special interest in them and had them baptized as Catholics. At the end of the war, when the children's relatives in New Zealand and Israel tried to reclaim them, their caretaker refused to return them. Years of endless legal proceedings went by while the boys grew up as Catholics, ignorant of their family history. When the World Jewish Congress and the Catholic Church finally reached an agreement about their custody, the children were nowhere to be found. Their caretaker/appropriator had smuggled them into Franco's Spain. During the next five months, their case made headlines in all the major French newspapers and their fate remained unknown. Finally in June 1953, eight years after their relatives had started searching for them, the children were found; earlier that year, the Grenoble judicial court had recognized that they had been kidnapped, and at the end of July they rejoined their family in Israel. As adults, they have expressed their satisfaction in having been raised by their relatives and having had the opportunity to return to the Jewish faith.[4]

In Australia and in the United States, indigenous people have long suffered such attempts by the dominant group to absorb their children. In Australia, some of the children were so young when taken that they did not remember where they had come from or who their parents were. The white government, which saw the Aboriginal way of life as a "positive menace to the State," decided that the children should adopt the values and belief system of the dominant white culture. Laws and procedures ensured that children could be removed without parental consent as a matter of the "child's moral or physical welfare": it became the parents' burden to demonstrate "that a child had a right to be with them, not the other way around." A child could be taken away simply "for being Aboriginal."[5] Cut off from their families and communities, many children became ashamed of the color of their skin and drifted into lives of isolation, despair, and alcoholism. These practices supposedly ended in 1969 with the abolition of the Aborigines Welfare Board, but during this century the government took one out of six or seven Aboriginal children from their families. In 1997 a government-appointed inquiry recognized that the practice had been genocide. The report described the creation of a "stolen generation": light-skinned aboriginal children had been handed out to white families for adoption, dark-skinned children put in orphanages. The report recommended that a national day of mourning be observed and that the government compensate all those affected.[6]

In the United States, Native American children were indoctrinated to be subordinate to the white majority. Attendance at mission schools was mandatory on many reservations. The children were compelled to undergo instruction in Christianity and English, while indigenous religion and languages were prohibited. When the U.S. commissioner on Indian affairs in 1886 determined that, in the words of one recent scholar, day schools "afforded students far too much proximity to their families and communities—and thus a continuing interaction with their own cultures,"[7] the government opened boarding schools where the children could be effectively isolated from their culture of origin. The students were not allowed to visit home; and after their training was complete, they were placed with white families for three years. The system often worked as it had been intended, and the children saw their true families again only when they were sent back to their communities at age seventeen or eighteen. Their long years away made many of them functional outcasts; in some cases they became agents of the white power structure, trying to "undermine and eventually replace the traditional forms possessed by their peoples."[8]

Article II of the United Nations Convention on the Prevention and Punishment of the Crime of Genocide defines "genocide" as follows:

> Genocide means any of the following acts committed with intent to destroy, in whole or in part, a national, ethnical, racial or religious group, as such: a) Killing members of the group; b) Causing serious bodily or mental harm to members of the group; c) Deliberately inflicting on the group conditions of life calculated to bring about its physical destruction in whole or in part; d) Imposing measures intended to prevent births within the group; e) *Forcibly transferring children of the group to another group* [my emphasis].[9]

By this definition, it seems that in all the cases discussed above except that of East Germany, genocide occurred. However, some have criticized the United Nations for defining genocide too narrowly, arguing that political groups should be included in the list of possible victims. If this wider definition were accepted, the East German case would fit as well.[10]

In Argentina, human rights organizations have often used the term *genocide* to describe the crimes committed by the state. As we have seen, children were forcibly separated from their families, and their parents, the so-called subversives, were disappeared. The UN report on the disappearance of children in Argentina (discussed below) stopped short of calling the Argentine case "genocide" but stated that "the activities of the appropriators can be *compared* to those described in the Convention on the Prevention and Punishment of the Crime of Genocide" (my emphasis). The report called not only for effective domestic legislation to deal with the captive children but also for international cooperation in designing mechanisms to help find those children outside Argentina and return them to their legitimate families.[11]

SEGUNDA DESAPARICIÓN

In Argentina the judicial delays and obstacles that the Grandmothers faced after locating the stolen children made it possible for another form of abuse to take place. In several cases, the kidnappers escaped to other countries with the children. The Grandmothers coined the term *segunda desaparición* (second disappearance) to describe this new turn of events. By 1987 the Grandmothers knew of at least seven children who had been taken from Argentina to live in Paraguay with their captors.[12] Paraguay, on Argentina's border, was then governed by the longest-ruling dictatorship in the hemisphere—the notoriously corrupt regime of General Alfredo Stroessner, which ran the country from 1954 to 1989. Paraguay was one of the members of Operación Cóndor, the network of Southern Cone security forces that collaborated to ensure the kidnapping of "subversives" and their forced return to their countries of origin.[13] That the government of Paraguay, famous for its own human rights abuses, would side with the kidnappers was a given. It was one of the most logical places for them to go into hiding.

Thus military physician Norberto Atilio Bianco and his wife, Nidia Susana Wherli (see chapter 1), fled to Paraguay in 1986 after Argentine authorities ordered genetic testing to determine the identity of the two children whom they claimed as theirs. Major Bianco was accused of kidnapping them after they were born in the Campo de Mayo hospital during their mother's captivity. The judge in charge of the case traveled to Paraguay, where he argued for the extradition of the appropriators and the restitution of the children to their legitimate families. The Paraguayan authorities allowed neither him nor the Argentine ambassador to see the children or their kidnappers. Accusing the Grandmothers of Marxist-Leninist leanings typical of "subversive" groups, the attorney general proclaimed:

> We Paraguayans are, by nature, against any type of pressures. . . . Defending the human rights of the accused, we must reject the request for extradition. . . . [T]he defense is right in qualifying this as political persecution[;] . . . the intervention of the Grandmothers of the Plaza de Mayo in the judicial matters of our country must be avoided. While the influence of that pressure group in the Argentine Republic is considerable, here it must be rejected in order to respect our political sovereignty, based on nonintervention in internal matters and the self-determination of peoples.[14]

Prompted by the Grandmothers, the Argentine delegate to the OAS, Leandro Despouy, denounced the second disappearance of Argentine children. Despouy pressed the OAS to broaden the PanAmerican Convention of Human Rights to provide additional protection to the rights of children, invoking as well the Montevideo Treaty, which mandates the extradition of those accused of kidnapping. Only in early 1997 were Major Bianco and his wife finally extradited.[15]

At the United Nations, the Grandmothers urged the Human Rights Commission to form an expert group that would investigate the situation and ensure that there were no further second disappearances, and the forty-three countries constituting the commission unanimously agreed to nominate such a group.[16] The Economic and Social Council of the United Nations, which endorsed the commission's decision, authorized the secretary general to provide all the assistance necessary for its implementation. In April 1988 Theo van Boven, a Dutch diplomat and former director of the UN Center for Human Rights, was appointed to carry out the task.[17] Van Boven proceeded to inform the Argentine and the Paraguayan governments of his plans to visit both countries and asked for cooperation from the authorities. While the Argentine government responded positively to his request, the Paraguayan government let him know that "the question of the children was under examination by the courts and that under these circumstances a visit to Paraguay was not opportune because it could be considered as interference in the judicial process."[18] Consequently, the UN report on the situation of the children was based only on van Boven's visit to Argentina, including his consultations there with members of human rights organizations, psychologists, health professionals, and government officials. He fully confirmed the Grandmothers' views:

> Promptness and effectiveness in the handling of evidence and in taking measures to return the children to their legitimate families depended on the judges in charge of the proceedings. Some acted promptly, but many delayed cases unnecessarily by procedural means and by refusing to implement measures requested by the children's families. In many cases, years went by before the judges ordered haemogenetic tests to determine a child's real identity, thus establishing the commission of offenses of abduction, detention and concealment of minors and of the suppression of records and forgery of public documents. As a matter of fact, abductors usually registered the children as their own and forged the documents required to establish their identity.
>
> Several judges failed to take the necessary measures to prevent the alleged abductors from fleeing, leaving the country or hiding so that the latter managed to remove themselves from the judges' jurisdiction. In a number of cases where such measures were ordered, the authorities responsible for keeping watch on the abductors did not appear to have carried out court orders properly, since several of the abductors managed to leave the country and are now living in Paraguay, where they have taken the children.[19]

The Argentine authorities challenged the van Boven report, and at their prompting some members of the Human Rights Commission objected to it, thus preventing it from receiving the full discussion and general attention it deserved.[20] At the national level, the Grandmothers asked President Alfonsín in November 1988 to pressure the government of Paraguay and to appoint a special public defender to expedite the legal work on behalf of the disappeared children. This resulted in the creation of a four-member commission of federal prosecutors to help investigate and resolve these cases.[21]

Two stories in particular drew considerable attention from the media because of the wide-ranging and complex ethical and political questions they raised. The cases of Mariana Zaffaroni and the twins Gonzalo and Matías Reggiardo Tolosa illustrate the tragic effects of judicial lethargy on the lives of these children and their legitimate families. Growing up in the homes of their kidnappers and absorbing their values, these children were put in an unbearable situation. Because they were isolated from information and support that would have provided an alternative vision of the world, their life experiences were molded by the military and police communities in which they were immersed. As the repressors attempted to turn these children into their own and to become the "new parents" that General Camps had envisioned, they led the children to violently reject their legitimate families' values and ideals. One of the leaders of a revolt against the Alfonsín government in 1987, Colonel Mohamed Alí Seineldín, acknowledged what had taken place: "We did for them the best that we could; we gave them our own homes and our own families."[22] And the youngsters incorporated the worldview of the repressors.

PIECES OF A PUZZLE

Mariana Zaffaroni was eighteen months old when she was kidnapped with her parents in San Isidro, a Buenos Aires suburb, in September 1976. The family had sought refuge in Argentina from persecution for their political activities in their native Uruguay. Their disappearance in Argentina offers yet another example of how the repressive forces of the two countries coordinated their terrorist activities.

The two grandmothers, Marta Zaffaroni in Brazil and María Ester Gatti in Uruguay, became very active with the Grandmothers' Association as they searched for the child. During their investigations, they also found that Mariana's mother was three months pregnant when she had been kidnapped. In 1979 Marta Zaffaroni went to Chile to look for Mariana. She hoped that since the Julien Grisonas children (also from Uruguay; see chapter 3) had been found in Chile, Mariana might also have been taken there, but her visit bore no fruit. In 1983 Marta Zaffaroni was able to meet with an Argentine intelligence officer, a member of the SIDE directed by General Otto Paladino, who was in charge of the secret transfer of Uruguayan prisoners from Buenos Aires to

Montevideo, Uruguay. The officer told her that Mariana was being well taken care of in the hands of one of his friends, also a member of SIDE. But he refused to tell where the child was or to identify the appropriator.

In May 1983 Mariana's grandmothers published an advertisement in the newspaper *Clarín,* asking the Argentine population for help in their search. Twenty days after the ad appeared, CLAMOR, in Brazil, received an anonymous tip with the name and address of the kidnapper. The two grandmothers went to Buenos Aires, where they were able to see Mariana as she was leaving school: they had no doubt about the child's identity. However, her birth certificate registered her as Daniela Romina Furci, the daughter of Miguel Angel Furci and Adriana González, and her birth date had been changed.

The Grandmothers started legal proceedings to reclaim Mariana. Three different judges refused to work on the case; a fourth finally ordered genetic testing in June 1985. At that point, Furci showed up at the police station; he claimed that his wife had left him, taking the child with her, and that he did not know their whereabouts. A few days later, he was nowhere to be found. Furci had been active in the Automotores Orletti, the secret concentration camp to which practically all Uruguayan citizens kidnapped in Argentina were taken. Testimony from a survivor of the camp established that Mariana and her mother had been seen there. In Uruguay the flight of the Furcis provoked a wave of indignation, and 80,000 signatures demanding justice were collected and sent to President Alfonsín.[23]

At that point Mariana's maternal grandmother, María Ester Gatti, received a telegram and two letters signed by Mariana, then ten years old. Hostile in tone, the letters accused her of being an atheist and a member of the Uruguayan Communist Party. Raising ethical issues and matters of family and religion, they reflected a confused and extreme right-wing perspective, and revealed the environment in which the child was being raised—or, more accurately, indoctrinated. Her grandmother comments:

These letters tell me clearly what kind of a person Furci is, when he makes a child sign such letter. Using the name of the child to sign a letter that is a true mélange, mixing the Bible with the manuals of the armed forces. . . . When I get these letters I ask myself: What do they teach her? How do they teach her? Which values are they giving her? It is evident that all that they are teaching her does not have anything to do with what her parents would have taught her, nor with what she would have learned had she been with any of her grandparents.[24]

In 1989, after the Furcis secretly returned to Buenos Aires, the Gatti grandmother and Furci met in an attempt to negotiate a solution. When that proved impossible, the authorities again tracked down Furci. In June 1992 the genetic testing was carried out, and the couple was arrested soon after. Furci was sentenced to seven years in prison and Adriana González to three. They were found guilty of kidnapping, illegal imprisonment of a minor, and falsification of documents. The midwife who had signed the birth certificate admitted that she had lied and had never attended the birth. In passing sentence, the judge stated: "There is no precedent that I know of for this type of case—the secret police systematically stealing the fruit of the womb of the people they tortured and killed. If anything, we owe it to these children to tell them the truth and punish the crime."[25] However, he allowed Mariana to remain with the Furcis' family, awarding custody to Adriana González's mother. Adriana González herself was released after only three months of prison, and eighteen-year-old Mariana rejected the attempts of her legitimate grandmothers to establish a connection with her. She was not willing to listen to the truth about her origins. She told the judge that she did not want to see her maternal grandmother because "each time I see her she says things that hurt too much."[26]

Maria Ester Gatti reflects:

She evidently does not understand the situation or does not want to understand it so as not to suffer. She rejects many of the things that we tell her. She realizes that if she accepts them many of the ideas and beliefs she holds would crumble. And that will provoke guilty feelings, pain and emotions that could cause depression. What she is doing now is defending her life . . . she does not want to suffer anymore. She wants to live, how can I say it? in peace.[27]

Mariana maintains a close relationship with Furci and visits him often in prison, but María Ester Gatti feels that she has provided Mariana with the knowledge she needs, the pieces of a puzzle that will enable her eventually to construct her own story. Gatti believes that when Mariana marries and creates her own family, she will need to confront her history. For the moment, she keeps her distance, respecting Mariana's wishes.[28]

Estela de Carlotto presents the point of view of the Grandmothers:

> With the optimism that characterizes us, we say: Mariana knows who she is. She has been restituted, even if she does not live with her family of origin. She has her own documents, knows her real name. She will travel through life with that name, and, as she faces questions and doubts about her history, she has the information for her to one day make a choice: she can choose freedom with her family or she can stay with her parents' murderers. In any case, whatever she decides, she will be an adult, choosing her own destiny. We Grandmothers do not have a crystal ball, nor can we think that we are omnipotent and can control the personal journey of every child we find.[29]

DOES KIDNAPPING CREATE RIGHTS?

In late May and early June of 1994, the story of Gonzalo and Matías Reggiardo Tolosa was covered relentlessly by the Argentine media. A well-launched TV campaign by conservative media personalities, front-page articles in newspapers, and numerous radio shows all put the case of "the twins" (as it was popularly called) at the center of the nation's attention. Their saga reveals the repression's horrors, the atmosphere of impunity that followed the end of the regime, and the mainstream media's complicity in creating a nightmare for them and their legitimate family.

In February 1977, a joint police and military commando unit kidnapped María Rosa Tolosa and Juan Enrique Reggiardo, both twenty-four-year-old architecture students, and Antonia Oldani de Reggiardo, Juan Enrique's mother. They all remain disappeared. María Rosa was seven months pregnant at the time. The following month, an anonymous telephone call informed the Tolosa family that the couple were in a concentration camp run by the army, outside Buenos Aires. The message suggested they contact Monsignor Grasselli (see chapter 3), secretary to the influential Monsignor Tortolo, general vicar of the armed forces. Monsignor Grasselli confirmed that the couple was indeed in a concentration camp and added that María Rosa would most likely deliver in a clinic where the army usually took the kidnapped pregnant women. Shortly thereafter, another phone call informed the Tolosa family that the birth had taken place.

Survivors of La Cacha, the camp in question, testified to the family's presence, the normal progress of María Rosa's pregnancy, and her removal to a different location to give birth. In an attempt to confuse and mislead those who might be searching for the children, the camp guards informed the other prisoners that María Rosa had delivered *female* twins.[30] In fact, at the nearby women's prison in Olmos, María Rosa delivered male twins by cesarean, probably on April 27. She was most likely killed soon after the delivery. The twins were registered as born on May 16 in a Buenos Aires hospital to Alicia Beatriz Castillo, wife of Samuel Miara.[31]

Also known as "Covani" and "El Turco González" (González the Turk), Samuel Miara was an active member of the police force, infamous for his cruelty in several concentration camps. In the camps he chose who, among the prisoners, would be "transferred" and executed. Survivor Nora B. Durante identified him as the man who had raped her in El Banco.[32] Ana María Careaga (see chapter 1), seven months pregnant at the time, reported that he would kick her in the womb during interrogation sessions. Another survivor, Carlos D'Agostino, recounted Miara's brutal treatment of Jewish prisoners.[33] Miara also used his position to amass personal wealth. Looting the homes of his victims, he would refill his stock of domestic appliances for his business. In addition, he was believed to be involved in several kidnappings in which hefty ransoms were paid to save the lives of his victims.[34]

In 1984 the Grandmothers accused Miara of kidnapping the twins. By the time the judge ordered genetic testing done on the Miara couple, they were nowhere to be found. At the time of this second disappearance, the boys were eight years old.[35] In early 1987 the Grandmothers informed the Ministry of the Interior that the Miaras were living in Asunción, the capital of Paraguay. Judge Miguel Pons traveled there and, armed with irrefutable evidence, ordered the Miaras extradited and jailed. In Paraguay the Miaras were living comfortably, socializing with their fellow kidnapper Major Norberto Bianco, and enjoying the protection of the Paraguayan police.

Finally in May 1989, two months after the overthrow of General Stroessner, Interpol was able to seize the Miaras, who were then extradited to Argentina with the twins. In October doctors and scientists at the National Genetic Data Bank demonstrated a probability higher than 99.99 percent that the children, now twelve years old, were the sons of Reggiardo and Tolosa.[36] In spite of the test results and the confession from Miara and his wife that they were not the boys' natural parents, the judge, following the advice of the children's court-assigned defender—Dr. Carlos Tavares, who had defended General Videla in the junta's trial—gave custody to the Miaras. Tavares successfully challenged the genetic testing on procedural grounds.

In 1990, after a new judge, Ricardo Weschler, took over the case, two appellate court decisions affirmed the validity of the genetic tests and the identity of the twins as members of the Reggiardo Tolosa family. However, the twins continued to live with the Miaras. Concerned about the children's psychological well-being, one of the federal prosecutors charged by President Alfonsín to expedite and resolve cases of child disappearances requested a professional opinion on the assignment of custody to the Miaras. It was rendered by Dr. Ricardo Rodulfo, a psychoanalyst and a professor of clinical psychology of children and adolescents at Buenos Aires University: "To hide the truth about one's origin constitutes a true psychic catastrophe that breaks the continuity of the generational web in which the child rests. . . . [W]e believe that to have the proof of the legitimate origin of these minors and to delay their restitution not only is without justification; it also becomes a day-to-day form of new violence."[37] But Judge Weschler dismissed Rodulfo's concerns: "There is no doubt that the Miaras are not the parents, but for now I will not make any decision regarding custody. What is going on is that the children are doing well. Those . . . are psychologists. I am a father and a judge. That is what is important."[38]

In May 1993 an important new development took place: one judge annulled the birth certificates of the twins, while another ruled that the children would carry the last name of their true parents but keep the first names given to them by their kidnappers in order to "avoid confusion." The twins, now sixteen years old, continued to live with Beatriz Miara.[39] In August the International Commission of Human Rights of the OAS, prompted by a complaint from the Grandmothers, called on the Argentine government to resolve the twins' custody issue. It pressed the government at least to put the twins in a foster home temporarily and to provide them with psychological counseling by a professional chosen by their legitimate family. The decision about restitution was now in the hands of yet another judge, Jorge Ballesteros.[40]

In November 1993 Judge Ballesteros moved the twins into a foster home, and in December he ruled that they would live with Eduardo Tolosa, their maternal uncle. Furthermore, he prohibited contact with the Miaras. In a short time, the twins met their paternal grandfather, uncles, aunts, and other relatives, and started the process of learning about their family. The judge's decision was based on Article 8 of the United Nations International Convention on the Rights of the Child—the right to preservation of identity, an article for which the Grandmothers had lobbied extensively at the United Nations (see chapter 7).

Enter the mainstream media. Over the following months, the lives of the twins were scrutinized by the same agencies of mass communication that had kept silent about their kidnapping and their parents' disappearance. It turned out that the youngsters had difficulties with their uncle. Their different political perspectives caused friction, and they accused him of not allowing them to attend their private Catholic school and of trying to limit their freedom. In spite of Judge Ballesteros's admonition that to protect their psychic and physical health the twins should not participate in media events, producers from a succession of high-visibility TV shows pounced on them.

Beginning with an appearance on a show hosted by a right-wing politician, the twins appeared on some of the most popular prime-time programs; they consistently expressed their desire to live with the Miaras, because "they gave them all their love." Carefully chosen images and words—Beatriz Miara embracing the twins, shots from the movie *The Official Story* (an Oscar-winning Argentine movie about a woman who suspects that her adopted daughter is the child of a disappeared), the right music, and the incessant use of key terms such as "mother country," "freedom," "rights," and "father"—manipulated the audiences to favor the Miaras.[41] Avoiding any reference to the history of the case, the TV programs criticized the judge's decision to restitute the twins to their family and expressed sympathy for the kidnappers, calling them "love parents" and even inventing a new term to describe them: "historical parents." No mention was made of the legitimate parents, and the Grandmothers were negatively portrayed. A box was delivered to Judge Ballesteros's home containing two grenades ready to explode.[42]

Soon thereafter, the judge reversed his decision. The twins went to live with a foster family, were allowed to visit the Miaras, and returned to the private school they had previously attended. Their uncle, Eduardo Tolosa, gave up custody. While denying that he had ever curtailed their freedom, he recognized that in the seven months that they were with him "he might have committed mistakes." He also pointed out that it was impossible in only seven months for the twins to fully absorb the truth of what had happened to them. Tolosa expressed his hope that "one day the twins will realize that they have been victims of the dictatorship, just like their parents."[43]

One of Argentina's best-known journalists, Horacio Verbitsky, underscored the unusual treatment that the media had given to the twins' case by comparing it to the recent kidnapping of a newborn baby in a Buenos Aires hospital. The same newspapers and magazines that extolled the "historic parents" vehemently condemned the abduction of the newborn, offered thousands of dollars as reward for information, and demanded swift and harsh punishment to make examples of the lawbreakers.[44] The analysis of Julio Strassera, the prosecutor of the 1985 trial of the military commanders, was even more pointed: he saw the appearances of the twins on television as part of a campaign to legitimize the crime of kidnapping, noting that the journalists involved had had excellent relations with the repressive regime. He maintained that it all amounted to an attack on the restitution process, which had worked extremely well for all the children who had been found and returned to their families. To him, the twins were like the children of divorced parents who tell the judge they want to live with one parent or the other, with the difference that in the latter case "the information is not publicized nor is there an effort to demonstrate, through the TV, that one parent is good and the other is bad." Strassera also stressed that if the judicial system had worked properly the twins' situation would have been resolved five or six years earlier.[45]

Grandmother Estela de Carlotto comments:

> We believe there is a campaign out there, the work of what I call "the club of the appropriators," which targeted this case, trying the break the backbone of our organization. . . . They spread lies about our work and try to create a positive image of the kidnappers, even those who were involved in the murders of the children's parents. I point my finger to the yellow press because they have helped to create this situation, calling the kidnappers "parents" before millions of spectators. I think that they hope to stop us, so that the hundreds of children still missing will not be allowed to be reunited with their families and learn their true history.[46]

Finally, in December 1994, Judge Ballesteros condemned Samuel Miara to seven and a half years in prison and Alicia Beatriz Miara to three years. Because Miara had been in pretrial detention since 1991 and because Argentine law counts each day of detention without sentence as two days of time served, one day after sentencing—and with unusual speed—the judicial system allowed Miara to walk free. At the end of 1994, Gonzalo and Matías were living with a foster family, saw the Miaras weekly, and had no contact with their uncle or their grandfather.[47]

APPROPRIATION IS NOT ADOPTION

In a report prepared for the First Argentine Congress on Adoption in 1986, the Grandmothers articulated some of the important differences between appropriation and adoption. They called attention to the fact that in adoption, the parents or other relatives freely and consciously give up their parental rights, while the mothers and fathers of the children who disappeared or those born in captivity were in no position to exercise their rights as parents. The children's relatives, unaware of these "adoption proceedings," of the children's whereabouts, or indeed of their very existence, were equally unable to participate in the process.

Judge Juan M. Ramos Padilla, a judge who acted swiftly and honorably in these cases, commented sadly in one of his rulings that the appropriation of minors in Argentina carried a penalty of three to ten years in prison, while armed car robbery was punished with nine to twenty years. He, too, stressed the difference between appropriation and adoption: "The situation with which we are dealing, which is surrounded by fraud and forgery, and in which there is no law or truth but only the absolute power of the abductors, undermines what should be a parent-child relationship. As a result, it damages the child's psyche and the society as a whole, which sees a mockery being made of such important values as truth, justice, identity, and family." Moreover, he dismissed the argument that the abducted children had been well provided for, surrounded with material comfort, and treated as "their own" by the appropriators: "That the children might have been given good care, luxury, and even affection does not constitute mitigating circumstances. . . . This situation might be compared to that of a domestic animal, which is afforded every luxury and even affection, but solely for the purpose of its master's satisfaction."[48]

As renowned psychologist and psychoanalyst Eva Giberti comments:

> While we professionals try to spin ideas, the grandmothers keep on rescuing the children who, unlike adopted children, *were not abandoned by their parents,* but were snatched. . . . When I speak about slavery in regard to these children I am not using a metaphor: their chance to choose to continue the

> story of their lives as it was planned by their original families has been nullified. . . . [I]nstead of continuing with the likely story of their lives, together with their relatives, they have been *subjected to a mutation.*[49]

She points out that if the hundreds of children that disappeared were to tell their stories, enormous social upheaval would result. Fear of that possibility drives the state-sanctioned effort to transform and neutralize the children's experiences by allowing their appropriators to keep them and by negating what really happened. As a result, the children pay a price, becoming "absent to themselves, foreigners to their original identity." Giberti believes that the rescue of these children is not only a matter of justice but also a necessary act to repair a damaged social equilibrium; otherwise, a kind of social insanity will continue.[50]

Giberti also notes that the appropriations have forced the professional community dealing with adoptions to address new questions and dilemmas. Families that had adopted children in good faith started to wonder about the children's origins, and the children themselves raised questions about their history. It became increasingly clear that the experience of the Grandmothers would have an impact on the laws regarding custody and adoption and that a new area of work was opening up for the organization (see chapter 7).

CAPTIVE CHILDREN ARE AT RISK

The Grandmothers note that kidnapped children and children born in captivity are at risk for many reasons: the violent separation from their mothers, the concealment of their history, the systematic and continuous lies on which their family life is based, and their deliberate isolation from the networks of social information that would enable them to learn about their country's recent past—and thus about themselves.[51] These factors, the Grandmothers argue, endanger the physical and mental health of the children; only restitution can create the optimal conditions for the healthy development of the children.

Theo van Boven's report came to the same conclusions:

> [The children] live at present in family settings which, in view of the atrocities committed in the past and the involvement therein of the heads of those families, are an affront to internationally recognized humanitarian and human rights principles. Under such circumstances, they are being denied the opportunity to develop physically, mentally, spiritually and socially in a

> healthy and normal manner and in conditions of freedom and dignity[;] . . . they risk not being brought up in a spirit of tolerance, friendship among peoples, peace and universal brotherhood. In fact, they continue to be treated as the "booty" of a "dirty war" and this situation persists as long as their right to keep their identity and to live with their legitimate families is not recognized and made effective. . . . [T]he author of the present report has come to the firm conclusion that nearly without exception the return of the child to the legitimate family is in "the best interests of the child."[52]

Psychoanalyst Fernando Ulloa, former president of the Buenos Aires chapter of the Argentine Psychiatric Association, supervised the psychological treatment of some of the children restituted to their families. He observed that the great majority of the found children, in spite of the terrible wounds that they suffered, benefited greatly from the restitution process. He also expressed his concerns about the children still in captivity: "Those that present themselves as parents, having been appropriators and kidnappers, control an atrocious secret . . . the effects of which are quite terrible. When a family lives in such a situation, the truth emerges in subtle ways, through doubts and hesitations. . . . It can be affirmed that the appropriated children know the truth." The emotional dynamics that permeate the appropriator/victim relationship are far from healthy:

> Many times the appropriators show a display of intense love that has all the connotations of fetishistic love. That display of love of their "trophy children" is the only means they have to negate their crime. It is as if they are saying, "It is not true that we are criminals when we offer so much love and dedication to these children." This is, paradoxically, the most sinister effect. The children are subjected to the tremendous contradiction of having to live, on one hand, with those signals which simulate love, but that in reality cover up for a crime of which they are the victims. That is what is called the fetishist effect: when through this simulation of love, even if felt, a veil is extended over the crime.[53]

Alicia Lo Giúdice, a psychoanalyst and child psychologist who has worked with some of the restituted children, similarly warns of how damaging appropriation can be:

> The child becomes an object for the appropriators. In the case of a child who was kidnapped when she was almost two, she was able to keep her name because she kept insisting on it, but the kidnappers tried to have her repress the

memory of her life up to that moment. She was already talking, was toilet-trained, and they tried to force her to forget about her mother and father. They tried to turn her into a newborn, to negate her previous life, to make her believe that she was not who she had been. This is a very powerful intervention in the life of a child whose psyche is in the process of formation. That is why the situation is so serious. The Grandmothers' position was to say no, this is what happened, let's face it, let's find the children and set the truth straight.[54]

OPEN LETTER TO A JUDGE

As the saga of the Reggiardo Tolosa twins developed, Adriana Calvo de Laborde—a member of the Association of Ex-Detained-Disappeared and one of the few women who gave birth in captivity and was not killed (see chapter 1)—wrote an open letter to one of the judges involved in the twins' case. She reminded him that she had been kidnapped when she was six and a half months pregnant and that, blindfolded and handcuffed, she gave birth to her daughter on the floor of a police car. At that moment, she swore to herself that she would dedicate her life to ensuring that the truth was known and justice won. She had shared her captivity with many other courageous women, six of whom also were pregnant. None of them survived. She wrote to Judge Wechsler that she was witness to those mothers' desire that their children be with their legitimate families. In her own case, she noted, nobody could convince her that had she been killed, her daughter would have been better off in the hands of the repressors.[55]

In 1995 Calvo de Laborde's daughter, Teresa, celebrated her eighteenth birthday and spoke of what her life might have been if she had been kept captive:

> It is a miracle that my mother could deliver me and that I was not stolen. I believe I am one of the few cases in which they left a newborn with her mother and did not give her to families related to the security forces. If that had happened, my life would have been very different: they would have given me another kind of education and way of thinking. Maybe I would be living with a military man and his wife, and I would love them. But I would not know the truth, because in those cases you never know the truth. If I was living with a father who tells me that he stole me or he bought me, who tortured or was a friend of torturers, I don't know if I could love him.[56]

The children still captive do not have a voice. The process of recovering their identity and their truth may take many more years. This is why the National Genetic Data Bank will keep blood samples of their relatives up until the year 2050. Some of the children may have heard the message of the Grandmothers. Some of them will, undoubtedly, begin to question their history and their origins. The Grandmothers believe that eventually, as the children become young adults, some will come forward and begin searching for their legitimate families. Indeed, this is already starting to happen: as the next chapter explores in more detail, more than a hundred young people have contacted the National Commission for the Right to Identity and asked for help in finding the truth about their origins. As one of them, a nineteen-year-old man, has said: "For now, what I want is to know the truth. Afterward I will decide what to do."[57] The Grandmothers are waiting to assist and support them in their search.

SEVEN

A NEW STRATEGY

The Right to Identity

When they stole the children they tried to change what is natural. . . .A person is born with a certain history; one cannot insert oneself in another's history. We know this because of the children we have recovered. They all have said that they knew there was something wrong, that they felt pressure on their heads and anguish in their hearts. That is what the found children told us.

Berta Schubaroff

The creation in 1987 of the National Genetic Data Bank marked an important moment in the evolution of the work of the Grandmothers. The bank provided the Grandmothers with the scientific expertise they needed to bolster their cases and prove to the judicial system the affiliation of the children found. But it was not enough. Legal obstacles to their work arose constantly. For example, the grandmother of Ximena Vicario found herself without legal standing because of an antiquated law regarding custody that prohibited nonparental relatives (grandparents, uncles or aunts, and siblings) from being interested parties in custody cases. Only after the Grandmothers brought pressure to bear on legislators was the law eventually changed.[1]

Moreover, when cases under investigation ended up in court, the appropriators frequently refused to let the children be tested at the bank, and often judges failed to question either the legitimacy of the adoptions or the patently false birth certificates that were produced. The Grandmothers realized from the very beginning that the courts alone, even when working properly, were not enough: the existing adoption law and its regulations helped cover up children's disappearances and protect the kidnappers. Something more fundamental was needed to protect the rights of the disappeared children.

Already in 1986, at the first Argentine Congress of Adoption, the Grandmothers challenged the closed adoption system, because maintaining secrecy about origins made possible the illegitimate adoptions.

That secrecy, they maintained, was also damaging to children who had been adopted legally: given the publicity that surrounded the work of the Grandmothers, these children would be bound to wonder about their origins and the fate of their parents. The Grandmothers argued for new ideas and legal instruments to make adoptions truly protective of the welfare of *all* children. Children had to be told the truth about their history. They also criticized the Argentine adoption law for facilitating illegal adoptions by not requiring that the biological parents be present during the proceedings.[2]

THE UNITED NATIONS CONVENTION ON THE RIGHTS OF THE CHILD AND THE RIGHT TO IDENTITY

In 1985, influenced by the Grandmothers' arguments, the Argentine government presented to the United Nations Working Group drafting a convention on the rights of the child an article regarding the rights of children to their identity and life with their families of origin. The Convention on the Rights of the Child was adopted in November 1989 by the General Assembly, and by September of the following year it had obtained the twenty ratifications needed to gain the force of international law. By the end of 1997, the convention had been ratified by 191 states, becoming in the process the most widely accepted human rights treaty in history. As of May 1998, only the United States and Somalia among the UN member states had not yet ratified it.[3]

The convention's primary focus is on "the best interest of the child." Its fifty-four articles cover a wide range of areas, from children's right to be free from sexual and economic exploitation to their right to proper nutrition, housing, education, and health care. The articles fall under three headings: provision (the right to get one's basic needs fulfilled), protection (the right to be shielded from harmful acts or practices), and participation (the right to be heard on decisions affecting one's own life). It constitutes the most important body of international legislation on children's rights, and its norms are binding for those governments that have ratified it.[4]

The 1989 convention broke new ground in creating new rights, such as Article 8 on the preservation of the identity of the child, and in introducing new legal concepts—such as Article 21 on adoption, which recognized "that intercountry adoption may be considered as an alternative means of a child's care, if the child cannot be placed in a foster or an adoptive family or cannot in any suitable manner be cared for in the child's country of origin."[5] The Grandmothers, who played a key role in formulating and developing the language of Article 8, worked closely with the Argentine Ministry of Foreign Affairs in drafting it—a remarkable feat for women lacking any formal training in international law.[6]

The original wording proposed by the Argentine government was very strong:

> The child has the inalienable right to retain his true and genuine personal, legal, and family identity. In the event that a child has been fraudulently deprived of some or all of the elements of his identity, the State must give him special protection and assistance with a view to re-establishing his true and genuine identity as soon as possible. In particular this obligation of the State includes restoring the child to his blood relations to be brought up.[7]

The final version reflected the compromises necessary to have the article endorsed by the other members of the working group. Representatives of some countries did not want to be obliged to include the concept of "identity" in their national laws. Others did not want to create conflict with reproductive technologies such as artificial insemination or in vitro fertilization. Still others questioned whether Article 8 would be compatible with laws allowing abortions.[8]

As adopted, Article 8 declares:

> 1. States Parties undertake to respect the right of the child to preserve his or her identity, including nationality, name and family relations as recognized by law without unlawful interference.
> 2. Where a child is illegally deprived of some or all of the elements of his or her identity, States Parties shall provide appropriate assistance and protection with a view to speedily re-establishing his or her identity.[9]

Though not as specific as the original draft, Article 8 fills an important legal void by forcing the state to respect the right of the child to preserve his or her identity and to take action to restore that identity when it has been put in jeopardy. Argentina's National Congress ratified the convention in October 1990, though it took exception on four questions: the moment when life begins, international adoptions, family planning, and children in armies. Incorporated into Argentine jurisprudence, the Convention on the Rights of the Child has become part of the body of law regarding children.[10]

Significantly, because the concept of identity is not defined in the convention, it remains somewhat ambiguous. Although elements—"nationality, name and family relations as recognized by law"—are explicitly named in Article 8, this list is not exhaustive; thus different interpretations of the "right to identity," incorporating different elements, could arise in the future. Legal scholar George A. Stewart breaks down identity into four interpretive categories:

> Familial identity includes natural parents, family and ancestors as well as family name. Tribal identity is intended here to include ethnic, cultural and religious identity. Biological identity includes medical and genetic information about oneself and one's ancestors and blood relatives, and also historical data such as place and time of birth and records of events important to the person. Political identity is nationality.[11]

Issues of identity and its various interpretations open up a discussion in international law that may have far-reaching implications for human rights movements worldwide.

The convention stipulated that a UN Committee on the Rights of the Child be established to monitor and help governments bring their national laws and practices into conformity with the convention. The committee, which consists of ten members of varied professions and nationalities, reviews reports on the implementation plans from the countries that have ratified the convention. Similarly, the Grandmothers, who had actively supported the passage of an international convention protecting children, worked vigorously in implementing the measure as they educated both the public and professionals about it. The incorporation of the convention in Argentine law aided their efforts to make broad changes in the adoption system and in particular to end the secrecy that characterized adoption proceedings.[12]

Estela de Carlotto comments:

Here, people think of us as "searchers of identity." Abroad, Article 8 of the Convention is called "the Argentine article" because we fought for it. We, supported by many people in Argentine society and even in the government, succeeded in incorporating it in our Constitution. And it was not only Article 8, but also Articles 7 and 11, articles that speak of the right of children to be themselves, to have their family and identity, and how the state has the obligation to restore it to them. Article 11 states that children who have been taken illegally out of their country of origin have to be returned to that country. So, there is support for the return of the children who have been taken abroad, those "second disappearances" carried out by the military, the police, or their accomplices.[13]

In 1990 the Grandmothers pointed out to President Menem that because Argentina had ratified the Convention on the Rights of the Child, he was obligated to ensure that the disappeared children recover their identity. Yet his upcoming presidential pardon of the members of the juntas would in effect legitimize the children's captivity, condemning them to ignorance of their real families and to life with their parents' murderers.[14] Eighteen months after his election, Menem remained silent about the disappeared children. The Grandmothers held the government responsible for its inaction and stated that it was plain common sense and within reason to expect that the *Estado de Derecho* (democratic state) ought to intervene and repair the damage that the *Estado Terrorista* (terrorist state) had done. They therefore called on the international human rights community to hold the Argentine government to its commitment that the right to identity become a reality.[15] In turn, the right to identity became the legal foundation on which the Grandmothers built their arguments.

The case of Emiliano Carlos Tortrino Castro became the test case in the Argentine judicial system for recognizing and applying the right to identity. It centered on the issue of compulsory genetic testing of the youngster to ascertain his biological affiliation. Emiliano had disappeared with his mother, María Carmen Tortrino, in March 1977, when he was eight months old; his father had disappeared a few months before. The child had a visible identifying characteristic: a cleft palate. Immediately after his disappearance, the two families started to search for him. After a few days, Grandfather Tortrino learned that a child with a cleft palate had been found in the streets and put under a judge's guard. In April the judge gave the child to a couple, authorizing them to give him their name. In a matter of weeks the child had lost his identity; in less than six months, the adoption was completed.

In 1988, with the help of two prosecutors nominated by President Alfonsín, the Grandmothers got involved in the case; they offered to provide witnesses and demanded that genetic testing be performed on the child to determine his identity. The adoptive couple challenged the judge's order requiring such tests, and the attorney general sided with them, arguing not only that he wanted to "protect the intimacy" of Emiliano but that mandatory testing threatened the "physical and psychic integrity of the minor."[16] In 1995 the case reached the Supreme Court, which issued no decision on mandatory genetic testing; it declared the case closed, citing the statute of limitations. The Grandmothers responded by launching a national and international campaign to collect a million signatures to send to the Human Rights Commission of the OAS to protest the Supreme Court's ruling.[17]

Human rights lawyers such as Alcira E. Ríos—professor of civil family law at the Universidad de Buenos Aires and one of the Grandmothers' legal advisors—support mandatory genetic testing of the children:

> I believe that the testing has to be mandatory in the case of the children. It cannot be mandatory for adults because it would be contrary to the constitutional principle of self-incrimination. But the minor has been the victim of a crime, and the judge is obliged to investigate the crime, and if he needs the testing he has to order it. The judge has to decide since the minor is not able to give informed consent. And here it would not be self-incrimination because the child is a victim, not accused of any crime.[18]

Finally, in December 1996, the Supreme Court agreed with Alcira Ríos's reasoning: it ruled that mandatory testing can be ordered even if the "adoptive" parents or the child are opposed to it. This decision, which represents a significant victory for the Grandmothers, will help resolve some of their cases presently in court.[19]

The case of Simón Antonio Riquelo, in neighboring Uruguay, has raised similar issues. In 1976 Simón, twenty days old, was taken from his mother, Sara Méndez Lompodio, when she was kidnapped in Buenos Aires. After spending four years in jail, Sara, together with the Grandmothers, started the long search for her child. In 1987 Sara and the child's father, Mauricio Gatti (who died of a heart attack in 1991), found a boy in Montevideo whom they believed to be their son. The boy had been adopted by a relative of the military officer in charge of Sara's kidnapping. The court in Uruguay ruled legitimate the opposition of the adoptive parents to the blood test, and Sara took her case to the Supreme Court. At the end of 1997 the Court ruled against her. There is nothing else Sara can do within the Uruguayan judiciary. It is likely that in the future, she will pursue her case at the international level.[20]

THE NATIONAL COMMISSION FOR THE RIGHT TO IDENTITY

In 1991 the government opened the archives containing information on the Nazis who had been living in Argentina since World War II. Human rights organizations immediately demanded that the archives containing information on the Argentine disappeared also be made available. The military and security spokesmen claimed that there were no files on the disappeared and that the last de facto president, General Reynaldo Bignone, had ordered the burning of the archives. The Grandmothers pointed out that even if there were no formal archives, there were plenty of "living archives"—such as General Ramón Camps, who was responsible for the death of over 5,000 people.[21]

In July 1992, the Grandmothers met with President Menem and they insisted that the government create a commission to search actively for the disappeared children. One result of this meeting was that the Office of Human Rights was upgraded to undersecretariat status, which conferred a wider range of action and decision making on its director, Alicia Pierini. Most important, the government formed the National Commission for the Right to Identity, whose purpose is "to impel the search of the disappeared children and to determine the whereabouts of children kidnapped and disappeared of known identity and of children born while the mother was illegally detained, and to fulfill the commitment made by the state when it ratified the Convention on the Rights of the Child."[22]

The commission is composed of seven members—two prosecutors designated by the attorney general, two members chosen by the Grandmothers (who, to maintain their independence and freedom to criticize, did not want to sit on the commission themselves), and three members of the Undersecretariat of Human Rights, including its director.[23] A critical element in its success is that the commission, like the National Genetic Data Bank, is not restricted to working solely on the disappeared victims of state terrorism. It also investigates the cases of children who have lost their identity in other ways, such as through illegitimate adoptions and the traffic of children. Since the commission's inception, over one hundred young people have approached it for help in identifying their origins and establishing their family history.[24]

The Grandmothers were thus able to bring to the commission's attention the most pressing cases—including those of the Reggiardo Tolosa twins, Emiliano Carlos Tortrino Castro, and Major Norberto Atilio Bianco and his wife—which the commission could use its power to resolve, maneuvering through the legal morass and judicial delays. The commission's own investigations have uncovered forty additional cases of disappearances of pregnant women and children, which had not been previously reported to the Grandmothers' organization.[25] The Grandmothers' lawyers found that the commission facilitated their task, as its constant exchanges with the judicial system's representatives gave the prosecutors a deeper understanding of the cases' complexities.

However, the Grandmothers understood that despite some progress, they needed to remain vigilant. In December 1993, together with a number of other organizations working on behalf of children's rights, they created a separate committee to monitor the implementation of the Convention on the Rights of the Child in Argentina.[26] Having succeeded in including the right of identity in the convention and in Argentine law, the Grandmothers sought to ensure that the Argentine judicial system incorporated this new right in its practice.

FIRST SUCCESS: ANNULMENT OF AN ADOPTION

In 1991, because of the newly created right to identity, a "full" adoption was annulled for the first time in Argentina.[27] After genetic testing demonstrated that the child's identity had been forged, Judge Héctor Armando Nattero declared Ximena Vicario's adoption null and void. Alcira Ríos explains:

> Many of the disappeared children have been "fully" adopted. Adoption law in Argentina establishes the loss of biological identity and inclusion in the adoptive family. And it is irrevocable. When we asked for the annulment of Ximena Vicario's adoption, many people raised their eyebrows, because in this country there had never been an annulment of a full adoption. This is the first case. The basis for this was the right of identity. Once the testing showed who she was, it followed that there had been fraud in the adoption process; and since family rights are paramount, her adoption was annulled. They all agreed—the judge, the Judicial Chamber, and the Supreme Court. This opens the way for annulments of other adoptions. The children themselves, when they become adults, can request that their adoptions be annulled. That is why this decision was so important. And now the right to identity has constitutional rank because the Convention for the Rights of the Child has been incorporated into the newly reformed national Constitution.[28]

The legal decision requiring that the Reggiardo Tolosa twins recover their name and be issued legal documents with that name was also based on the right to identity. After the genetic testing demonstrated that they were not the children of policeman Samuel Miara and that there was no biological relationship between them and him, the court restored their identity and appointed a guardian. Miara no longer had any rights over them.

Over seventy-five cases are currently being pursued by the Grandmothers in which genetic testing needs to be performed to assess the children's identity. Once their true identities are ascertained, their adoptions too might be annulled. As the Grandmothers had argued, full recognition of the right to identity by the Argentine judicial system was and is essential to recovering who the found children really are.

IMPACT ON ADOPTION LEGISLATION

The Grandmothers' experience in struggling to recover the disappeared children, together with the introduction of the right to identity into the new Constitution, is changing how adoption is regarded in Argentina. The Grandmothers oppose not adoption itself but the legal regulations, procedures, and practices that are not in the best interest of the children. Chicha Mariani expresses their views forcefully:

> I believe that adoption is a totally legitimate institution and that it is absolutely necessary—with the caveat that children should not be sold or taken away from their families, as has happened here. I also believe that a child has a right to her or his identity. I do think that international adoptions should not exist and that they are an abominable practice. In 1983, in Geneva, for the first time we talked with representatives of an international adoption agency and we realized what was going on: they had photo albums offering children, as if it were a natural thing. That horrified us.... I think that to transfer a child is like transferring a plant from one environment to another. The plant dries up if you change the environment. Likewise, the child suffers from discrimination. I think it is a terrible thing to take children from their country, to change their environment. Roots are a powerful thing and the proof is in the thousands of cases of people looking for their roots, wanting to find out their origins.[29]

The thinking of the Grandmothers converges with that of Maria Josefina Becker, deputy director of the Brazilian Child Welfare Agency, FUNABEM (Fundação Nacional para o bem-estar do menor abandonado). Becker articulates a Latin American viewpoint on international adoption:

> Another question surrounding international adoption concerns the paucity of real knowledge as to the medium and long range consequences of such adoption, especially with regard to children of different ethnic and racial origins. We can assume that in most cases the baby or small child will really be loved and accepted by the adoptive parents, who will do everything possible to protect and shield the child against any form of discrimination. However, one day the child will become an adolescent and in time a young adult. The fact that the child has been adopted by a family does not necessarily mean that he or she has been adopted by a society or by a country. What problems will the young black, or person of indigenous or racially mixed features, experience in the formation of his or her identity, in relationships with his or her peers, and in becoming integrated into the daily life of the society? . . . We must also think of the right of the adolescent to know his or her own roots. How will they react to the fact that a decision to deprive them of one nationality and grant them another was made without their having any say whatsoever?[30]

These new questions and new thinking arise directly from the Grandmothers' struggles. They presented their work and discussed the right to identity at the Second Interdisciplinary Adoption Symposium in the Southern Cone, held in Buenos Aires in November 1994; another participant in the same workshop, a professional in the field of adoption, underscored their call for change:

> The institution of adoption deserves a new ideology that rescues the value of freedom, the importance of truth, and respect for personal rights, especially the right to identity. . . . The knowledge of one's own genesis is an essential factor for the construction of the self of the adoptee. . . . [I]t is necessary to have a new ideological and legal definition of adoption, more flexible, more open, more respectful for the dignity and individuality of each person, as unique beings, with a right to a life worth living.[31]

Influenced by the Grandmothers and supported by a few professionals and politicians, legislators began in 1994 to draft new adoption legislation that would take into account the right to identity. Graciela Fernández Meijide, a member of Congress, is one of the proponents of the new law:

In general, adoption legislation tends to stress the rights of adults, instead of the rights of children. Our law emphasizes the right of the child. It demands that children be told the truth, that they are adopted. The judge is supposed to keep all the information about the biological family so that when the child is sixteen, he or she has access to that information and can search for their families if they want. . . . Sometimes we think it is cruel to tell a person the truth (first as a child, but later as an adult). But that view reflects a colonialist attitude. Only the colonizer refuses to respect the identity of the colonized. It does not matter what the origin of an adoption is. It can be a perfectly legal adoption, as when a child is orphaned or abandoned. Or an adoption following a crime, as under the dictatorship, when children were stolen. Or an adoption following the sale of a child, a horrible practice, more and more common in our country. Regardless of the adoption situation, it is hypocritical not to tell the truth. It is a lack of respect of children's full humanity and their right to their identity.[32]

The new legislation will also specify that illegality in the adoption process is sufficient grounds for annulment. Grandmother Antonia Segarra elaborates on this point:

When it is proven that a child has been stolen, of course the adoption has to be annulled. Those who stole the child should be arrested and the child reunited with her or his family. We wanted this to become law and to be an established principle in jurisprudence, so that we do not have to fight for each case separately. We are not against adoptions, but our grandchildren were stolen; their parents did not abandon them and we have not abandoned them either. We have looked for them since the very beginning.[33]

The newly drafted legislation was approved by the House of Representatives in 1994 and by the Senate in early 1997. In its final version the law gives adopted children the right to know that they are adopted and full access to their adoption records at age eighteen. While the new legislation does not explicitly prohibit international adoptions, it requires a five-year residency period in Argentina for those wishing to adopt. If enforced, this condition will make international adoptions practically impossible. The Argentine government maintains that before international adoptions can even be considered, a body of law to protect children needs to be developed; otherwise those adoptions can become a cover-up for the sale and trafficking of children.

OTHER IMPORTANT CONSEQUENCES OF THE RIGHT TO IDENTITY

Illegal adoptions and trafficking of children are serious problems in Latin America.[34] In Argentina, according to a 1989 investigative report from Defence of Children International, during the years of the dictatorship, the sale and traffic of children reached its peak; but the practice has continued, with an estimated 12,000 illegal adoptions per year. One adoptive mother reported, "In 1986 I was told of a boutique at the back of a store; it looked like an adoption agency, and it had been operating since the Proceso. The sister of an acquaintance of mine bought a baby for $8,000."[35]

In the interior of the country, in some of the poorest areas, it is not uncommon to have witnesses give false testimony about births. Sister Martha Pelloni, a well-known community activist, in testimony before the Permanent Assembly for Human Rights accused members of the judicial system of participating in the illegal adoption and traffic of children.[36] A 1993 report by the superior court of Corrientes province acknowledged that children were given away without any oversight or regulation. Sister Martha stated to the court:

> From the moment I arrived in Goya, in Corrientes province—and I knew nothing about the issue—I started to get calls from distraught relatives regarding children who are now in Italy, France, Germany, and the United States. When I asked the callers to identify themselves, I always received the same answers: fear and tears. I asked myself: Who are the provincial authorities responsible for people reacting this way?[37]

In 1994 the case of Carlitos García in Chaco province attracted enormous attention. The child was adopted by a Spanish bullfighter and his wife, in flagrant violation of Argentine adoption law. The judge involved had participated in an unusually high number of adoptions, given the population and number of births in the region.[38] The case became symbolic of the ease with which international adoptions took place despite the government's opposition. An international adoption agency based in Oslo, Norway, was reported to operate in Argentina and to have arranged for more than 3,000 children from Latin America and Asia to be adopted in Europe.[39] Even worse, drug traffickers have been implicated in the sale of children.[40]

A national network to fight the traffic of children has recently emerged. The private foundation Identidad de Origen (Identity of Origin), started by former Buenos Aires province senator Ricardo Ivoskus, has launched a campaign to lobby Congress against any type of legislation that may lead to the acceptance of international adoptions. Ivoskus, who has taken a leading role in this fight, has exposed the corruption in the judicial system that has allowed illegal adoptions to take place.[41] Grandmother Elsa Oesterheld laments: "Foreigners come here and buy children, that happens all the time. In our talks, we tell people about the National Genetic Data Bank, as a tool in the fight against the traffic of children, where parents of stolen children can deposit their blood, so that the children can one day trace their origins."[42]

The right to identity can and probably will be invoked in connection with the newly developed technologies of assisted reproduction. In her book *De la cigüeña a la probeta* (*From the Stork to the Test Tube*) Argentine feminist Susana Sommer asks, "What will be the answer when those born of in vitro fertilization or surrogacy ask about their identity?"[43] Children conceived through artificial insemination, in vitro fertilization, and other reproductive technologies who want to know their history will be able to claim the right to identity in requesting information about their genetic origins.[44] As these new reproduction modalities become more common in Argentina, legal experts, ethicists, and feminists will have the difficult task of reconciling them with the right to identity.[45]

In the United States as well, the secrecy surrounding adoption and issues of identity has become controversial. A sealed records policy still exists in most U.S. states, and the origin of adoptees continues to be a well-guarded secret. Adoption agencies, courts, and hospitals refuse to divulge any family information to adoptees or to birth parents searching for their biological kin. The birth certificates of adopted children do not reflect their true history.[46] Author and adoption counselor Betty Jean Lifton has poignantly described the adopted child's search for roots and struggle to form an authentic self after experiencing disconnection and losses that society usually fails to acknowledge.[47] A network of members of the adoption triad—adoptees, birth parents, and adoptive parents—is now working actively for a healthy adoption system with open adoption and open records, one that recognizes the adoptees' rights to the knowledge of their origins.[48] However, since the United States has not ratified the United Nations Convention on the Rights of the Child, adoptees cannot support their demands for change by claiming the right to identity.

The ability to claim memory and one's history are essential to that right. Erik Erikson has shown us that identity develops both from immediate life involvements and from one's larger sense of history and continuity with the past.[49] The Grandmothers' work accords with his views and introduces into the international legal sphere the principle that human beings are not isolated units, that feelings of belonging and connection are necessary components of a healthy identity.

The fight for human rights starts with everyday issues. Guided by love for their children and grandchildren, the Grandmothers started their searches—first as individuals dealing with their personal tragedies, later as part of a movement. Eventually their work transcended the particular, resulting in the creation of a new ethical and legal principle that has now been incorporated in international human rights legislation. As Eleanor Roosevelt convincingly wrote in 1958:

> Where, after all, do universal human rights begin? In small places, close to home—so close and so small that they cannot be seen on any maps of the world. Yet they ARE the world of the individual persons; the neighborhood . . . ; the school or college . . . ; the factory, farm or office. . . . Unless these rights have meaning there, they have little meaning anywhere. Without concerned citizen action to uphold them close to home, we shall look in vain for progress in the larger world.[50]

Inspired by the Grandmothers' example, citizens in other countries are taking action. Currently in El Salvador, relatives of children who disappeared during the civil war have organized themselves to denounce the disappearances and to find the children. The Asociación Pro-Búsqueda de los Niños (Association for the Search of Children) has documented the disappearance of 156 children and identified 24. One of the recent stories is particularly striking: Gina Marie Craig (her adopted name) was taken by Salvadoran soldiers and adopted by an American couple from Ohio. The child kept insisting that she knew her family was alive. Genetic testing has proved her right, and she is now trying to reconnect with her large family in a rural area in El Salvador. "No one believed me, but I always knew it in my heart," said Gina

Marie in a 1996 interview. There are probably dozens of children with similar stories.[51] In practically all the countries around the world that ratify the Convention for the Rights of the Child, the right to identity will affect their adoption practices and procedures and help prevent the traffic and sale of children.

Estela de Carlotto summarizes the successes of the Grandmothers in creating new mechanisms and practices that will aid all children:

Without being doctors or lawyers, only grandmothers, and with the priceless collaboration of professionals committed to our cause, we were able to defeat the perverse design of those who stole our grandchildren. . . . Because of our initiative, since 1987 we have in Buenos Aires the National Genetic Data Bank, unique in the world[;] . . . this Bank will keep our blood and those of our families until the year 2050. . . . In the legal arena we succeeded in changing those obsolete laws that viewed children and their families through a colonial lens: the adoption law, the custody law, etc. . . . In the international order we were able, together with other national and international organizations, to include Articles 7, 8, 11, and 12 in the Convention for the Rights of the Child. And in the psychological arena, we have opened the national and international debate about the right of a child to live with her or his family of origin.[52]

EIGHT

THE POLITICS OF MEMORY

My terror of forgetting is greater than my terror of having too much to remember. Let the accumulated facts about the past continue to multiply. Let the flood of books and monographs grow, even if they are only read by specialists. Let unread copies lie in the shelves of many libraries, so that if some be destroyed or removed others will remain. So that those who need can find that this person did live, those events really took place, this interpretation is not the only one.
Yosef H. Yerushalmi,* Zakhor *(1989)

After the fall of the military regime in 1983, President Alfonsín's amnesty laws and Menem's presidential pardons allowed those guilty of atrocities to go free. These actions both ensured impunity and strengthened the conspiracy of silence, making it possible for belief in the "official story" to continue. In the few prosecutions, the criminals' connections with the power structure, together with the long judicial delays, meant that they either received light sentences or had the cases against them dropped.

In late 1994 the Menem government passed law 24.411, which offers economic compensation to the relatives of those murdered or disappeared. The Grandmothers, like all the other human rights organizations except the Mothers of the Plaza de Mayo, interpret this law as the government's acknowledgment of the genocide perpetrated by the state during the dictatorship, and they have endorsed it. However, no legal sanctions are planned for those responsible for the crimes.[1] In 1995 former navy captain Adolfo Francisco Scilingo confessed to taking part in the murder of political prisoners who had been drugged and thrown from aircraft into the Río de la Plata.[2] In the same year, the chief of the army, Lieutenant General Martín Antonio Balza, publicly admitted to the kidnapping, murder, and torture carried on by the armed forces during the repression but denied the existence of lists containing information about the disappeared, and the Argentine bishops announced that they would "examine their conscience" about the role of the church during the dictatorship.[3] None of these declarations resulted in any action whatsoever.

THE CULTURE OF IMPUNITY

Under the banner of "pacification" and "reconciliation," a culture of impunity has flourished in Argentina. The regime's unpunished crimes have created a climate in which people increasingly see police violence, lack of an independent judicial system, and endemic governmental corruption as normal, everyday aspects of Argentinian life.[4] As has frequently been demonstrated throughout the world, impunity is the enemy of democracy, because it prevents social reconciliation. When the prerequisites for authentic reconciliation—truth and justice, acknowledgment of the crimes committed, and punishment—are not met, forgiveness is impossible. Reconciliation cannot be dictated from above.[5]

As an act of violence, impunity also has serious consequences for individuals and families trying to heal from the psychosocial trauma caused by human rights abuses during the dictatorship. The repression has damaged at least three generations: the parents of the disappeared, the disappeared, and the children of the disappeared. And the long-term effects of growing up in an atmosphere that legitimizes crime and denies reality are likely to harm the mental and spiritual well-being of future generations of Argentines.[6]

In May 1990, the People's Permanent Tribunal—an international group—met in Buenos Aires to discuss the case of Argentina as part of its sessions on crimes against humanity in Latin America.[7] After hearing testimonies from victims of the repression and reviewing extensive documentation, the tribunal noted, "Under the justification of pardoning, forgetting, or reconciling, the structures, mechanisms, and attitudes of the past remain intact in the present. They allow the continuation of crimes against humanity, while simultaneously destroying the possibility of civilized coexistence between people."[8] Impunity, according to the tribunal, fulfilled at least three purposes: it protected those who had committed crimes, allowed history to be written from the point of view of the oppressor, and shifted the blame for the economic and social chaos created by the dictatorship onto the most marginalized and exploited segments of the population. It had become a structural element of the Argentine reality, perpetuating an unequal distribution of power and the exploitation of workers, whose status, rights, and working conditions were deteriorating rapidly. Moreover, the tribunal pointed to the danger that impunity has created for the consolidation of democracy in Argentina: "Accompanied by the great majority of the Argentine people, we denounce as totally erroneous the project to achieve peace and democratic coexistence by negating the values on which this coexistence is built: life, liberty, equality, truth, and justice."[9]

The economic situation in Argentina has been—and is—devastating for major segments of society. The free-market-oriented economic policies introduced by Finance Minister Domingo Cavallo during the Menem administration (and continued by his successor, Roque Fernández) opened the economy to international competition and investment. Inflation was drastically reduced and government agencies were aggressively privatized. The country has been struggling with recession, unemployment has reached a staggering 20 percent, and important social benefits have been reduced or eliminated. These unpopular measures have been denounced by opposition parties and labor unions, which believe the poor are being squeezed to protect investors and international agencies—the same sectors that benefited most from the dictatorship.[10]

High-ranking members of the Menem administration have been at the center of scandals involving allegations of drug trafficking and extortion. For example, in "Swiftgate" President Menem's brother-in-law Emir Yoma was accused of trying to obtain money from Swift-Armour, a transnational meatpacking corporation.[11] A lethargic court investigation has not produced definitive results.

Nor is corruption limited to the upper levels of government. Police brutality and corruption are rampant in Argentina. Many officers now in positions of authority had participated directly in the repression; since they were under the control of the military, they enjoyed total impunity. Under democracy, the police have stressed the need for "security" and for waging a "war on crime." The structures of repression created by the dictatorship thus continue to shape current police operations. Some of the worst police abuses have been carried out against young people; and they have been denounced by the progressive media and human rights organizations, as well as provoking vigorous community organizing.[12]

The judiciary seems little better. In Catamarca province, the case of María Soledad Morales, a seventeen-year-old girl found murdered who obviously had been tortured and mutilated, has rocked the country by revealing the degree of corruption in the province's judicial system. The governor of Catamarca and two of his closest associates came to figure prominently in the case; not surprisingly, it remains unsolved. Weekly silent marches, organized by Carmelite nun Sister Martha Pelloni, the former headmistress of María Soledad's school, have attracted up to 30,000 participants.[13] The director of the Center for Legal and Social Studies, Martín Abregú, summarized the situation: "The case has inflamed Argentina. It's a case of passion and politics, cover-ups and killers. But mostly it's struck a chord because people are sick of impunity in this country."[14]

The lack of trust in the judicial system has become endemic, notes political scientist Atilio H. Borón: "The judicial system is in shambles. Only those few with money and resources can make some use of it. It is not independent; it is very closely linked to the centers of political power. If the decision of a judge does not agree with those in power, it gets changed. The Supreme Court is addicted to the government. Interior Minister Carlos Corach himself has said that he runs the Court by telephone."[15]

In 1992 and 1994 the bloody bombings in Buenos Aires of the Israeli Embassy and the Argentine Israelite Mutual Association (AMIA) brought outcries from around the world. Though neither case has been solved, there is strong evidence of police involvement, at least in the AMIA case.[16] And in early 1997 the burned body of José Luis Cabezas, a thirty-six-year-old photojournalist working for the news magazine *Noticias,* was found in his car in a resort town. His magazine had published investigative reports on alleged corruption in the provincial police.[17]

These are just some of the most obvious examples of what the Grandmothers call "the current impunity in action."

THE POLITICS OF REMEMBERING

In analyzing the mechanisms that impede the development of democracy in Latin America, Eduardo Galeano uses the expression "the kidnapping of history": "For those who are starving, the system denies them even the nourishment of memory. So that they don't have a future, it steals their past. *Official history is told by, for, and of the rich, the white, the male, and the military.*"[18] The work of the Grandmothers provides a strong counterpoint to the kidnapping of history in Argentina.

As historian Yosef Hayim Yerushalmi writes in describing the history of the Jews: "What we call 'forgetting' in a collective sense occurs when human groups fail—whether purposely or passively, out of rebellion, indifference, or indolence, or as the result of some disruptive historical catastrophe—to transmit what they know out of the past to their posterity."[19] By telling their stories and by pursuing the truth, the Grandmothers work to prevent such failure, ensuring that those responsible for atrocities do not win a victory over history. The Grandmothers' everyday work, their personal testimonies, and the pictures of the disappeared that they publish regularly in their newsletter challenge the country's pervasive historical amnesia. It keeps the victims from becoming an anonymous mass. Every time the Grandmothers find a disappeared child, a detailed picture emerges of how the dictatorship implemented a methodology of terror that targeted society's most vulnerable members. Each story contains a thread that connects the police, the military, and the intelligence services to the disappearances. Nonetheless, the perpetrators have denied the evidence and have tried, unsuccessfully, to silence the Grandmothers.

U.S. psychiatrist Judith Herman has analyzed the relationship between crime and silence:

> In order to escape accountability for their crimes, perpetrators will do everything in their power to promote forgetting. Secrecy and silence are the perpetrator's first lines of defense, but if secrecy fails, the perpetrator will aggressively attack the credibility of the victim and anyone who supports the victim. If the victim cannot be silenced absolutely, the perpetrator will try to make sure that no one listens or offers aid. To this end, an impressive array of arguments will be marshalled, from the most blatant denial to the most sophisticated rationalizations. After every atrocity one can expect to hear the same apologies: it never happened; the victim is deluded; the victim lies; the victim fantasizes; the victim is manipulative; the victim is manipulated; the victim brought it upon him- or herself (masochistic); the victim exaggerates (histrionic), and, in any case, it is time to forget the past and move on.[20]

The Grandmothers challenge silence and denial by bearing witness to the crimes of the dictatorship: they defy the numbing and the active forgetting that the culture of impunity fosters. The Grandmothers have zeroed in on the politics of memory, on what is remembered and how it is remembered, and on the distortion of the historical record. They know that silence and forgetting play into the hands of the powerful and that personalizing the disappeared and naming the murderers are the first steps in the recovery of truth.

Grandmother Delia Califano speaks of her everyday telling:

> I need to transmit what I know. When I go to the beach, if somebody sits close to me, I find a way to tell my story. It is a way to keep memory alive. I feel it complements our public work, the speaking up we do on the radio and TV. When somebody sits next to me in a train and we start talking about the high cost of living and the fear that the military might step in, I bring up the disappearances. I am always searching for a way to let others know what happened.[21]

The Grandmothers' determination to *not* forget and to continue documenting the methodology of terror led them to help found the Latin American Federation of Associations for Relatives of the Detained and Disappeared (FEDEFAM), started in 1981 in Costa Rica. Grandmother María Alexiu de Ignace was FEDEFAM president from 1991 to 1993. FEDEFAM, which has lobbied the United Nations and the OAS to recognize forced disappearances as a crime against humanity, has strongly opposed the amnesty laws and the presidential pardons in Argentina and other Latin American countries.[22] In 1993, at the United Nations, FEDEFAM sponsored the testimony of one of the found children, Laura Scaccheri, who after eight years was restituted to her legitimate family. Laura asked the Human Rights Commission to support the restitution of the Reggiardo Tolosa twins to their family, challenging the notion that the twins themselves should be the ones to decide with whom to live:

> Now I live with my family. With them, I can ask questions, search, look back bit by bit, cry and laugh with love and, above all, without lies. If my restitution and that of fifty other children happened, why is it so difficult for the others? . . . Like for instance, the current case in Argentina of the Reggiardo Tolosa twins in which it is claimed that they should be the ones to choose. That means delegating to children what adults should be doing. Can a child that has been living with someone for years choose to leave? I don't think so. In my own case it was very difficult to understand that they had lied to me for so long, that they lied about everything.[23]

LOOKING TO THE FUTURE

Because they want the past to be remembered, the Grandmothers speak often about the importance of collective memory. However, as the creation of the National Genetic Data Bank demonstrates, their focus is on the future. Increasingly, they have emphasized working with the young, because it is the next generation that will inherit the country and will continue their work. The Grandmothers know that workers, community groups, students—all those who question the injustices of the system—might well become the next targets of repression, if democracy does not take a firm hold in Argentina.

In 1990 the Grandmothers published a book of prose and poetry, *Algún día . . .* (*Someday . . .*), by two young women, Mariana Eva Pérez and Yamila Grandi, who hope someday to find their siblings born in captivity. Both their mothers were pregnant when they were abducted.[24] Mariana Eva Pérez was fifteen months old when her parents disappeared. She tells what she knows about her brother:

From the testimony of a woman who was in the ESMA, the camp where my mother was taken, we know that my mother delivered my brother on November 15, 1978, that he weighed a little over three kilos, and that the delivery was normal. We also know that she was allowed to keep the baby for three to four days, which is unusual because generally they took the babies away as soon as they were born. After the delivery, apparently she was scared that she would be tortured and killed. She left the ESMA with my brother in her arms and that is the last we know of her. She had named him Rodolfo Fernando. So, I know I have a brother and that is the one the Grandmothers are searching for.

I grew up with my grandparents, who gave me a lot of love. They always told me the truth. When I was eight or nine years old they took me to the National Genetic Data Bank to deposit my blood. That was very confusing. My grandmother explained that it was to help identify my brother. I was really glad with that news, I always wanted a brother. However, I got sad when I realized I could not meet him. I finally decided that I would play my part in the search, that I would support the Grandmothers. After that decision, when I would go the Bank, I would say, decisively, "Here is my arm, please go ahead."[25]

Her grandmother Argentina Pérez recalls:

Mariana has always been very spontaneous. Her first-grade teacher told me that one day she stood up and said: "Teacher, can I say something?" When she said yes, Mariana told the class: "I want my schoolmates to know that my parents are disappeared." Then all the children started to ask what that meant, and the teacher had to explain about the disappearances.[26]

Mariana adds:

I thought it was important to let them know about my history, because when I like someone I want them to know who I am. And I don't just care about my brother. I care also about the other children who disappeared. When I can, I go to see the Grandmothers to find out what they are doing and if there is something I can do to help.

In 1992, the Grandmothers celebrated their organization's fifteenth anniversary with a three-day international seminar on the issues of identity, affiliation, and restitution. At the closing ceremony, after the various panels and addresses by sociologists, physicians, psychologists, social workers, and lawyers, the found children and the siblings of children born in captivity spoke. Mariana fully understands the importance of their role:

At the end of the seminar, we spoke about the future of the Grandmothers, and we said that their work has to continue. If they are unable to continue because they get too old or too sick, we will take over. The future of the Grandmothers is in our hands. We all agreed about that. We told the Grandmothers not to worry. Their work will not be over when they are gone. Our goal is to continue until we find the last child, and even after that. So that people will not forget what happened here, so that history does not repeat itself. As soon as the dictatorship was over, some people wanted the Mothers and the Grandmothers to shut up, they did not want them talking about the past. That is why it is so important that we keep the memory alive.

The voices of the young are beginning to be heard in Argentina. In October 1995, high school students protested over the use of the infamous ESMA facilities for a swimming contest. The youngsters pointed out that thousands of people had been tortured and killed in the ESMA and that to try to legitimate its use by hosting a sports event there was an affront to the memory of the disappeared. Out of 120 expected participants, only 20 showed up.[27] More generally, many now attending schools and universities are commemorating the students who disappeared during the dictatorship and are committing themselves to the values for which so many of them were killed. They are refusing to accept unemployment, poverty, lack of education and health services, poor housing, and all the other injustices of the present Argentine society.[28] In October 1996, inspired by the Mothers of the Plaza de Mayo/Línea Fundadora, students at the Colegio Nacional de Buenos Aires (Buenos Aires National School, the city's most prestigious public high school) publicly commemorated ninety former students who had been killed or disappeared during the dictatorship. The event, "Bridge of Memory," and an exhibit on the lives of the disappeared students attracted hundreds of people.[29]

In 1995 about seventy young people between the ages of sixteen and twenty started a new human rights organization. They are children of those who disappeared or were assassinated during the dictatorship. They call themselves HIJOS (Hijos por la Identidad y la Justicia, contra el Olvido y el Silencio; Children for Identity and Justice, against Oblivion and Silence). Among their basic demands are the annulment of the amnesty laws and the presidential pardons, so that their parents' murderers can be prosecuted, and restitution of the disappeared children made to their families of origin. Miguel Santucho, a twenty-year-old member, describes the organization:

HIJOS is a very heterogeneous group. There are different political perspectives, different ages and cultures. In our group we do not have a hierarchy; we don't have representatives or a president. We carry out our work in committees, we meet in assembly once a week, and we try very hard to reach decisions by consensus. We came together to create HIJOS because we felt that there was something missing in our lives. My mother disappeared. I only know a few things about her, and I can't fill that void. I realize that the reason that she disappeared is that at the social level she represented something that the dominant class wanted to eliminate. Her bonds with other people needed to be destroyed. By recovering those social bonds, I will be able to reclaim part of my identity and obtain justice. . . . We are an independent organization, but we are aware that our existence today is possible thanks to the twenty years of struggle of the Mothers, the Grandmothers, and the other organizations.[30]

At the June 27, 1996, celebration of the "first thousand Thursdays" of the Mothers of the Plaza de Mayo, HIJOS was a highly visible and welcome presence. One member of HIJOS declared to the press: "For us, HIJOS, this march of the Mothers represents the contact with our history and the struggle of our parents. Those who believed in the victory of death were wrong: twenty years afterward, here we are to say 'presente.'"[31]

On October 29, 1996, the first anniversary of Antonio Bussi's assumption to power as governor of Tucumán province, HIJOS organized protests in Tucumán and Buenos Aires. Bussi, a well-known commander during the dirty war, had been in charge of the clandestine detention camps in that province. Trained by the Pentagon, Bussi had learned in Vietnam the counterinsurgency techniques he later applied in Tucumán. Calling it a "Day of National Shame," HIJOS marched to the Plaza de Mayo, accompanied by human rights activists. Representatives of the political parties were conspicuously absent from the event.[32] HIJOS has received threats and some of its members have been arrested. The organization met with Minister of the Interior Carlos Corach to request a "preventive" habeas corpus for its members, making the government responsible for eventual attacks on them. The minister offered them police protection but they refused, saying, "We don't want policemen on our doorsteps. They are the same people that murdered our parents. What we want is that the security forces be purged."[33]

The Grandmothers' struggle for the identification and restitution of their disappeared grandchildren is, like most women's work, essential, everyday, and down-to-earth. The qualities that they bring to the public arena—fortitude, patience, and vigilance—are central to establishing a real democracy. In keeping historical memory alive, the Grandmothers have assumed a role that grandmothers often play in the life of their communities: telling the stories that create a sense of identity and common purpose among family members. Their refusal to give in to complacency and silence affirms the continuity of life and provides hope. By recovering the identity of their grandchildren, they are beginning the essential process of constructing a historical and inclusive Argentine social identity, an identity that is itself necessary to heal a deeply damaged society and lay the foundation for a living democracy.

Against forgetting, against unfinished business, nobody can speak more eloquently than the Grandmothers of the Plaza de Mayo:

We must not forget or be silent. Our duty is to keep alive the memory, to keep talking tirelessly about the horrors of the Argentine genocide. We will not let any episode, insignificant as it may seem, go by without expressing our views. We will clarify and spread the truth, the whole truth, to enlighten the minds of those who still refuse to understand.[34]

AFTERWORD

It is a beautiful spring in Buenos Aires in 1997. The Grandmothers celebrate their twentieth anniversary by hosting a three-day congress with the theme "Youth and Identity" in a downtown theater. The congress starts with an homage to the twelve founding Grandmothers, including a film that shows photographs of the children and pregnant women who were disappeared. Human rights activists, lawyers, scientists, psychologists, religious leaders, and journalists participate.

The children of the disappeared tell their stories in many of the sessions, eliciting, without exception, an overwhelmingly enthusiastic response from the audience. In the lobby of the theater an exhibit of photographs and posters documents the work of the Grandmothers and celebrates their accomplishments. On the second night, a concert with famous actors, musicians, and singers energizes the public.

I meet Grandmother Cecilia Pilar Fernández de Villas and I am confronted with a story that astonishes me. In July 1977 her seven-month-pregnant daughter, Cecilia Marina, along with Cecilia Marina's husband, Hugo Renaldo Penino, were kidnapped from their home in Buenos Aires. Survivors of the ESMA testified that Cecilia Marina delivered a baby boy who was "given" to one of her kidnappers, Navy Captain Jorge Vildoza, currently a fugitive. In 1983 and early 1984, *six years* after her disappearance, and a few months *after* the restoration of democracy, Cecilia Marina contacted her family by phone several times. In each conversation she asked for news about her son. Her family taped one of the conversations in which she said that her night guardians allowed her to make the calls, that she was held in captivity with others, and that she believed she would soon be set free. Her family brought her case to the attention of the new constitutional government to no avail. She, as well as her son and husband, remain disappeared. There have been no further phone calls.

Cecilia Pilar has recently returned from Spain. In my conversations with her I learn of the growing international outrage at the genocide and state terrorism perpetrated in Argentina. Cecilia Pilar was among the first to testify in the current inquiry in Madrid on the disappearance of 425 Spanish citizens and Spanish descendants during the dictatorship. More than a hundred members of the military and the police are being investigated. Spanish Judge Baltasar Garzón has already issued an order to capture and extradite General Leopoldo Galtieri, the president of the third junta.

Other European countries are following suit. Survivors of the camps and relatives of the disappeared provide ample testimony of the atrocities committed by the regime. Though in Argentina he is a free man, Alfredo Astiz has been condemned in France to life imprisonment for his participation in the disappearance of two French nuns (see chapter 2). The Italian government is moving ahead with a trial that implicates the ex-commanders of the three juntas and eighty-nine members of the military in the disappearance of Italian citizens living in Argentina. If the Argentine government rejects the requests for extradition (as in the case of Galtieri it already has), those found guilty would be sought by Interpol should they leave the country. Argentina would then become a huge prison and the perpetrators, international pariahs. The message is clear: the truth refuses to be buried and the absence of justice will not go unchallenged. The struggle against impunity continues, now in an international setting.

The congress ends on a high note. The Grandmothers give commemorative medals to recognize those who have accompanied and supported them for twenty years, both in Argentina and abroad. The impassioned presence of so many young people has filled the theater with a sense of hope. The promise of both continuity and renewal is in the air. The work of the Grandmothers goes forward unabated.

In July 1998, as this book was going to press, I learned that General Jorge Rafael Videla, age seventy, president and army commander of the first junta and one of the leaders of the 1976 coup, had been arrested. He was charged with abducting children whose parents disappeared and then putting them up for adoption—a crime that could bring a sentence of twenty-five years in prison. Arrests, on similar charges, of other prominent members of the military regime were expected to follow.

APPENDIX ONE

BIOGRAPHICAL SKETCHES OF GRANDMOTHERS INTERVIEWED

Elsa Pavón de Aguilar

Elsa Pavón de Aguilar was born in the city of Buenos Aires in 1936, the daughter of a poor single mother who was a nonpracticing Catholic. She went to elementary school for only a year and a half and later worked as a maid. When she was seventeen she married her employer, a forty-seven-year-old man. Their four children were raised Jewish, the faith of her husband. After separating from him and then becoming a widow at age thirty-three, she remarried and was widowed again at forty-nine. She completed her education as an adult, obtaining degrees in nursing and laboratory technology.

In 1978 the oldest of her children, Mónica, disappeared with her husband and their twenty-three-month-old daughter, Paula, in Uruguay, where they had gone to escape political persecution. At that point, Elsa retired from her work to devote herself to the search for her missing family members. In 1983 the Grandmothers found Paula living in Buenos Aires with a police family under a false identity. After a year of work to demonstrate her identity and after genetic testing, Paula was returned to her family of origin.

As part of her work with the Grandmothers, Elsa waged a successful six-year battle to get Paula's identity documents revised to reflect her real name. Elsa has recently completed a degree in social psychology and lives in Buenos Aires with Paula.

Otilia Lescano de Argañaraz

Otilia Lescano de Argañaraz was born into a middle-class Catholic family in 1914 in Santiago del Estero, a province in the North of Argentina. When she was fifteen she moved to Córdoba province, where she worked for many years as a music teacher in an impoverished rural school and was active with the Teacher's Union. She was married and widowed twice, and had five children from her first marriage. Her family has a long tradition of activism in the Radical Party, one of the two main political parties in Argentina.

In 1976 her son César, a member of an armed guerrilla group, ERP, was killed in an attack on the Villa María barracks. In 1977 her daughter María de las Mercedes, six months pregnant, was kidnapped with her husband in the city of Mar del Plata. From testimonies of survivors of the same camp where her daughter was imprisoned, Otilia believes that she delivered the baby while in captivity. She has not had further information about her daughter, her son-in-law, or the child.

Otilia joined the Grandmothers shortly after her daughter's disappearance and has been a mainstay of the organization in Córdoba, struggling with the lack of resources and with the conservative climate of the province. She has represented the Grandmothers at the annual Encuentro de Mujeres (National Women's Meeting) that take place in Argentina. She lives in Córdoba with one of her grandchildren.

Emma Spione de Baamonde

Emma Spione de Baamonde was born into a middle-class Catholic family in the city of Buenos Aires in 1915. After finishing elementary school, Emma took courses in weaving, cooking, and home economics. Married at twenty-five, Emma had three children; she was widowed at age seventy-four. She worked for many years as a volunteer with the Argentine League against Cancer, in particular helping patients who came to Buenos Aires from the provinces cope with the hospital experience.

One of her sons, Miguel Angel, disappeared in 1976. His wife and three-year-old child, Martín, disappeared a year and a half later, in 1978. For five years Emma and the Grandmothers engaged in an extensive search for the child with no success, but in 1983 a judge informed her that Martín was well and had been living in the house of a maternal aunt. The family had denied that they had the child, wanted no contact with Emma, and labeled her son a "communist." Emma was able to reconnect with her grandchild. No information about the whereabouts of her son and daughter-in-law ever emerged.

Emma started working with the Grandmothers in the 1970s; after her husband died she lived in the Grandmothers' office for two years, turning it into her second home. She received many death threats while she was living at the office and finally, after the office was broken into, went back to her home. She lives with her daughter in Buenos Aires.

Delia Giovanola de Califano

Delia Giovanola de Califano was born in 1926 in La Plata, the capital of Buenos Aires province, into a middle-class Catholic family. Married at nineteen, she became a widow at thirty-seven and had to hold three jobs in order to support herself and her son. She worked as a teacher and was the director of an elementary school. She remarried when she was forty-three years old.

Her son, Jorge Oscar Ogando, and his wife, Stella Maris Montesano, disappeared in 1976; Stella Maris was eight months pregnant. From the testimony of a woman who was in the same detention camp as her son and daughter-in-law, Delia knows that her grandchild was born in the camp, and that he was a blond, blue-eyed boy. An anonymous letter informed CONADEP where her son and daughter-in-law are buried, but Delia has been unable to locate their graves. Because her son was an adopted child, only the relatives from his wife's family have deposited their blood in the National Genetic Data Bank.

She is one of the founders of the Association. Health problems prevented Delia from working with the Grandmothers for two years. After total hip replacement in 1994 she returned to continue her work with the organization. She lives with her second husband and a granddaughter in Buenos Aires province.

Estela Barnes de Carlotto

Estela Barnes de Carlotto was born in Buenos Aires in 1930 into a middle-class Catholic family. Early on, she decided to work in education and she held her first job as an elementary school teacher when she was twenty-one. She taught for twenty-seven years and was the principal of a school. Married in 1954, she had four children.

In 1977 her husband, Guido, was kidnapped. He appeared twenty-five days later after Estela raised the ransom money that his abductors requested. After three months, Estela's oldest daughter, Laura, a member of the Montoneros organization, disappeared. She was two and a half months pregnant. Survivors of the same camp where Laura was imprisoned testified that she delivered a male child in June 1978 and that she named him Guido. In August 1978 Laura was assassinated and her body was delivered to her family. Estela immediately retired from her job to dedicate herself to the search for her grandchild. There has been no further information regarding the child.

Estela joined the Grandmothers' organization in 1978. She was the vice president until 1989, when she became the president. Estela has spoken about the work of the Grandmothers in many parts of the world and testifies yearly on the disappeared children at the UN Human Rights Commission meetings in Geneva, Switzerland. She lives in La Plata with her husband.

Haydée Vallino de Lemos

Haydée Vallino de Lemos was born in Buenos Aires in 1919 to a working-class Catholic family. She completed elementary school, worked for many years as a seamstress, was married, and had three children. Her husband, a shirtmaker, died broken-hearted soon after the abduction of two of their children. She has not been involved in politics but she cares deeply about the unemployed, the lack of economic justice, and the struggles of the old and the poor. When Haydée asked her remaining daughter where she got her ideas about the world, she replied, "From you, mother," and pointed out the ways in which Haydée had stressed social conscience and responsibility toward society during their childhood.

In 1977 her son Mario Alberto and her daughter Mónica María, eight months pregnant, disappeared. Mónica María delivered a baby girl while in captivity. The child, María José, was given to a policewoman and her husband, who registered her as their own. After ten years she was identified by the Grandmothers; after the genetic testing demonstrated her identity, María José was returned to her legitimate family. She is now connected to a large extended family that includes an older sister.

As one of the founding Grandmothers, Haydée has been involved with the organization since 1977. She lives with her two granddaughters, who participate in human rights activities and care about social justice much in the same way their parents did.

María Isabel Chorobik de Mariani

María Isabel Chorobik de Mariani (known to her friends as "Chicha") was born in the province of Mendoza in 1923 to a middle-class Catholic family. She grew up in a peaceful and loving home where her parents fostered her interest in the arts. She pursued a teaching career and for twenty-five years chaired the department of aesthetics in a high school where she taught music, visual education, and art history. In her twenties, she married a musician, Enrique José Mariani, and they had a son.

In 1976 her daughter-in-law, Diana Teruggi, was murdered and her three-month-old granddaughter, Clara Anahí, was kidnapped in La Plata. Her son, Daniel, a member of the Montoneros organization, went underground but was captured and killed in 1977. Chicha retired from teaching and devoted herself to the search for her granddaughter. She received reliable information that her granddaughter had been "adopted" by a "powerful" family.

Chicha is one of the founders of the Grandmothers' organization and was its president for over ten years. She has traveled extensively on behalf of the organization and has spoken at many international human rights gatherings and conferences. She was officially recognized for her work on human rights by the French government in 1989. Also in 1989, she retired from active participation in the organization, though she continues to search for her missing granddaughter. She lives in La Plata with her mother.

Raquel Radío de Marizcurrena

Raquel Radío de Marizcurrena was born in 1931 in Villa Ramayo, a small town in Buenos Aires province; she was one of seven children in a Catholic working-class family. She was five years old when her mother died and twelve when she lost her father. She finished elementary school but was unable to continue her education because she had to help her older sister take care of the family. Married at twenty-one, Raquel had two sons and became a homemaker. She was widowed at age fifty-seven. She is very concerned about social justice and admired Eva Perón for her work in behalf of the poor.

In 1976, on her son Andrés's twenty-fourth birthday, the police broke into her home and abducted him and his wife, Liliana Beatriz, four months pregnant. All inquiries about them and about her grandchild have been unsuccessful.

Raquel believes that her grandchild is with an influential and rich family, because in several magazines covering society news she has seen pictures of a boy who looks exactly like her husband when he was a child. She is one of the founders of the Grandmothers' Association and was involved in identifying Pablito Moyano, one of the found children who was returned to his family of origin. She lives with her remaining son in Acasuso, in Buenos Aires province, and works at the Grandmothers' office every day.

Amelia Herrera de Miranda

Amelia Herrera de Miranda was born in a small town in Córdoba province in 1923, to a working-class Catholic family. She completed elementary school, worked as a seamstress, was married in her twenties, and had three children. She lost one of her children, a son, in a motorcycle accident.

In 1976 her daughter Amelia, her son-in-law, Roberto Francisco Lanuscou, and their three children disappeared. She later found out that their house had been demolished by the joint forces of the police and the army, that her son-in-law was killed with a grenade and her daughter shot in the head. Two of the children died in the fire that destroyed their home. According to the neighbors, the third child, a six-month-old girl, was taken away in an ambulance.

In 1982 Amelia was approached by the Grandmothers, who had information about some unmarked graves that seemed to fit the profile of Amelia's daughter and her family. After exhumation of the graves it was ascertained that the graves were indeed those of her daughter, son-in-law, and two of the children, ages four and five. There were no traces of the youngest child. Amelia has been active in the Grandmothers' Association since then. Finding the remains of her daughter and two of her grandchildren was very important to her, and that success has helped sustain her focus on finding her missing granddaughter.

Amelia's husband, Juan Miranda, one of the few men who have become active in the Grandmothers' organization, died in 1995. Amelia lives alone in Buenos Aires.

Nélida Gómez de Navajas

Nélida Gómez de Navajas was born in the city of Buenos Aires in 1927 into a middle-class Catholic family. Married at twenty-one and widowed at age forty-three, she had two children. She taught school for ten years and then held an administrative position in a savings association for twenty-seven years until her retirement.

After her daughter Cristina, a sociologist, disappeared in 1976, Nélida found a letter from Cristina to her husband saying that she had missed two periods and that she thought she was pregnant. Cristina was married to Julio César Santucho, a brother of Mario Santucho—the leader of the ERP, one of the two major guerrilla groups in Argentina. Survivors of the same clandestine camp where Cristina was taken reported that she was savagely tortured because of her connection to the Santucho family. There has not been any further information concerning Cristina or the child.

Nélida has traveled extensively on behalf of the Grandmothers' Association, taking their message particularly to Spain, where she has an extended family, and to Italy. A devout Catholic, she is disappointed with the role of the Argentine Catholic Church during the dictatorship.

She has been active in the Grandmothers' organization since the early 1980s, and she lives with her son in Buenos Aires.

Elsa Sánchez de Oesterheld

Elsa Sánchez de Oesterheld was born in the city of Buenos Aires in 1925 to a middle-class Catholic family whose members were conscious of their working-class origins. She loved the humanities and literature and was a voracious reader. She completed secondary school, was married at age twenty-two, and had four daughters. Her husband, a freethinker and a humanist, was the well-known science fiction writer Héctor Germán Oesterheld.

By 1977 all four of Elsa's daughters as well as her husband had been taken by the dictatorship. She was able to recover the body of one of her daughters but has not received any information regarding the other members of her family. Two of her daughters were pregnant: Diana, six and a half months, and Marina, eight months.

Elsa believes that the leadership of the Montoneros, one of the two main guerrilla groups in Argentina, behaved irresponsibly and took advantage of the young, indoctrinating them and not giving them time to reflect. Elsa tried, in vain, to alert her husband and her children about the contradictions between their humanist beliefs and the ideology of the Montoneros. But they refused to listen.

In 1985 the Grandmothers contacted Elsa after learning that two of her missing daughters had been pregnant. Elsa traveled in Latin America in behalf of the Grandmothers; participating in conferences on human rights has given her an awareness of the richness and vastness of human rights struggles in other countries, not just in Argentina. She has been particularly invigorated by the vitality of the women's movement and the indigenous peoples' movement in Latin America. She lives alone in Buenos Aires.

Argentina Rojo de Pérez

Argentina Rojo de Pérez was born in 1923 in the province of Córdoba to a working-class Catholic family. She left school and started working after fifth grade, when she was twelve years old. When she was nineteen she completed her elementary education. She married in her late twenties and helped her husband run his business, selling groceries, fruits, and vegetables. They had one son.

Argentina and her husband were threatened and attacked in their home several times during the 1970s. In 1978 her son, José Manuel, and her daughter-in-law, Patricia Julia Roisinblit (daughter of Rosa Roisinblit, currently the vice president of the Grandmothers' Association), disappeared; both were members of the Montoneros organization. Her daughter-in-law was eight months pregnant. Their fifteen-month-old daughter, Mariana, was left behind. Testimony from survivors of the same camp where Patricia had been imprisoned revealed that in November 1978 she had given birth to a baby boy and that she had named him Rodolfo Fernando. There has been no further information about the disappeared couple or the child.

Argentina heard of the Grandmothers' organization through Rosa Roisinblit. Argentina was widowed in 1989 when she was sixty-six years old and lives in Buenos Aires with her granddaughter, Mariana.

Rosa Tarlovsky de Roisinblit

Rosa Tarlovsky de Roisinblit was born in 1919 in the province of Santa Fé to a Jewish immigrant family. Her father had become a wealthy landowner but after World War I lost his fortune because of the recession. Her parents and her oldest sister were committed Zionists. After finishing elementary school, Rosa, at fifteen, studied midwifery. She also became an expert surgeon's assistant. She married in her early thirties and had a daughter, Patricia Julia. Rosa was widowed at age fifty-three, several years before the coup.

In 1978 Patricia, a medical student, and her husband, José Manuel Pérez—both members of the Montoneros organization—disappeared. The uncertainty about their fate, and that of the baby boy Patricia was said to have delivered in captivity, was mentioned in the preceding biographical sketch.

Rosa started working with other Grandmothers in 1979 and has traveled widely on behalf of the organization, attending international conferences and making presentations on the topic of children and human rights. She is currently the vice president of the Grandmothers' Association, lives alone in Buenos Aires, and is in close contact with her granddaughter, Mariana.

Antonia Acuña de Segarra

Antonia Acuña de Segarra was born in 1934 in the province of Tucumán to a single mother from a Catholic middle-class family. Her mother married when Antonia was a small child, and she developed a good relationship with her stepfather. She completed high school in Buenos Aires and married in her early twenties. She had three children.

Her older daughter, Alicia Estela, two and half months pregnant, disappeared with her companion, Carlos María Mendoza, in 1978. A few days later her other daughter, Laura Beatriz, disappeared together with her companion, Pablo Torres; she was eight months pregnant. Finally, her son, Jorge, also disappeared. There has been no further information about any of them.

Antonia lives in the resort city of Mar del Plata, but since her children had been living in Buenos Aires she went there to search for them. She soon connected with the Grandmothers and decided to work with the group, because it was the only organization searching for children and their parents. Antonia has attended all the FEDEFAM meetings since 1983, presenting the case of the disappeared children of Argentina. Her involvement with FEDEFAM has increased the Grandmothers' understanding of the atrocities committed in other countries of Latin America and has helped foster a special bond and solidarity between them. Antonia and her husband continue to live in Mar del Plata.

Reina Esses de Waisberg

Reina Esses de Waisberg was born in Buenos Aires in 1919, one of seven children in a middle-class Jewish family. She completed elementary school and went to work at age sixteen when her father's business went bankrupt. After her mother died from an illegal abortion when Reina was eighteen, she took care of her siblings. She married in her early twenties and had two children. Devoting herself to family and home, she led a very comfortable life while her husband was alive. She became a widow in her fifties, several years before the coup.

In 1977 her son Ricardo and his companion, Valeria Belaustegui Herrera, members of ERP, were abducted from their home with their fifteen-month-old daughter, Tania. Valeria was two months pregnant at the time. She was seen eight months pregnant in one of the clandestine detention centers. Tania was returned to Reina, but security forces subsequently tried to kidnap her again. The support of Mónica Pastora Aranda, Reina's household helper, and the intervention of a relative who was a member of the military prevented a second abduction.

Tania's maternal grandmother, Matilde Herrera (one of the authors of *Identidad: Despojo y restitución*), was active with the Grandmothers. When Matilde died in 1990, Tania prompted Reina to join the Association. Reina lives in Buenos Aires with Tania and Mónica Pastora Aranda.

Alba Lanzillotto

Alba Lanzillotto was born in 1928 in La Rioja, a province in the North of Argentina, one of seven children in a Catholic middle-class family. She married the poet and journalist Ariel Ferraro and had two children. She was widowed at age sixty-one. Alba worked as a high school teacher and felt that it was one of her responsibilities as a teacher to awaken a sense of justice and equality in her students. This and her militancy in behalf of the poor—following the example of Monsignor Angelelli, the progressive bishop of La Rioja assassinated in 1976—earned her a two-week prison term. After coming out of prison in 1977, Alba went into exile in Spain, where she lived until 1984.

Alba was nineteen years old when her twin sisters, Ana María and María Cristina, were born, and she was like a mother to them. Both sisters disappeared in 1976, when Ana María was eight months pregnant.

Ana María was married to Domingo Menna, an important member of ERP. Alba has received information indicating that the child was born and that it was a boy.

On her return from Spain, Alba joined the Grandmothers and started working on the newsletter. She has represented the Grandmothers in the monthly meetings of a Senate commission dealing with the reform of the laws of custody and adoption. Alba and her family maintain close ties with the three surviving children of her disappeared sisters. Alba lives in Buenos Aires with her daughter, son-in-law, and grandchildren.

Nya Quesada

Nya Quesada was born in a small town in the province of Buenos Aires in 1920 to a humble family with anarchist political beliefs. Peace, solidarity, and a belief in humanity were stressed as the most important values of life. She had a carefree and happy childhood and greatly enjoyed reading.

After finishing her elementary education, she pursued a career in the arts; she has been an actress all her adult life. She was married in her twenties to actor and graphic artist Antonio Bai and they had one daughter, Adriana Mirta Bai Quesada, who became an architecture student.

Adriana, her husband, and their two-and-a-half-year-old son, Nicolás, disappeared in 1978. Twenty days after the abduction, Nya's sister Menchu, a well-known theater and TV actress, received a phone call from a juvenile court where Nicolás had been abandoned. The child had been taken to the home of one of the secretaries of the court; and after seeing a TV program on which Menchu's name had been mentioned, he had screamed that she was his aunt. An unusually sensitive judge returned the child to his legitimate family.

Nya's husband, who suffered from asthma, was distraught over his daughter's disappearance and never regained his strength. He died in 1980. In 1981 one of Nya's friends received a phone call from a woman who identified herself as Adriana and who mentioned episodes from their past that only Adriana would have known about. Nya still hopes, against all odds, to see her daughter again. She regrets that her busy acting schedule does not allow her to be as active as she would like with the Grandmothers' Association. She lives in Buenos Aires with her sister Menchu and with Nicolás.

Elena Santander

Elena Santander was born in Buenos Aires in 1929 into a middle-class Catholic family. After finishing elementary school Elena helped her mother at home and later started working as a seamstress. She married in her twenties and had three children. She became a widow in her forties, a few years before the coup.

In 1975 Elena's home was looted and she was abducted with her son, Alfredo Moyano, and his wife, María Asunción Artigas. They were held for five days, during which she witnessed the torture of Alfredo. In 1977 Alfredo and María Asunción, who was two months pregnant, were abducted again. From testimonies of survivors of the same camp where they were taken, Elena learned that her daughter-in-law had delivered a baby girl.

The Grandmothers identified Elena's granddaughter, María Victoria, in 1987, thanks to the information provided by one of the girl's teachers. She had been appropriated by the brother of the policeman in charge of the camp, who had registered her as his daughter. After genetic testing demonstrated María Victoria's identity she was returned to her family of origin and went to Uruguay to live with her maternal grandparents.

Elena worked with the Grandmothers' Association for many years even though her health deteriorated after the abduction of her son and his family. She lived in Buenos Aires with a brother and died in February 1996.

Berta Schubaroff

Berta Schubaroff was born in the city of Buenos Aires in 1928 to Jewish working-class parents who had emigrated from Russia. She completed her secondary education in an arts school and loved drawing, painting, and music. Berta was married in her early twenties to poet and journalist Juan Gelman, had two children, and devoted herself completely to her family. After ten years of marriage she decided to separate from her husband because she had a feeling that "beyond marriage and children there was something else."

In 1976 her twenty-year-old son, Marcelo Ariel; her daughter, Nora Eva; and her son's wife, María García Irureta Goyena, who was seven and a half months pregnant; disappeared. Her daughter was released after three days but her son and daughter-in-law remained in captivity.

In 1989 the remains of her son were found in an unmarked grave in a cemetery in Buenos Aires. Through a contact in the Vatican, Juan Gelman learned that their grandchild had been born in a camp. Since the note he received was written in English and it referred to "the baby," it is not known if it was a boy or a girl.

Berta and her daughter went into exile in Spain in 1979. At the end of 1984, back in Argentina, she joined the Grandmothers' organization and since that time has been active with the group. Berta is an accomplished sculptor, working mostly with ceramics and clay. She lives in Buenos Aires with her daughter and her grandson.

Sonia Torres

Sonia Torres was born in the province of Córdoba in 1929 to an upper-middle-class Catholic (nonpracticing) family. Her father was a dentist and a member of the Argentine Senate. She wanted to study architecture but her parents did not allow it, saying that it was a career for men. They suggested that she study pharmacy, a more appropriate career for a woman. While a pharmacy student she was married and eventually had three children. Sonia separated from her husband after fourteen years. Though she was not a *peronista,* Sonia admired Eva Perón for her commitment to social justice and the poor.

In 1975 Sonia and her children were arrested. Sonia and her youngest child were released after a few days. The other two were kept and tortured for almost a month. In 1976 her daughter Silvina Mónica, an economics student who was seven months pregnant, was abducted with her companion, Daniel Orozco. Sonia found out that her daughter delivered a son and that she had been at La Perla camp, one of the most infamous clandestine detention centers in Córdoba. Although Sonia's investigation led her to the identity of the woman who turned her daughter in, she has not been able to find out any further information regarding her missing daughter and her family.

After the disappearances, Sonia went to Buenos Aires and developed her connection with the Grandmothers' Association. Sonia continues to work with the Grandmothers and occasionally attends their meetings in Buenos Aires. She owns and manages a pharmacy in Córdoba, where she lives alone.

APPENDIX TWO

DECLARATION OF PRINCIPLES AND AFFIDAVIT OF THE GRANDMOTHERS OF THE PLAZA DE MAYO, JULY 21, 1982

Since October 1977, we, the undersigned grandmothers,[1] constitute a group that arose spontaneously as a consequence of the disappearances of our children and grandchildren, or of our daughters or daughters-in-law who were pregnant at the time. We presented petitions before the corresponding authorities, such as the security forces who had taken part in the "operativos," and finally we came together at the Plaza de Mayo to join in the complaint of so many mothers whose children had disappeared. While we searched for our children, demanding the protection of law and justice for them, we knew that the search for the grandchildren should be directed toward specific locations: foundling homes, youth institutions, orphanages, juvenile courts, etc. With that knowledge, there in the Plaza de Mayo, facing the Government House, which never responded to our inquiries and complaints, we, the mothers of the mothers, decided to band together in order to petition on behalf of the disappeared young children, thus creating the Movement of the Grandmothers. As time went by and considering our continued condition as victims, despite our incessant complaints, we have resolved to constitute the Civilian Association called "Abuelas de Plaza de Mayo." We are not motivated by any political objective. No one has called us together, no one directs us or uses us. We are against violence and against any type of terrorism, private or state. We desire peace, brotherhood, and justice. For the future of Argentina we wish that a democratic system prevail, one respectful of the fundamental rights of humankind. Believers or not, we adhere to the moral principles of Judeo-Christianity. We reject injustice, oppression, torture, assassination, kidnapping, arrests without due process, detentions followed by disappearances, persecution for religious, racial, ideological, or political motives. Concerning our detained-disappeared sons and daughters, we demand that they be returned alive and that a complete clarification be made of all events that transpired from the time of their detention and later during their disappearance. Regarding our grandchildren, we ask that the fate handed to each and every one of the disappeared children in the Argentine Republic since 1975 be clarified, as well as the fate of the babies born in detention camps where their young mothers were taken while pregnant, and that these children be reintegrated with their family members, and all their rights respected: right to life, right to maintain their true identity, right to live with their legitimate family. We know there are many many Argentine homes in the same situation as ours. Therefore, we have decided to form a Civilian Association that shall be called "Abuelas de Plaza de Mayo," so we may aid each other and offer assistance to the victims of the events described above. In order to reach our goal, which is that the authorities of the country, civil, military, and judicial, restore the children to their family members until their parents, now disappeared, be also liberated, we will make inquiries, initiate actions, write and circulate publications such as we will consider appropriate, with due respect for the laws and public order. We wish to work to build an Argentina where Justice shall exist. Where no one can be detained and made to disappear as has happened with our children and grandchildren. Where a system of laws shall prevail and where one may live in an atmosphere of freedom, tolerance, and mutual respect. Where all the rights of children shall be respected and universally acknowledged.[2]

NOTES

CHAPTER ONE. NOT JUST ONE MORE COUP

1. Quoted in John Simpson and Jana Bennett, *The Disappeared and the Mothers of the Plaza* (New York: St. Martin's Press, 1985), 76.

2. Raquel Angel, "Una fecha marcada a sangre y fuego—Memoria de un día trágico," *Madres de Plaza de Mayo,* March 1986, 4–5.

3. In *The Invention of Argentina* (Berkeley: University of California Press, 1991), Nicolas Shumway traces a current in Argentine political thought that sees the country as a "sick" entity whose "health" can only be improved by "drastic surgery," like coups and the elimination of "subversives" (166).

4. Paul Lewis, "The Right and the Military Rule, 1955–1983," in *The Argentine Right: Its History and Intellectual Origins, 1910 to the Present,* ed. Sandra McGee Deutsch and Ronald H. Dolkart (Wilmington, Del.: Scholarly Resources, 1993), 147–70. See also Jean-Pierre Bousquet, *Las Locas de la Plaza de Mayo* (Buenos Aires: El Cid Editor, 1982), 37–38.

5. Quoted in Simpson and Bennett, *The Disappeared,* 33. On the topic of Borges, see also Lawrence Weschler, *A Miracle, a Universe: Settling Accounts with Torturers* (New York: Penguin Books, 1990), 18.

6. Emilio F. Mignone, *Derechos humanos y sociedad: El caso argentino* (Buenos Aires: Centro de Estudios Legales y Sociales/Ediciones del Pensamiento Nacional, 1991), 63.

7. Quoted in Daniel Frontalini and María Cristina Caiati, *El mito de la guerra sucia* (Buenos Aires: Centro de Estudios Legales y Sociales, 1984), 22.

8. Amnesty International, *Argentina: The Military Juntas and Human Rights—Report of the Trial of the Former Junta Members* (London: Amnesty International, 1987), 14; Juan E. Méndez, *Truth and Partial Justice in Argentina: An Update,* An Americas Watch Report (Washington, D.C.: Americas Watch, 1991), 7, 11. General Videla served both as commander of the army and president from March 1976 to March 1981. The second junta members (March 1981 to December 1981) were Lieutenant General Roberto Viola, pres-

ident and army commander; Admiral Armando Lambruschini, navy commander; and Brigadier General Omar Graffigna, air force commander. The third junta members (December 1981 to June 1982) were Lieutenant General Leopoldo Galtieri, president and army commander; Admiral Jorge Anaya, navy commander; and Brigadier General Basilio Lami Dozo, air force commander. After the Malvinas/Falklands defeat a "caretaker" junta was put together; Lieutenant General Reynaldo Benito Bignone was appointed to preside over the transition to elected civilian government.

9. David Rock, *Argentina, 1516–1987: From Spanish Colonization to Alfonsín* (Berkeley: University of California Press, 1987), 346–47.

10. Ibid., 349–53. Many women were active in the predominantly male guerrilla organizations. For a fascinating study of their role and their experiences, see Marta Diana, *Mujeres guerrilleras: La militancia de los setenta en el testimonio de sus protagonistas femeninas* (Buenos Aires: Planeta, 1996).

11. Rock, *Argentina,* 358–60.

12. Ibid., 363. See also Ignacio González Janzen, *La Triple A* (Buenos Aires: Editorial Contrapunto, 1986).

13. Martin Edwin Andersen, *Dossier Secreto: Argentina's Desaparecidos and the Myth of the "Dirty War"* (Boulder, Colo.: Westview Press, 1993), 118–19.

14. Frontalini and Caiati, *El Mito,* 72.

15. Mignone, *Derechos humanos y sociedad,* 54.

16. Both quoted in Penny Lernoux, *Cry of the People: The Struggle for Human Rights in Latin America—The Catholic Church in Conflict with U.S. Policy* (New York: Penguin Books, 1991), 164. General Viola and General Galtieri, members of the second and third juntas, received training at the U.S. Army's School of the Americas in Fort Benning, Georgia (information provided by SOA Watch in Washington, D.C.).

17. Mignone, *Derechos humanos y sociedad,* 64.

18. "Doctrina de la Seguridad Nacional (DSN)," *FEDEFAM,* November 1984, 22.

19. Quoted in Frontalini and Caiati, *El mito,* 11.

20. Eduardo Luis Duhalde, *El estado terrorista argentino* (Buenos Aires: Ediciones El Caballito, 1983), 118–25.

21. Ibid., 114–15; Amnesty International, *Report of an Amnesty International Mission to Argentina, 6–15 November 1976* (London: Amnesty International, 1977), 41–42. According to AI, in 1976 there were about 12,000 registered refugees in Argentina. Many refugees were tortured and deported to their countries of origin. Others were assassinated, including two prominent Uruguayan politicians, Senator Zelmar Michelini and Héctor Gutiérrez Ruiz (former president of the Chamber of Representatives), and former Bolivian president Juan Torres.

22. Iain Guest, *Behind the Disappearances: Argentina's Dirty War against Human Rights and the United Nations* (Philadelphia: University of Pennsylvania Press, 1990), 63–64.

23. Jacobo Timerman, *Prisoner without a Name, Cell without a Number* (New York: Vintage Books, 1982), 102.

24. Noam Chomsky and Edward S. Herman, *The Washington Connection and Third World Fascism,* vol. 1 of *The Political Economy of Human Rights* (Boston: South End Press, 1979), 265–66. See also Andersen, *Dossier,* 146.

25. Barbara Stallings, *Banker to the Third World: U.S. Portfolio Investment in Latin America, 1900–1986* (Berkeley: University of California Press, 1987), 100, 234.

26. Both quoted in Guest, *Behind the Disappearances,* 28.

27. Ibid.

28. William L. Shirer, *The Rise and Fall of the Third Reich: A History of Nazi Germany* (New York: Simon and Schuster, 1960), 957–58.

29. Amnesty International, *"Disappearances": A Workbook* (New York: Amnesty International, 1981), 17–30.

30. "El método de las desapariciones," *Testimonios,* September 20, 1984, 4–5.

31. Asamblea Permanente por los Derechos Humanos, *Las cifras de la guerra sucia* (Buenos Aires: Asamblea Permanente por los Derechos Humanos, 1988), 17.

32. Noemí Ulla and Hugo Echave, *Después de la noche: Diálogo con Graciela Fernández Meijide* (Buenos Aires: Editorial Contrapunto, 1986), 83.

33. Quoted in Raúl Veiga, *Las organizaciones de derechos humanos* (Buenos Aires: Centro Editor de América Latina, 1985), 122.

34. Mignone, *Derechos humanos y sociedad,* 66, and interview by author, Buenos Aires, December 16, 1994.

35. Ibid., 91.

36. Quoted in ibid., 69.

37. *Nunca Más: The Report of the Argentine National Commission on the Disappeared* (New York: Farrar, Straus, and Giroux, 1986), 413. See also Familiares de Desaparecidos y Detenidos por Razones Políticas, *Abogados desaparecidos* (Buenos Aires: Familiares de Desaparecidos y Detenidos por Razones Políticas, 1988).

38. Quoted in Mignone, *Derechos humanos y sociedad,* 56.

39. *Nunca Más,* 245–46.

40. Duhalde, *El estado,* 95.

41. *Nunca Más,* 11–12.

42. Ibid., 51, 199.

43. "Los Campos," *Testimonios,* September 20, 1984, 5–11.

44. *Nunca Más,* 25.

45. Ibid., 73.

46. Amnesty International, *Testimony on Secret Detention Camps in Argentina* (London: Amnesty International, 1980), 18.

47. *Nunca Más,* 273, 308.

48. Timerman, *Prisoner without a Name,* 148.

49. Quoted in Marcelo M. Suárez-Orozco, "The Treatment of Children in the 'Dirty War': Ideology, State Terrorism and the Abuse of Children in Argentina," in *Child Survival: Anthropological Perspectives on the Treatment and Maltreatment of Children,* ed. Nancy Scheper-Hughes (Dordrecht: D. Reidel, 1987), 234.

50. *Nunca Más,* 307–8.

51. Horacio Verbitsky, *The Flight: Confessions of an Argentine Dirty Warrior,* trans. Esther Allen (New York: New Press, 1996), esp. 17–57.

52. Laura Beatriz Bonaparte, *Militares en la Argentina y su método de tortura interminable* (Copenhagen: Rehabilitation and Research Center for Torture Victims, 1984).

53. *Nunca Más,* 222.

54. Ibid., 223.

55. Ibid., 215.

56. Alipio Paoletti, *Como los Nazis, como en Vietnam* (Buenos Aires: Edición Cañón Oxidado, 1987), 31, 69.

57. For an analysis of sexual torture of female political prisoners, see Ximena Bunster, "Surviving Beyond Fear: Women and Torture in Latin America," in *Surviving Beyond Fear: Women, Children, and Human Rights in Latin America,* ed. Marjorie Agosín (Fredonia, N.Y.: White Pine Press, 1993), 98–125.

58. *Nunca Más,* 37.

59. Paoletti, *Como los Nazis,* 303, 93.

60. Ibid., 92, 93, 101.

61. Ibid., 297.

62. Quoted in María Seoane and Héctor Ruiz Núñez, *La Noche de los Lápices* (Buenos Aires: Planeta-Edición Definitiva, 1992), 183.

63. Quoted in Tina Rosenberg, *Children of Cain: Violence and the Violent in Latin America* (New York: William Morrow, 1991), 89.

64. Amnesty International, *Report, November 1976,* 38.

65. *Nunca Más,* 337.

66. Ana María Careaga, interview by author, Buenos Aires, December 26, 1994.

67. However, some pregnant women were killed with their babies in their womb. Abuelas de Plaza de Mayo, *Niños desaparecidos en la Argentina desde 1976* (Buenos Aires: Abuelas de Plaza de Mayo, 1990), 128–30, names Adriana Gatti Casal, Hilda Inés Olivier de Santilli, Ana María del Carmen Pérez de Azcona, and Liliana Sofía Barrios de Castro. And an unidentified burned female corpse with a nine-month-old fetus still attached to the umbilical cord was found in Cañuelas in 1976, together with other six bodies, the result probably of a mass execution (correspondence with Alejandro Inchaurregui, September 5, 1995).

68. *Nunca Más,* 297–98, 295.

69. Ibid., 288–89.

70. Ibid., 294–95.

71. "Fué ubicado en Paraguay el prófugo Mayor Bianco," *Informaciones,* no. 13 (April–May 1987): 18–20; "El pasado que vuelve," *Página 12,* March 7, 1997.

72. *Nunca Más,* 271–72.

73. Ibid., 290–92; and Adriana Calvo de Laborde, interview by author, Buenos Aires, December 27, 1994.

74. Alicia Partnoy, *The Little School: Tales of Disappearance and Survival in Argentina* (Pittsburgh: Cleis Press, 1986), 124.

75. Emilio F. Mignone, *Witness to the Truth: The Complicity of Church and Dictatorship in Argentina, 1976–1983,* trans. Philip Berryman (Maryknoll, N.Y.: Orbis Books, 1988), 2, 20, 19. The four resisting priests were Enrique Angelelli, bishop of La Rioja; Jaime de Nevares, bishop of Neuquén; Miguel Hesayne, bishop of Viedma; and Jorge Novak, bishop of Quilmes.

76. Quoted in ibid., 5–6, 11, 36.

77. Ibid., 54.

78. Ibid., 57, 110–18; quotation, 111.

79. Ibid., 46, 42.

80. Ibid., 44–45. Mignone met with Pio Laghi three times after the disappearance of his daughter and portrays him as aware of the repressive nature of the system, but afraid to speak up. Pio Laghi acknowledged to Mignone that the government was in the hands of criminals; but when Mignone quoted him to Admiral Massera two years later, Massera said: "I find it odd that Laghi would say that: we get together to play tennis every two weeks" (45).

81. Quoted in ibid., 107.

82. Ibid., 132–33, 143.

83. Judith Laikin Elkin, "Quincentenary: Colonial Legacy of Anti-Semitism," *Report on the Americas* 25, no. 4 (February 1992): 4–7; Robert Weisbrot, *The Jews of Argentina: From the Inquisition to Perón* (Philadelphia: Jewish Publication Society of America, 1979), 15–56, 200–201.

84. Ronald H. Dolkart, "The Right in the Década Infame, 1930–1943," in Deutsch and Dolkart, *The Argentine Right,* 87.

85. Simon Wiesenthal, *The Murderers among Us: The Wiesenthal Memoirs,* ed. Joseph Wechsberg (New York: McGraw-Hill, 1967), 337–38. Wiesenthal states that after World War II, Buenos Aires became the terminal port of a clandestine organization, ODESSA, which took care of Nazi criminals, providing them with false identification and helping them to settle in the country. See also Jorge Camarasa, *Los Nazis en la Argentina* (Buenos Aires: Editorial Legasa, 1992), and Ann Louise Bardach, "Argentina Evades Its Nazi Past," *New York Times,* March 22, 1997.

86. Weisbrot, *The Jews of Argentina,* 252. For example, a young Jewish student, Graciela Narcisa Sirota, was kidnapped and tortured in 1962. One of her kidnappers carved a three-inch swastika on her right breast and explained, "This is in revenge for Eichmann." When her father went to the police he was turned away; even when the identity of the kidnappers became known, the police refused to file charges.

87. Morton M. Rosenthal, "Argentinian Jews in Danger," *ADL Bulletin,* November 1976, 4–5.

88. Ibid., 5. These included works by Mussolini, Hitler, and Goebbels.

89. Quoted in Weisbrot, *The Jews of Argentina,* 10.

90. Timerman, *Prisoner without a Name,* 73–74.

91. *Nunca Más,* 72.

92. Ibid.

93. Ibid., 69.

94. Ibid., 71.

95. Edy Kaufman and Beatriz Cymberknopf, "La dimensión judía en la represión durante el gobierno militar en la Argentina (1976–1983)," in *El antisemitismo en la Argentina,* ed. Leonardo Senkman (Buenos Aires: Centro Editor de América Latina, 1989), 258–59.

96. Marcos Aguinis, *Un país de novela: Viaje hacia la mentalidad de los argentinos* (Buenos Aires: Planeta, 1988), 177.

CHAPTER TWO. THE FALL OF THE REGIME

1. Martin Edwin Andersen, *Dossier Secreto: Argentina's Desaparecidos and the Myth of the "Dirty War"* (Boulder, Colo.: Westview Press, 1993), 175–83.

2. Ibid., 182.

3. ANCLA bulletin, March 16, 1977, "La situación laboral"; reprinted in *Rodolfo Walsh y la prensa clandestina 1976–1978,* ed. Horacio Verbitsky (Buenos Aires: Ediciones de la Urraca, 1985), 94–96.

4. Iain Guest, *Behind the Disappearances: Argentina's Dirty War against Human Rights and the United Nations* (Philadelphia: University of Pennsylvania Press, 1990), 101, 489.

5. Horacio Verbitsky, "Una experiencia de difusión clandestina y participación popular," in Verbitsky, *Rodolfo Walsh,* 6. See also Andrew Graham-Yooll, *A Matter of Fear: Portrait of an Argentinian Exile* (Westport, Conn.: Lawrence Hill, 1982), 90–97.

6. Rodolfo Walsh, "Escuela de Mecánica de la Armada/Historia de la guerra sucia en la Argentina," in Verbitsky, *Rodolfo Walsh,* 13–36.

7. From *Cadena Informativa,* in Verbitsky, *Rodolfo Walsh,* 38.

8. Verbitsky, "Una experiencia de difusión clandestina," 11.

9. Raúl Veiga, *Las organizaciones de derechos humanos* (Buenos Aires: Centro Editor de América Latina, 1985), 75.

10. The name of the Mothers' founder is spelled differently in various sources. I am using the spelling that appears in Madres de Plaza de Mayo, *Nuestros hijos* (Buenos Aires: Editorial Contrapunto, 1987), 1:11, as suggested by Hebe Bonafini, president of the Mothers.

11. The Plaza de Mayo is flanked by the presidential palace (Casa Rosada), the cathedral, and several ministries. Because it is surrounded by buildings representing the structures of power, rallies at the plaza have a particularly charged appeal.

12. Jean-Pierre Bousquet, *Las Locas de la Plaza de Mayo* (Buenos Aires: El Cid Editor, 1982); "Historia de las Madres," *Madres de Plaza de Mayo,* January 1985, 6; Jo Fisher, *Mothers of the Disappeared* (Boston: South End Press, 1989); Marysa Navarro, "The Personal Is Political: Las Madres de Plaza de Mayo," in *Power and Popular Protest: Latin American Social Movements,* ed. Susan Eckstein (Berkeley: University of California Press, 1989), 241–58; Marguerite Guzmán Bouvard, *Revolutionizing Motherhood: The Mothers of the Plaza de Mayo* (Wilmington, Del.: Scholarly Resources, 1994); Matilde Mellibovsky, *Círculo de amor sobre la muerte* (Buenos Aires: Ediciones del Pensamiento Nacional, 1990).

13. Quoted in Veiga, *Las organizaciones,* 35.

14. Ibid., 42.

15. Noemí Ulla and Hugo Echave, *Después de la noche: Diálogo con Graciela Fernández Meijide* (Buenos Aires: Editorial Contrapunto, 1986), 82–83.

16. Arlette Welty-Domon, *Sor Alicia: Un sol de justicia* (Buenos Aires: Editorial Contrapunto, 1987), 27–28.

17. Uki Goñi, *Judas: La verdadera historia de Alfredo Astiz—el infiltrado* (Buenos Aires: Editorial Sudamericana, 1996). Among the twelve there were three Mothers: Azucena Villaflor de DeVincenti, María Eugenia Ponce de Bianco, and Esther Ballestrino de Careaga. The other nine were Alice Domon, Léonie Duquet, Gabriel Eduardo Horane, José Julio Fondevilla, Nélida Raquel Bulit, Angela Auad de Genovés, Horacio A. Elbert, Patricia Oviedo, and Remo Berardo.

18. Welty-Domon, *Sor Alicia,* 113–22.

19. Aída de Suárez, quoted in Fisher, *Mothers of the Disappeared,* 89; Azucena, quoted in Mellibovsky, *Círculo de amor,* 118.

20. The Grandmothers trace the birth of their Association to an informal gathering that took place in October 1977 at a demonstration during the visit of U.S. Secretary of State Cyrus Vance to Argentina. María Isabel Chorobik de Mariani (one of the founders of the Association), however, currently believes that their first meeting was in November, because that was the month of Cyrus Vance's trip to Argentina. Interview by author, La Plata, December 9, 1994.

21. Alyson Brysk, *The Politics of Human Rights in Argentina: Protest, Change, and Democratization* (Stanford: Stanford University Press, 1994), 45–51.

22. Guest, *Behind the Disappearances,* 174–75.

23. Bousquet, *Las Locas,* 155.

24. Organización de los Estados Americanos (OEA), Comisión Interamericana de Derechos Humanos, *Informe sobre la situación de los derechos humanos en Argentina* (Washington, D.C.: Organización de los Estados Americanos, 1980), 7.

25. A study of the NN burials in Buenos Aires province during the 1970s and early 1980s revealed a significant increase during the junta government. Also, the age, gender, and time and cause of death of these bodies closely matched reported disappearances. See Clyde Collins Snow and María Julia Bihurriet, "An Epidemiology of Homicide: *Ningún Nombre* Burials in the Province of Buenos Aires from 1970 to 1984," in *Human Rights and Statistics,* ed. Thomas B. Jabine and Richard P. Claude (Philadelphia: University of Pennsylvania Press, 1992), 329–63.

26. "Lo que la OEA no publicó," *Testimonios,* April 12, 1984, 3–7.

27. Emilio F. Mignone, interview by author, Buenos Aires, December 16, 1994.

28. Jorge Camarasa, Rubén Felice, and Daniel González, *El juicio: Proceso al horror* (Buenos Aires: Sudamericana/Planeta, 1985), 108–9.

29. Guest, *Behind the Disappearances,* 74.

30. Ragnar Hagelin, *Mi hija Dagmar* (Buenos Aires: Sudamericana/Planeta, 1984).

31. Paul Heath Hoeffel and Juan Montalvo (a pseudonym for Argentine scientist César Chelala), "Missing or Dead in Argentina," *New York Times Mag-*

azine, October 21, 1979, 44–45 ff; "Los campos de concentración," *Testimonios,* September 20, 1984, 5. See also Commission Argentine des Droits de l'homme, *Argentine: Dossier d'un génocide* (Paris: Flammarion, 1978).

32. Amnesty International, *Testimony on Secret Detention Camps in Argentina* (London: Amnesty International, 1980); Guest, *Behind the Disappearances,* 69.

33. Veiga, *Las Organizaciones,* 132.

34. Guest, *Behind the Disappearances,* 239.

35. OEA, *Informe,* 136–45.

36. Bousquet, *Las Locas,* 177–78.

37. Fisher, *Mothers of the Disappeared,* 110.

38. Gary W. Wynia, *Argentina: Illusions and Realities* (New York: Holmes and Meier, 1986), 113–14.

39. Bousquet, *Las Locas,* 163–64.

40. Camarasa, Felice, and González, *El juicio,* 50–51.

41. María Sonderéguer, "Aparición con vida (El movimiento de derechos humanos en Argentina)," in *Los nuevos movimientos sociales,* vol. 2, *Derechos humanos. Obreros. Barrios,* ed. Elizabeth Jelin (Buenos Aires: Centro Editor de América Latina, 1985), 19.

42. Veiga, *Las organizaciones,* 46.

43. Quoted in ibid., 41.

44. These are my own recollections as a child going to school in Argentina in the 1940s and 1950s. The islands are off the coast of Argentina in the South Atlantic Ocean. Argentina has always called them "Malvinas," while the British call them "Falklands."

45. Wynia, *Argentina,* 3–29. In this chapter there is an interesting transcript of a telephone conversation between Galtieri and President Reagan in which Reagan warns Galtieri about the possible effects of the war on Argentina-U.S. relations.

46. Sonderéguer, "Aparición con vida," 23.

47. Ibid., 24–26; Andersen, *Dossier Secreto,* 304. See also Centro de Estudios Legales y Sociales, *Autoamnistía: Legalizar la impunidad* (Buenos Aires: Centro de Estudios Legales y Sociales, n.d.).

48. Juan E. Méndez, *Truth and Partial Justice in Argentina: An Update,* An Americas Watch Report (Washington, D.C.: Americas Watch, 1991), 11.

49. Asamblea Permanente por los Derechos Humanos, *Derechos humanos, democracia y el futuro de la APDH* (Buenos Aires: Asamblea Permanente por los Derechos Humanos, 1985), 15.

50. Asamblea Permanente por los Derechos Humanos, *Las cifras de la guerra sucia* (Buenos Aires: Asamblea Permanente por los Derechos Humanos, 1988), 26. See also Alyson Brysk, "The Politics of Measurement: The Contested Count of the Disappeared in Argentina," *Human Rights Quarterly* 16 (1994): 676–92.

51. Emilio F. Mignone, *Derechos humanos y sociedad: El caso argentino* (Buenos Aires: Centro de Estudios Legales y Sociales/Ediciones del Pensamiento Nacional, 1991), 71. See also Americas Watch, *The State Department Misin-*

forms: A Study of Accounting for the Disappeared in Argentina, An Americas Watch Report (New York: Americas Watch, 1983), 4.

52. "Desaparecidos: El Gobierno difundió 290 nuevos nombres," *Clarín,* April 1, 1995.

53. Mignone, *Derechos humanos y sociedad,* 161. Also, in 1986 the CELS published a list of 692 names of repressors involved in the clandestine detention camps; see Centro de Estudios Legales y Sociales, *Terrorismo de estado: 692 responsables* (Buenos Aires: Centro de Estudios Legales y Sociales, 1986).

54. *Nunca Más: The Report of the Argentine National Commission on the Disappeared* (New York: Farrar, Straus, and Giroux, 1986), 286.

55. Mignone, *Derechos humanos y sociedad,* 154–55.

56. Camarasa, Felice, and González, *El juicio,* 67.

57. Ibid., 94–101.

58. Ibid., 187–88.

59. "El sentido ético de la vida es no matar," *El Diario del Juicio,* June 11, 1985.

60. Camarasa, Felice, and González, *El juicio,* 193–95.

61. Quoted in Amnesty International, *Argentina: The Military Juntas and Human Rights—Report of the Trial of the Former Junta Members* (London: Amnesty International, 1987), 46; see Camarasa, Felice, and González, *El juicio,* 11–17. General Videla and Admiral Massera were condemned to life imprisonment. General Agosti was sentenced to four years and six months, General Viola to seventeen years, and General Lambruschini to eight years in prison. They were all perpetually disqualified from holding public office. The other four generals—Graffigna, Galtieri, Anaya, and Lami Dozo—were exonerated.

62. "Ley de Punto Final—El no de Abuelas," *Informaciones,* no. 11 (January 1987): 3–4.

63. "Un llamado a la memoria colectiva," *Informaciones,* no. 14 (June–July 1987): 3.

64. Méndez, *Truth and Partial Justice,* 48.

65. Ibid., 49.

66. Ibid., 50.

67. Bouvard, *Revolutionizing Motherhood,* 201–2.

68. Ibid., 205. See also Amnesty International, *Argentina—The Attack on the Third Infantry Regiment Barracks at La Tablada: Investigations into Allegations of Torture, "Disappearances," and Extrajudicial Executions* (New York: Amnesty International, 1990).

69. Méndez, *Truth and Partial Justice,* 65–67.

70. Ibid., 68–69.

71. Tribunal Permanente de los Pueblos, *La impunidad juzgada: El caso argentino* (Buenos Aires: Fundación Servicio Paz y Justicia, 1992), 104.

CHAPTER THREE. THE GRANDMOTHERS ORGANIZE

1. Abuelas de Plaza de Mayo, *Niños desaparecidos en la Argentina desde 1976* (Buenos Aires: Abuelas de Plaza de Mayo, 1990), 126–27; *Nunca Más:*

The Report of the Argentine National Commission on the Disappeared (New York: Farrar, Straus and Giroux, 1986), 314; Equipo Argentino de Antropología Forense, *Breve reseña sobre el caso de la familia Manfil* (Buenos Aires: Equipo Argentino de Antropología Forense, n.d.); and Alejandro Inchaurregui, correspondence with author, September 5, 1995. Alba Lanzillotto, the current secretary of the Grandmothers' Association, provided the number of disappeared children and pregnant women as of September 22, 1997.

2. Quoted in Amnesty International, *The Missing Children of Argentina: A Report of Current Investigations* (New York: Amnesty International, 1985), 3.

3. Emilio F. Mignone, *Derechos humanos y sociedad: El caso argentino* (Buenos Aires: Centro de Estudios Legales y Sociales/Ediciones Del Pensamiento Nacional, 1991), 116–17. Also, interview by author, Buenos Aires, December 16, 1994.

4. A document issued during the dictatorship by the Ministry of Interior gave instructions on what to do with the children of the detained and disappeared. The document was destroyed by the army shortly before the return to democracy. See "Conferencia de prensa sobre destrucción de documentación, impunidad y reivindicación del terrorismo de Estado," *Informaciones,* no. 21 (November 1988–January 1989): 28.

5. Judith Filc, *Entre el parentesco y la política: Familia y dictadura, 1976–1983* (Buenos Aires: Editorial Biblos, 1997).

6. Hernán Dinamarca and Marisol Santelices, *¿Donde están?: La historia de los 13 niños uruguayos desaparecidos* (Montevideo: Ediciones La República, 1989).

7. Asociación Pro-Búsqueda de los Niños, "Los niños desaparecidos: Un reto de la posguerra," paper distributed at XIII Congreso de FEDEFAM, November 20–25, 1995, San Salvador.

8. María Isabel Chorobik de Mariani, interview by author, La Plata, December 9, 1994. Subsequent quotations from her are taken from this interview, unless otherwise noted.

9. At one of their early gatherings, a Mother had picked up a rusty nail from the ground and put it on her lapel. "It is a symbol of suffering, like the nails of Christ," she said. After that, other Mothers started to use nails to recognize each other. See *Madres de Plaza de Mayo,* February 1985, 15.

10. Haydée Vallino de Lemos, interview by author, Buenos Aires, November 5, 1993.

11. Raquel Radío de Marizcurrena, interview by author, Buenos Aires, November 25, 1993. Subsequent quotations from her are taken from this interview, unless otherwise noted.

12. Delia Giovanola de Califano, interview by author, Buenos Aires, October 29, 1996.

13. Julio E. Nosiglia, *Botín de guerra* (Buenos Aires: Cooperativa Tierra Fértil, 1985), 90. The twelve original Grandmothers were María Isabel Chorobik de Mariani, Beatriz H. C. Aicardi de Neuhaus, Eva Márquez de Castillo Barrios, Alicia Zubasnabar de de la Cuadra, Vilma Delinda Sesarego de Gutiérrez, Mirta Acuña de Baravalle, Haydée Vallino de Lemos, Leontina Puebla de Pérez, Delia Giovanola de Califano, Raquel Radío de Marizcurrena, Clara

Jurado, and María Eugenia Cassinelli de García Irureta Goyena. They were later joined by Julia de Grandi.

14. Ibid., 91.

15. Rosa Tarlovsky de Roisinblit, interview by author, Buenos Aires, November 17, 1993. Subsequent quotations from her are taken from this interview, unless otherwise noted.

16. Nosiglia, *Botín de guerra,* 92.

17. Matilde Herrera and Ernesto Tenembaum, *Identidad: Despojo y restitución* (Buenos Aires: Editorial Contrapunto, n.d), 23.

18. Quoted in ibid., 24.

19. Nosiglia, *Botín de guerra,* 42.

20. Ibid., 113.

21. Ibid., 108–9.

22. Herrera, *Identidad,* 28.

23. Estela Barnes de Carlotto, interview by author, Buenos Aires, December 16, 1993.

24. Otilia Lescano de Argañaraz, interview by author, Buenos Aires, November 5, 1993.

25. Emma Spione de Baamonde, interview by author, Buenos Aires, November 4, 1993. Subsequent quotations from her are taken from this interview, unless otherwise noted.

26. Quoted in Nosiglia, *Botín de guerra,* 105.

27. Antonia Acuña de Segarra, interview by author, Buenos Aires, December 7, 1993.

28. Quoted in Nosiglia, *Botín de guerra,* 146.

29. Ibid., 32, 33.

30. Emilio F. Mignone, *Witness to the Truth: The Complicity of Church and Dictatorship in Argentina, 1976–1983,* trans. Philip Berryman (Maryknoll, N.Y.: Orbis Books, 1988), 14.

31. Quoted in Herrera, *Identidad,* 30.

32. Quoted in Nosiglia, *Botín de guerra,* 147.

33. Quoted in ibid., 103.

34. Nélida Gómez de Navajas, interview by author, Buenos Aires, November 9, 1993.

35. Abuelas de Plaza de Mayo/Grandmothers of Plaza de Mayo, *Missing Children Who Disappeared in Argentina between 1976 and 1983* (Buenos Aires: Grandmothers of Plaza de Mayo, 1988), 3.

36. Abuelas de Plaza de Mayo, *Los niños desaparecidos y la justicia* (Buenos Aires: Abuelas de Plaza de Mayo, 1988), 151–61.

37. Ibid., 151–52.

38. Abuelas, *Missing Children,* 26.

39. Jaime Wright, correspondence with author, August 24 and September 23, 1994. CLAMOR is not an acronym; the name derives from the text of Psalms 88.2: "Incline thine ear unto my cry." The founders of CLAMOR were Jan Rocha, Luiz Eduardo Greenhalgh, and Jaime Wright. CLAMOR was started in 1978. With the return of democracy in the Southern Cone in 1987, CLAMOR considered that its mission had been accomplished and disbanded.

40. Herrera, *Identidad,* 41, 43.

41. Nosiglia, *Botín de guerra,* 140–41.

42. Abuelas, *Niños desaparecidos,* 92.

43. Wright, correspondence with author.

44. Irene Barki, *Pour ces yeux-lá . . . La face cachée du drame argentin: Les enfants disparus* (Paris: Editions la Découverte, 1988), 168.

45. Magda Van Malder, secretary general of UFER, correspondence with author, May 7, 1995. UFER, based in Brussels, Belgium, is a federation of groups and individual members working for the promotion of intercultural and interracial understanding, cooperation, and exchange, in the spirit of the Universal Declaration of Human Rights. One of their representatives in Geneva, C. M. Eya Nchama, became a steadfast supporter and friend of the Grandmothers.

46. Quoted in César Chelala, "Grandmothers of the 'Disappeared,'" *Christian Science Monitor,* October 6, 1986.

47. Nosiglia, *Botín de guerra,* 198.

48. Quoted in Christopher Joyce and Eric Stover, *Witnesses from the Grave: The Stories Bones Tell* (New York: Ballantine Books, 1992), 226–27.

49. Victor B. Penchaszadeh, interview by author, New York, May 18, 1995. Paternity testing is done through the use of genetic markers such as red blood cell antigens and the white blood cell HLA antigens. HLA are used as standard markers because they are a highly variable genetic system, making it very unlikely that two unrelated individuals could share the same type. For more information, see Richard H. Walker, ed., *Inclusion Probabilities in Parentage Testing* (Arlington, Va.: American Association of Blood Banks, 1983).

50. Eric Stover, interview by author, Boston, August 9, 1994. Subsequent quotations from him are taken from this interview, unless otherwise noted. See also Rita Arditti, "Genetics and Justice: The Grandmothers of Plaza de Mayo Enroll Scientists in Their Struggle for Human Rights," *Woman of Power,* fall 1988, 42–44.

51. Quoted in Simson L. Garfinkel, "Genetic Trails Lead to Argentina's Missing Children," *Boston Globe,* June 12, 1989.

52. Joyce and Stover, *Witnesses from the Grave,* 221.

53. Ana María Di Lonardo, interview by author, Buenos Aires, December 15, 1993. Subsequent quotations from her are taken from this interview, unless otherwise noted.

54. Ana María Di Lonardo, Pierre Darlu, Max Baur, Cristian Orrego, and Mary-Claire King, "Human Genetics and Human Rights—Identifying the Families of Kidnapped Children," *American Journal of Forensic Medicine and Pathology* 5 (1984): 339–47.

55. Barbara Beckwith, "Science for Human Rights—Using Genetic Screening and Forensic Science to Find Argentina's Disappeared," *Science for the People* 19, no. 1 (January/February 1987): 6.

Grandparentage testing begins with blood testing of the grandparents (or aunts and uncles) and the child in question. By looking at selected genetic markers, doctors can establish if certain combinations of markers were inherited from the grandparents or if they arose by chance. Once the distribution of genetic markers in the Argentine population is taken into account, it is possible to determine if a child comes from a particular family with a certainty of up to 99.95 percent (this "probability of inclusion" never reaches 100 percent). Initially histocompatibility (HLA) typing was used. Later new techniques were added: DNA typing and mitochondrial DNA sequencing. Currently DNA testing is used regularly because of its greater accuracy. In 1988, when only the HLA system was used, a mistaken identification was made in the case of a girl. Critics of the Grandmothers used this case to launch an attack on genetic testing and on the work of the Association more generally.

For further information on the use of genetics to identify the kidnapped children, see Victor B. Penchaszadeh, "Abduction of Children of Political Dissidents in Argentina and the Role of Human Genetics in Their Restitution," *Journal of Public Health Policy* 13 (1992): 291–305, and "Genetic Identification of Children of the Disappeared in Argentina," *Journal of the American Medical Women's Association* 52, no. 1 (winter 1997): 16–27.

56. "Recibidas por Alfonsín," *Informaciones,* no. 8 (April 1986): 7–8.

57. Jorge Luis Berra, *Banco Nacional de Datos Genéticos: La identificación de los niños desaparecidos en la Argentina* (Buenos Aires: Abuelas de Plaza de Mayo, n.d.).

58. "La creación del Banco de Datos Genéticos," *Informaciones,* no. 13 (April–May 1987): 9–10.

59. "Se restituyó una niña nacida en cautiverio," *Informaciones,* no. 13 (April–May 1987): 14.

60. Ana María Di Lonardo, interview by author, Buenos Aires, October 31, 1996. In July 1996, Dr. Di Lonardo was awarded the title of Chevalier de l'Ordre National du Mérite by the French government. The award, created by General de Gaulle in 1963, recognizes individuals for distinguished activities in science, politics, and public service.

61. "Banco Nacional de Datos Genéticos," *Informaciones,* no. 20 (September–October 1988): 18.

62. "Entrevista con el presidente de la Nación, Dr. Raúl Alfonsín," *Informaciones,* no. 21 (November 1988–January 1989): 2–3.

63. "Niegan que se planee eliminar el Banco de Datos Genéticos," *Informaciones,* no. 27 (February–April 1990): 11. The article originally appeared in *La Prensa,* April 22, 1990.

64. "Allanamiento al Banco Nacional de Datos Genéticos," *Informaciones,* no. 31 (March–May 1991): 18.

65. Joyce, *Witnesses,* 239–56. Also, Mimí Doretti, telephone conversation, August 16, 1994.

66. Quoted in Eric Stover, "Scientists Aid Search for Argentina's 'Desaparecidos,'" *Science,* October 4, 1985, 56–57.

67. Clyde Snow, telephone conversation, January 24, 1996. Subsequent quotations from him are taken from this conversation, unless otherwise noted.

68. Joyce and Stover, *Witnesses from the Grave,* 225–26.

69. Victor B. Penchaszadeh, in "Implicaciones Sociales y Científicas de Nuestra Lucha," in *Filiación, identidad, restitución: 15 años de lucha de Abuelas de Plaza de Mayo,* ed. Estela Barnes de Carlotto, Alicia Lo Giúdice, Victor

B. Penchaszadeh, and Juan Carlos Volnovich (Buenos Aires: El Bloque Editorial, 1995), 32–34.

70. Mauricio Cohen Salama, *Tumbas anónimas: Informe sobre la identificación de restos de víctimas de la represión ilegal* (Buenos Aires: Equipo Argentino de Antropología Forense and Catálogos, 1992). In 1990 the EAAF identified the remains of María Adelia Garín de De Angeli, who was two months pregnant at the time of her disappearance in 1977. As in the cases of Liliana Pereyra and Laura Carlotto, it was determined that she had been killed after giving birth (271–72).

CHAPTER FOUR. FROM TERROR TO RESISTANCE

1. María del Carmen Feijoo and Mónica Gogna, "Women in the Transition to Democracy," in *Women and Social Change in Latin America,* ed. Elizabeth Jelin (London: Zed Books, 1990), 82.

2. Quoted in Eduardo Varela-Cid and Luis Vicens, *La imbecilización de la mujer* (Buenos Aires: El Cid Editor, 1984), 103.

3. Ibid., 3–4, 10–15.

4. Alicia Lombardi, *Las Madres de Plaza de Mayo: Un enfoque feminista* (Buenos Aires: ATEM, IV Jornadas de Mujeres, 1985); Jo Fisher, *Mothers of the Disappeared* (Boston: South End Press, 1989); Marysa Navarro, "The Personal Is Political: Las Madres de Plaza de Mayo," in *Power and Popular Protest: Latin American Social Movements,* ed. Susan Eckstein (Berkeley: University of California Press, 1989); 241–58; Marguerite Guzmán Bouvard, *Revolutionizing Motherhood: The Mothers of the Plaza de Mayo* (Wilmington, Del.: Scholarly Resources, 1994).

5. Elena Santander, interview by author, Buenos Aires, October 27, 1993. Subsequent quotations from her are taken from this interview, unless otherwise noted. In this respect the Grandmothers (as well as the Mothers) are an example of the "female consciousness" framework, proposed by historian Temma Kaplan to explain the political activism of otherwise "traditional" women. See Kaplan, "Female Consciousness and Collective Action: The Case of Barcelona, 1910–1918," *Signs* 7 (1982): 545–66.

6. Nya Quesada, interview by author, Buenos Aires, November 22, 1993.

7. Quoted in Norbert Lechner, "Some People Die of Fear: Fear as a Political Problem," in *At the Edge: State Terror and Resistance in Latin America,* ed. Juan E. Corradi, Patricia Weiss Fagen, and Manuel Antonio Garretón (Berkeley: University of California Press, 1992), 26. See also Marguerite Feitlowitz, *A Lexicon of Terror: Argentina and the Legacies of Torture* (New York: Oxford University Press, 1998).

8. Elsa Sánchez de Oesterheld, interview by author, Buenos Aires, November 10, 1993.

9. Berta Schubaroff, interview by author, Buenos Aires, November 18, 1993. Subsequent quotations from her are taken from this interview, unless otherwise noted.

10. Raquel Radío de Marizcurrena, interview by author, Buenos Aires, November 25, 1993. Subsequent quotations from her are taken from this interview, unless otherwise noted.

11. Haydée Vallino de Lemos, interview by author, Buenos Aires, November 5, 1993.

12. Otilia Lescano de Argañaraz, interview by author, Buenos Aires, November 5, 1993. Subsequent quotations from her are taken from this interview, unless otherwise noted.

13. Rosa Tarlovsky de Roisinblit, interview by author, Buenos Aires, November 17, 1993. Subsequent quotations from her are taken from this interview, unless otherwise noted.

14. Ignacio Martín-Baró, "Political Violence and War as Causes of Psychosocial Trauma in El Salvador," *International Journal of Mental Health* 18 (1989): 10–11.

15. Estela Barnes de Carlotto, interview by author, Buenos Aires, December 16, 1993. Subsequent quotations from her are taken from this interview, unless otherwise noted.

16. Mauricio Cohen Salama, *Tumbas anónimas: Informe sobre la identificación de restos de víctimas de la represión ilegal* (Buenos Aires: Equipo Argentino de Antropología Forense and Catálogos, 1992), 169–74.

17. Antonia Acuña de Segarra, interview by author, Buenos Aires, December 7, 1993. Subsequent quotations from her are taken from this interview, unless otherwise noted.

18. Elsa Pavón de Aguilar, interview by author, Buenos Aires, December 19, 1993.

19. Elizabeth Janeway, *Powers of the Weak* (New York: Alfred A. Knopf, 1980), 161–62.

20. Nélida Gómez de Navajas, interview by author, Buenos Aires, November 9, 1993. Subsequent quotations from her are taken from this interview, unless otherwise noted.

21. Amelia Herrera de Miranda, interview by author, Buenos Aires, November 1, 1993. Subsequent quotations from her are taken from this interview, unless otherwise noted.

22. Dorothy Dinnerstein, "What Does Feminism Mean?" in *Rocking the Ship of State: Toward a Feminist Peace Politics,* ed. Adrienne Harris and Ynestra King (Boulder, Colo.: Westview Press, 1989), 14.

23. Sonia Torres, interview by author, Córdoba, December 2, 1993. Subsequent quotations from her are taken from this interview, unless otherwise noted.

24. María Isabel Chorobik de Mariani, interview by author, La Plata, December 9, 1994.

25. Argentina Rojo de Pérez, interview by author, Buenos Aires, November 28, 1993.

26. Delia Giovanola de Califano, interview by author, Buenos Aires, October 29, 1996.

27. Alba Lanzillotto, interview by author, Buenos Aires, October 26, 1993. Subsequent quotations from her are taken from this interview, unless otherwise noted.

28. Reina Esses de Waisberg, interview by author, Buenos Aires, October 25, 1996. Subsequent quotations from her are taken from this interview, unless otherwise noted.

29. Judith Lewis Herman, *Trauma and Recovery* (New York: Basic Books, 1992), 192.

30. "Los niños desaparecidos y la conciencia argentina," *Informaciones,* no. 8 (April 1986): 2.

31. Sara Ruddick, *Maternal Thinking: Towards a Politics of Peace* (Boston: Beacon Press, 1989), 51.

32. Nancy Saporta Sternbach, Marysa Navarro-Aranguren, Patricia Chuchryk, and Sonia E. Alvarez, "Feminisms in Latin America: From Bogotá to San Bernardo," in *Rethinking the Political: Gender, Resistance, and the State,* ed. Barbara Laslett, Johanna Brenner, and Yesim Arat (Chicago: University of Chicago Press, 1995), 240–81; quotations, 242, 245.

33. Ibid.

34. "VIII Encuentro Nacional de Mujeres," *Informaciones,* no. 36 (January–December 1993): 20.

35. Lourdes Arizpe, "Foreword: Democracy for a Small Two-Gender Planet" in Jelin, *Women and Social Change,* xiv–xx.

CHAPTER FIVE. FINDING THE CHILDREN

1. Jaime Wright, correspondence with author, August 24, 1994.

2. Eduardo Luis Duhalde, *El estado terrorista argentino* (Buenos Aires: Ediciones El Caballito, 1983), 190.

3. Elsa Sánchez de Oesterheld, interview by author, Buenos Aires, November 10, 1993.

4. Estela Barnes de Carlotto, interview by author, Buenos Aires, December 16, 1993.

5. "Porque un niño secuestrado o nacido en cautiverio debe ser restituido a su legítima familia," *Informaciones,* no. 13 (April–May 1987): 26; "Segundo Seminario Nacional sobre 'niños desaparecidos, su restitución,'" *Informaciones,* no. 18 (March–May 1988): 3–8; Equipo Interdisciplinario de Abuelas de Plaza de Mayo, *El secuestro-apropiación de niños y su restitución* (Buenos Aires: Abuelas de Plaza de Mayo, 1989); Laura J. de Conte, in "Identidad, Filiación, Apropiación, Adopción y Restitución," in *Filiación, identidad, restitución: 15 años de lucha de Abuelas de Plaza de Mayo,* ed. Estela Barnes de Carlotto, Alicia Lo Giúdice, Victor Penchaszadeh, and Juan Carlos Volnovich (Buenos Aires: El Bloque Editorial, 1995), 91–101.

Psychologists working with the found children have found the theoretical perspective of French psychoanalyst Piera Aulangier on the relationship between the healthy psychic development of the child and the internal world of the parents—especially the mother—useful and relevant to their efforts. Alicia Lo Giúdice, interview by author, Buenos Aires, December 14, 1993.

6. Reina Esses de Waisberg, interview by author, Buenos Aires, October 25, 1996.

7. Tania María Waisberg, interview by author, Buenos Aires, October 30, 1996.

8. María Isabel Chorobik de Mariani, interview by author, La Plata, December 9, 1994.

9. Quoted in Matilde Herrera and Ernesto Tenembaum, *Identidad: Despojo y restitución* (Buenos Aires: Editorial Contrapunto, n.d.), 86. See also César Chelala, "100 Grandmothers, Still Searching," *Washington Post,* December 27, 1985. Uruguayan writer Eduardo Galeano wrote two short pieces inspired by what happened to Tamara: see "1983, Buenos Aires: Las abuelas detectives" and "1983, Lima: Tamara vuela dos veces," in *Memoria del fuego,* vol. 3, *El siglo del viento* (Mexico City: siglo veintuno editores, 1986), 321–23.

10. Quoted in Herrera and Tenembaum, *Identidad,* 86.

11. Lidia Castagno de Visentini, "Los verdaderos padres son los padres psicológicos," parts 1 and 2, *La Capital* (Rosario), March 29 and 30, 1984; "Verdad y Ley para los niños recuperados: Un diálogo con Francoise Dolto," *Psyche,* October 1986, 4–6. For a detailed rebuttal of these arguments, see Equipo Interdisciplinario de Abuelas de Plaza de Mayo, "Abuelas opinan sobre Dolto," *Psyche,* December 1986, 11–12, and Marie Pascale Chevance-Bertin, "Memóire pour l'impensable—le cas des enfants de disparus Argentins volés par des militaires ou des policiers," presented at Université Paris VII, 1986–87.

12. Estela de Carlotto, interview, Buenos Aires.

13. Ignacio Martín-Baró, "War and the Psychosocial Trauma of Salvadoran Children," in his *Writings for a Liberation Psychology,* ed. Adrianne Aron and Shawn Corne (Cambridge, Mass.: Harvard University Press, 1994), 122–35.

14. Quoted in "Preocupación por un memorandum de circulación interna en la Corte Suprema de Justicia de La Nación," *Informaciones,* no. 15 (August–September 1987):17.

15. For a detailed account of this case, see Juan Carlos Martínez, *La Abuela de Hierro* (Buenos Aires: Fundación Servicio Paz y Justicia, 1995).

16. "Dificultades en la Restitución," *Informaciones,* no. 8 (April 1986): 8–10.

17. "Adoption Dispute in Argentina," *Boston Globe,* January 4, 1989.

18. "Ximena Clama al Juez Fégoli," *Informaciones,* no. 26 (December 1989–January 1990): 12; "Ximena Vicario," *Informaciones,* no. 27 (February–April 1990): 7–10; "Comunicados: Sentencia judicial sobre la adopción de Ximena Vicario," *Informaciones,* no. 32 (June–November 1991): 10–11.

19. Tatiana Sfiligoy, interview by author, Buenos Aires, December 17, 1993. Subsequent quotations from her are taken from this interview, unless otherwise noted.

20. Elena Santander, interview by author, Buenos Aires, October 27, 1993.

21. Elsa Pavón de Aguilar, interview by author, Buenos Aires, December 19, 1993. Subsequent quotations from her are taken from this interview, unless otherwise noted.

22. Paula Eva Logares Grinspon, interview by author, Buenos Aires, December 20, 1994.

23. Nya Quesada, interview by author, Buenos Aires, November 22, 1993.

24. Haydée Vallino de Lemos, interview by author, Buenos Aires, November 5, 1993. Subsequent quotations from her are taken from this interview, unless otherwise noted.

25. María José Lavalle Lemos, interview by author, Buenos Aires, December 22, 1994. Subsequent quotations from her are taken from this interview, unless otherwise noted.

26. Herrera and Tenembaum, *Identidad,* 215–30; de Conte, in *Filiación, identidad, restitución.*

27. Nélida Gómez de Navajas, interview by author, Cambridge, Mass., October 30, 1989.

28. Estela de Carlotto, interview by author, Cambridge, Mass., October 30, 1989.

29. Ibid.

30. Herrera and Tenembaum, *Identidad,* 183.

31. Alicia Lo Giúdice, "La cajita: Subjetividad y traumatismo," paper presented at Pensar la Niñez: Primer Encuentro Psicoanalítico Interdisciplinario, Buenos Aires, November 1992.

32. Estela de Carlotto, interview, Cambridge, Mass.

33. Marcelo Bianchedi, interview by author, Buenos Aires, December 15, 1994.

34. Arturo Galiñanes, interview by author, Buenos Aires, November 18, 1993.

CHAPTER SIX. CAPTIVE MINDS, CAPTIVE LIVES

1. Marc Hillel and Clarissa Henry, *Of Pure Blood* (New York: McGraw-Hill, 1976), 157.

2. Quoted in ibid., 226.

3. Quoted in "E. Germany Took Infants, Data Say," *Boston Globe,* May 24, 1991.

4. Jacob Kaplan, *L'Affaire Finaly* (Paris: Les Editions du Cerf, 1993).

5. Peter Read, *The Stolen Generations: The Removal of Aboriginal Children in New South Wales, 1883 to 1969,* New South Wales, Ministry of Aboriginal Affairs (Sydney: Government Printer, 1982) 5, 6.

6. Alan Thornhill, "Australia Rues Removal of Aboriginal Children," *Boston Globe,* May 21, 1997; Commonwealth of Australia, *Bringing Them Home: Report of the National Inquiry into the Separation of Aboriginal and Torres Strait Islander Children from Their Families* (Sydney: Human Rights and Equal Opportunity Commission, 1997).

7. Jorge Noriega, "American Indian Education in the United States: Indoctrination for Subordination to Colonialism," in *The State of Native America: Genocide, Colonization, and Resistance,* ed. M. Annette Jaimes (Boston: South End Press, 1992), 380.

8. Ibid., 381.

9. United Nations, *Convention on the Prevention and Punishment of the Crime of Genocide* (New York: United Nations, 1991).

10. Kurt Jonassohn, "What Is Genocide?" in *Genocide Watch,* ed. Helen Fein (New Haven: Yale University Press, 1992), 17–26. See also Barbara Harff, "Recognizing Genocides and Politicides," in ibid., 27–41.

11. Theo van Boven, *Prevention of the Disappearance of Children* (n.p.: UN Economic and Social Council, Commission on Human Rights, 1988), 15.

12. "Texto de la presentación de Abuelas en la O.N.U.," *Informaciones*, no. 17 (December 1987–February 1988): 10–12.

13. Comisión de Familiares de Paraguayos Detenidos Desaparecidos en la Argentina, *Semillas de vida/Ñemity Ra* (Asunción, Paraguay: Comisión de Familiares de Paraguayos Detenidos Desaparecidos en la Argentina, n.d.), 19.

14. Quoted in "Novedades en el caso Bianco," *Informaciones*, no. 15 (August–September 1987): 12–13.

15. "Estudiará la OEA la situación de los hijos de desaparecidos," *La Prensa*, November 14, 1987; "El pasado que vuelve-extraditaron al ex-mayor Bianco," *Página 12*, March 7, 1997; Marta Gurvich, "The Dirty War's Family Secrets," *In These Times*, April 28, 1997, 27–30.

16. Andrea Rodríguez, "Hijos de desaparecidos, otro tema," *Informaciones*, no. 17 (December 1987–February 1988): 7–8. This article was originally published in *Página 12*, March 11, 1988.

17. Van Boven was a strong human rights advocate, and the Argentine government had blocked the renewal of his UN contract in 1982. See Hans Thoolen, introduction to *People Matter: Views on International Human Rights Policy*, by Theo van Boven (Amsterdam: Meulenhoff, 1982), 8.

18. Van Boven, *Prevention of Disappearance*, 1.

19. Ibid., 11.

20. Theo van Boven, correspondence with author, December 18, 1995. He also wrote:

> I was deeply disappointed at the time that the Argentine authorities and some members of the Sub-Commission prompted by the same authorities, objected to certain aspects of my report. In fact, the Argentine government wanted to use my report as a means to bring pressure on Paraguay and expected that I would come up with a black and white picture—Paraguay being the bad guy and Argentina the good guy. I made it clear in my report that Paraguay was obstructing the cause of justice but I also criticised to some extent the functioning of official mechanisms in Argentina, notably several parts of the judiciary. I still think this criticism was fully justified, but it was apparently not welcome to the Argentine authorities.

21. "Entrevista con el Presidente de la nación, Dr. Raúl Alfonsín," *Informaciones*, no. 21 (November 1988–January 1989): 2–3; "Abuelas en las Naciones Unidas," *Informaciones*, no. 22 (February–April 1989): 11–12.

22. Quoted in Juan Jorge Fariña and M. Brinton Lykes, "Cuestiones éticas y epistemológicas ante la experimentación psicológica con niños," in *Actas del Congreso Nacional de Etica* (Buenos Aires: Asociación Argentina de Investigaciones Eticas, Universidad de Buenos Aires, 1991).

23. Mariela Salaberry, *Mariana: Tú y nosotros—Diálogo con María Ester Gatti* (Montevideo: Ediciones de la Banda Oriental, 1993), 53–102.

24. Quoted in ibid., 96.

25. Nathaniel C. Nash, "Argentines Contend for War Orphans' Hearts," *New York Times*, May 11, 1993.

26. María Ester Gatti, telephone conversation with author, December 22, 1994.

27. Quoted in Salaberry, *Mariana*, 101.

28. María Ester Gatti, telephone conversation.
29. Estela Barnes de Carlotto, interview by author, Buenos Aires, December 22, 1994.
30. "De la apropiación a la verdad: La verdadera historia de un largo camino hacia la vida," *Informaciones,* no. 36 (January–December 1993): 50–52.
31. Andrea Rodríguez, *Nacidos en la sombra: La historia secreta de los mellizos Reggiardo Tolosa y el Subcomisario Miara* (Buenos Aires: Sudamericana, 1996), 46, 149.
32. A.R., "Una violación," *Página 12,* June 2, 1994.
33. Rodríguez, *Nacidos en la sombra,* 106, 121.
34. Julio Spina and Olga Viglieca, "Retrato de familia con secuestro," *El Porteño,* June 1989.
35. Rodríguez, *Nacidos en la sombra,* 141–42, 157–58. The Grandmothers, who then believed that the twins were the children of Adalberto Rossetti and Liliana Ross, a young medical student disappeared in 1976, referred to them as "Rossetti-Ross."
36. Ibid., 194.
37. Quoted in "Mellizos Reggiardo Tolosa," *Informaciones,* no. 29 (August–October 1990): 15.
38. Quoted in Jorge Llistosella, "Como enloquecer menores," *El Porteño,* May 1992.
39. Alejandra Rey, "Los Reggiardo Tolosa ya dejan de ser Miara," *Página 12,* May 19, 1993.
40. "La CIDH reclamó al gobierno por los mellizos Reggiardo Tolosa," *Página 12,* August 21, 1993.
41. See the booklet and film by Utpba (Unión de Trabajadores de Prensa de Buenos Aires), *La construcción de la noticia: Estudio de un caso de manipulación de la información* (Buenos Aires, 1994).
42. Rodríguez, *Nacidos en la sombra,* 248.
43. Quoted in "Tolosa renunció a la guarda de los mellizos y podrán visitar a Miara," *El Día* (La Plata), June 2, 1994.
44. Horacio Verbitsky, "El muro de Berlín," *Página 12,* June 5, 1994.
45. "Un caso muy difícil," *Página 12,* June 2, 1994; "Mellizos Reggiardo Tolosa: Denuncian campaña para justificar el secuestro," *El Día,* June 29, 1994.
46. Estela de Carlotto, interview, Buenos Aires.
47. Rodríguez, *Nacidos en la sombra,* 262–64.
48. Quoted in Abuelas de Plaza de Mayo, *Los niños desaparecidos y la justicia* (Buenos Aires: Abuelas de Plaza de Mayo, 1988), 106, 105.
49. Eva Giberti, *La adopción* (Buenos Aires: Sudamericana, 1987), 206–8, emphasis hers.
50. Ibid., 210.
51. "Primer Congreso Argentino de Adopción," *Informaciones,* no. 10 (September 1986): 4–8.
52. Van Boven, *Prevention of Disappearance,* 14.
53. Fernando Ulloa, "La verdad se filtra," *Página 12,* June 5, 1994.
54. Alicia Lo Giúdice, interview by author, Buenos Aires, December 14, 1993.

55. Adriana Calvo de Laborde, "Carta abierta al Dr. Wechsler," *Página 12,* January 2, 1992.

56. Quoted in Silvina Climis, "La vida pudo más," *Clarín,* April 16, 1995.

57. Quoted in "En busca de uno mismo," *Clarín,* April 2, 1995.

CHAPTER SEVEN. A NEW STRATEGY

1. "Proyectos—Abuelas de Plaza de Mayo," *Informaciones,* no. 28 (May–July 1990): 30.

2. "Primer Congreso Argentino de Adopción," *Informaciones,* no. 10 (September 1986): 4–8; "Jornadas interdisciplinarias sobre adopción," *Informaciones,* no. 24 (July–August 1989): 4.

3. Telephone conversation with the Legal Department of the United Nations in New York, April 29, 1998. President Clinton signed the convention in 1995, but only after approval by the Senate can it be incorporated into U.S. law. See Cynthia Price Cohen, "United States Signs the Convention on the Rights of the Child," *International Journal of Children's Rights* 3 (1995): 281–82.

4. Thomas Hammarberg, "The UN Convention on the Rights of the Child—and How to Make It Work," *Human Rights Quarterly* 12 (1990): 97–105.

5. United Nations, *United Nations Convention on the Rights of the Child* (New York: United Nations, 1990).

6. María Teresa Flores, in "Identidad, Filiación, Apropiación, Adopción y Restitución: Area Jurídica," in *Filiación, identidad, restitución: 15 años de lucha de Abuelas de Plaza de Mayo,* ed. Estela Barnes de Carlotto, Alicia Lo Giúdice, Victor Penchaszadeh, and Juan Carlos Volnovich (Buenos Aires: El Bloque Editorial, 1995), 143–44.

7. Quoted in George A. Stewart, "Interpreting the Child's Right to Identity in the UN Convention on the Rights of the Child," *Family Law Quarterly* 26 (1992): 223.

8. Jaime Sergio Cerda, "The Draft Convention on the Rights of the Child: New Rights," *Human Rights Quarterly* 12 (1990): 115–19.

9. *United Nations Convention on the Rights of the Child.*

10. Norberto Ignacio Liwski and Horacio David Pacheco, *Acerca de las reservas argentinas a la Convención Internacional De Los Derechos del Niño—Ley Nacional 23.849* (Buenos Aires: Sección Argentina de Defensa del Niño Internacional, 1991).

11. Stewart, "The Child's Right to Identity," 225–26.

12. "Encuentros en apoyo del proyecto sobre Derechos del Niño en las Naciones Unidas," *Informaciones,* no. 20 (September–October 1988): 15.

13. Estela Barnes de Carlotto, interview by author, Buenos Aires, December 22, 1994. Article 7 states:

> 1. The child shall be registered immediately after birth and shall have the right from birth to a name, the right to acquire a nationality, and, as far as possible, the right to know and be cared for by his or her parents.

> 2. States Parties shall ensure the implementation of these rights in accordance with their national law and their obligations under the relevant international instruments in this field, in particular where the child would otherwise be stateless.

Article 11 states:

> 1. States Parties shall take measures to combat the illicit transfer and non-return of children abroad.
>
> 2. To this end, States Parties shall promote the conclusion of bilateral or multilateral agreements or accession to existing agreements.
>
> *United Nations Convention on the Rights of the Child* (1990)

14. "Al Dr. Carlos Saúl Menem," *Informaciones,* no. 30 (November 1990–February 1991): 13.

15. "El obstinado silencio del Presidente," *Informaciones,* no. 30 (November 1990–January 1991): 12; "Comisión de Derechos Humanos de las Naciones Unidas—47 sesión," *Informaciones,* no. 31 (March–May 1991): 3–5.

16. Quoted in "Hijo de desaparecidos: Traban análisis genético," *Clarín,* February 2, 1995.

17. Alcira E. Ríos, correspondence with author, August 5, 1996, and interview, Buenos Aires, November 5, 1996.

18. Alcira E. Ríos, interview by author, Buenos Aires, December 27, 1994. See also Alcira E. Ríos, "La pericia immunogenética en los casos de los menores víctimas de desaparición forzada," paper presented to the National Commission on the Right to Identity (ca. 1996).

19. "Alegría de las Abuelas con la corte," *Clarín,* December 29, 1996.

20. For a detailed account of this case, see Carlos Amorín, *Sara Buscando a Simón* (Montevideo: Ediciones de Brecha, 1996). Also, Carlos Amorín, telephone interview by author, May 4, 1998.

21. It is by no means certain that all paper documentation was destroyed. In April 1997, former navy officer Adolfo Scilingo stated that secret files on the disappeared were hidden in a Swiss bank in 1983 by orders of the then–commander in chief of the navy, Admiral Rubén Franco. See "Ex-Argentine Officer Says 'Dirty War' Files in Swiss Vault," *Boston Globe,* April 5, 1997.

22. "Comisión Nacional por el Derecho a la Identidad de las Personas," *Informaciones,* no. 35 (August–December 1992): 20–22.

23. Alicia Pierini, interview by author, Buenos Aires, December 6, 1993.

24. Lita Abdala (a member of the commission chosen by the Grandmothers), interview by author, Buenos Aires, November 1, 1996.

25. Ibid.

26. "Comité Argentino de Seguimiento y Aplicación de la Convención Internacional sobre los Derechos del Niño," *Informaciones,* no. 36 (January–December 1993): 36.

27. Argentine law allows for two types of adoption: simple and full. "Simple" adoption confers rights to the adoptee as a member of the adoptive family but does not extinguish the rights and responsibilities of her or his family of origin. Adoptees are allowed to add the last name of their original family to their names, and the adoption is revocable. "Full" adoption results in the adoptee no longer

being a member of her or his family of origin. It is irrevocable, and the adoptee cannot recover affiliation with her or his family of origin. See Defensa de los Niños Internacional, *Venta y tráfico de niños en Argentina—Investigación* (Buenos Aires: Defensa de los Niños Internacional/Secretaría de Desarrollo Humano y Familia, Ministerio de Salud y Acción Social de la Nación, 1989), 68–70.

28. Alcira Ríos, interview, December 27, 1994.

29. María Isabel Chorobik de Mariani, interview by author, La Plata, December 9, 1994.

30. Maria Josefina Becker, "The Pressure to Abandon," *International Children's Rights Monitor* 5 (1988): 12–13.

31. Norma López Faura, "El derecho a la identidad biológica en la adopción," paper presented at the Second Interdisciplinary Adoption Symposium in the Southern Cone, Buenos Aires, November 5, 1994.

32. Graciela Fernández Meijide, interview by author, Buenos Aires, December 13, 1994.

33. Antonia Acuña de Segarra, interview by author, Buenos Aires, December 7, 1993.

34. See, for instance, Defence for Children International, *Protecting Children's Rights in International Adoptions: Selected Documents on the Problem of Trafficking and Sale of Children* (Geneva: Defence for Children International, 1989); María Elena Méndez de Díaz, Nora Miselem Rivera, and Jamileth Díaz Guerrero, *La adopción: El tráfico de menores en Honduras* (Tegucigalpa: Centro de Estudios de la Mujer, 1992); "Black Market in Adoptions Described in Guatemala," *Boston Globe,* September 14, 1997; "Detienen a una banda que robaba bebés y los vendía" and "El tráfico de menores, un gran negocio," *Clarín,* September 20, 1997.

35. Defensa de los Niños Internacional, *Venta y tráfico,* ii.

36. Mariana Carbajal, "Otra denuncia sobre bebés comprados en Corrientes," *Página 12,* December 27, 1994. Sister Martha Pelloni is nationally known because of her leadership in Catamarca province, where she organized the silent marches to protest the cover-up of the rape and murder of a young woman, María Soledades Morales, in 1990.

37. "Admiten que en Goya se trafican niños," *Página 12,* November 25, 1993.

38. "El paraíso de las adopciones," *Clarín,* December 12, 1994.

39. "Denuncian venta de bebés a Noruega," *La Voz del Interior* (Córdoba), November 30, 1993.

40. "Indagaron a los narcotraficantes que tenían al niño secuestrado," *La Nación,* March 27, 1994.

41. Carlos Rodríguez, "Exportados sin permiso," *Página 12,* September 10, 1996. See also Alfredo Silletta, *El grito de los inocentes: Tráfico y venta de niños en la Argentina—Adopciones ilegales, robo y prostitución infantil* (Buenos Aires: Corregidor, 1996).

42. Elsa Sánchez de Oesterheld, interview by author, Buenos Aires, November 10, 1993.

43. Susana E. Sommer, *De la cigüeña a la probeta: Los peligros de la aventura científica* (Buenos Aires: Planeta, 1994), 185.

44. Stewart, "The Child's Right to Identity," 232.

45. Gustavo A. Bossert, "Problemas jurídicos que se abren a partir de los avances científicos en materia de procreación," in *El derecho a la identidad: Los avances científicos, la regulación jurídica y los principios de la Convención sobre los Derechos del Niño (Ley 23.849),* ed. Alicia Pierini (Buenos Aires: EUDEBA, 1993), 93–117. See also Rita Arditti and M. Brinton Lykes, "Recovering Identity—The Work of the Grandmothers of Plaza de Mayo," *Women's Studies International Forum* 15 (1992): 461–71.

46. E. Wayne Carp, "The Sealed Adoption Records Controversy in Historical Perspective: The Case of the Children's Home Society in Washington, 1895–1988," *Journal of Sociology and Social Welfare* 19, no. 2 (June 1992): 27–57.

47. Betty Jean Lifton, *Lost and Found: The Adoption Experience* (New York: Harper and Row, 1988), and *Journey of the Adopted Self: A Quest for Wholeness* (New York: Basic Books, 1994).

48. See the newsletter *Chain of Life—A Progressive Adoption Newsletter* (P.O. Box 8081, Berkeley, CA 94707).

49. See Erik H. Erikson, *Childhood and Society,* 2nd ed. (New York: W. W. Norton, 1963).

50. Quoted in Blanche Wiesen Cook, "Eleanor Roosevelt and Human Rights: The Battle for Peace and Planetary Decency," in *Women and American Foreign Policy: Lobbyists, Critics, and Insiders,* ed. Edward P. Crapol (Wilmington, Del.: Scholarly Resources, 1992), 114.

51. Steve Fainaru, "El Salvador: Searching for a Stolen Past," three-part series, *Boston Globe,* July 14, 15, and 16, 1996. Gina Marie's story appears in the July 15 article, "'Imelda (Gina)' Struggles for Identity."

52. Estela Barnes de Carlotto, prologue to Pierini, *Derecho a la identidad,* 14.

CHAPTER EIGHT. THE POLITICS OF MEMORY

1. "Ley 24.411," *Informaciones,* no. 37 (January–December 1994): 24; Javier Calvo, "Dura interna por los desaparecidos," *Clarín,* December 8, 1996; María Adela Antokoletz, interview by author, Buenos Aires, December 8, 1994. There are currently two groups of Mothers of the Plaza de Mayo. In 1986, after the return of democracy, some members—critical of some of the positions of the organization and dissatisfied with the leadership of Hebe Bonafini, the president—broke away and formed their own organization. The new group, Mothers of the Plaza de Mayo/Línea Fundadora (Founders' Line), includes several Mothers who had been part of the original group as well as its former vice president, María Adela Antokoletz. The two groups differ on the issue of exhumations and identification of the remains of the disappeared and on the economic reparations to the families of the disappeared. Those led by Hebe Bonafini oppose the exhumations, believing that they divert attention from the murderers, and consider the economic reparations an insult to human dignity and to the disappeared. The Línea Fundadora, like the Grandmothers' Association, supports the exhumations and economic compensation to the families of the disappeared.

2. Horacio Verbitsky, *The Flight: Confessions of an Argentine Dirty Warrior,* trans. Esther Allen (New York: New Press, 1996).

3. Ricardo Kirschbaum, "Un cambio en la doctrina," *Clarín,* April 27, 1995; "'Examen de conciencia' por la represión ilegal," *Clarín,* April 30, 1995.

4. Alma Guillermoprieto, *The Heart That Bleeds: Latin America Now* (New York: Vintage Books, 1995), 119–50. See also Bell Gale Chevigny and Paul Chevigny, *Police Violence in Argentina: Torture and Police Killings in Buenos Aires,* An Americas Watch and Centro de Estudios Legales y Sociales Report (New York: Americas Watch; Buenos Aires: Centro de Estudios Legales y Sociales, 1991).

5. Charles Harper, "From Impunity to Reconciliation," in *Impunity: An Ethical Perspective,* ed. Charles Harper (Geneva: WCC Publications, 1996), viii–xviii.

6. Diana Kordon et al., *La impunidad: Una perspectiva psicosocial y clínica* (Buenos Aires: Sudamericana, 1995). See also Luis Pérez Aguirre, "The Consequences of Impunity in Society," in *Justice, Not Impunity* (Geneva: International Commission of Jurists, 1992), 107–20.

7. Tribunal Permanente de los Pueblos, *La impunidad juzgada: El caso argentino* (Buenos Aires: Fundación Servicio Paz y Justicia, 1992).

8. Ibid., 8.

9. Ibid., 103.

10. Jonathan Friedland, "Argentine Finance Chief Faces Dilemma," *Wall Street Journal,* July 29, 1996.

11. Guillermoprieto, *Heart That Bleeds,* 127.

12. See ibid., 119–50; Chevigny and Chevigny, *Police Violence in Argentina.* See also "Officers Charged in Buenos Aires," *Boston Globe,* August 30, 1996; "Argentina's Bereft Mothers: And Now, a New Wave," *New York Times,* November 18, 1997; and Paul Chevigny, *Edge of the Knife: Police Violence in the Americas* (New York: New Press, 1995), 181–201.

13. Norma Morandini, *Catamarca* (Buenos Aires: Planeta/Espejo de la Argentina, 1990).

14. Quoted in Jonathan Friedland, "Murder That Rocked Argentina Tears Up Its Justice System," *Wall Street Journal,* April 16, 1996. In 1997 the case of María Soledad Morales was reopened, and new information continues to pour in; see Andrea Osojnik, "Se cayó el muro de silencio," *Página 12,* September 26, 1997.

15. Atilio H. Borón, interview by author, Cambridge, Mass., March 19, 1996.

16. "Police Are Linked to Attack on Jews," *Boston Globe,* July 31, 1996; "Argentine Policeman Tied to 1994 Bombing," *Boston Globe,* November 15, 1997. For more information on the AMIA case, see Juan Salinas, *AMIA: El Atentado. Quiénes son los autores y por qué no están presos* (Buenos Aires: Planeta, 1997).

17. "La Pirámide, de luto por el asesinato de Cabezas," *Página 12,* September 26, 1997.

18. Eduardo Galeano, *We Say No: Chronicles, 1963–1991,* trans. Mark Fried et al. (New York: W. W. Norton, 1992), 215, emphasis his.

19. Yosef Hayim Yerushalmi, *Zakhor: Jewish History and Jewish Memory* (New York: Schocken Books, 1989), 109.

20. Judith Lewis Herman, "Crime and Memory," *Bulletin of the American Academy of Psychiatry Law* 23 (1995): 13.

21. Delia Giovanola de Califano, interview by author, Buenos Aires, October 29, 1996.

22. María Alexiu de Ignace, correspondence with author, September 22, 1996. FEDEFAM can be reached at Apartado Postal 2444, Carmelitas 1010-A, Caracas, Venezuela.

23. "Una niña desaparecida en Argentina habla ante la Comisión de Derechos Humanos," *Informaciones,* no. 36 (January–December 1993): 6.

24. Mariana Eva Pérez and Yamila Grandi, *Algún día . . .* (Buenos Aires: Abuelas de Plaza de Mayo, 1990).

25. Mariana Eva Pérez, interview by author, Buenos Aires, November 28, 1993. Subsequent quotations from her are taken from this interview, unless otherwise noted.

26. Argentina Rojo de Pérez, interview by author, Buenos Aires, November 28, 1993.

27. "Pocos alumnos en un torneo," *Clarín,* October 22, 1995.

28. Osvaldo Bayer, "El patio de los estudiantes vivos," *Página 12,* November 4, 1995.

29. Martín Granovsky, "Los chicos del Buenos Aires (que ya no están)," *Página 12,* October 23, 1996. On the Mothers of the Plaza de Mayo/Línea Fundadora, see note 1 above.

30. Miguel Hernán Santucho, interview by author, Buenos Aires, October 31, 1996. See also Sergio Ciancaglini and Martín Granovsky, *Nada más que la verdad: El juicio a las juntas* (Buenos Aires: Planeta, 1995), 338–39, and Juan Gelman and Mara La Madrid, *Ni el flaco perdón de Dios: Hijos de desaparecidos* (Buenos Aires: Planeta, 1997).

31. Quoted in "Habrá otros mil jueves," *Página 12,* June 28, 1996.

32. "Día de la Verguenza con los HIJOS marchando y los adultos en casa," *Página 12,* October 30, 1996.

33. "Víctimas de amenazas, los HIJOS le reclamaron al ministro Corach," *Página 12,* May 21, 1996.

34. "Acerca de la memoria—nunca lo olvides," *Informaciones,* no. 36 (January–December 1993): 22.

APPENDIX TWO. DECLARATION OF PRINCIPLES

1. Sixteen Grandmothers signed the declaration.

2. Translated by Cola Franzen; from the Grandmothers' archives.

BIBLIOGRAPHY

BOOKS AND ARTICLES

Abuelas de Plaza de Mayo. *Filiación, identidad, restitución: 15 años de lucha de Abuelas de Plaza de Mayo*, edited by Estela Barnes de Carlotto, Alicia Lo Giúdice, Victor Penchaszadeh, and Juan Carlos Volnovich. Buenos Aires: El Bloque Editorial, 1995.

———. *Missing Children Who Disappeared in Argentina between 1976 and 1983*. Buenos Aires: Abuelas de Plaza de Mayo, 1988.

———. *Niños desaparecidos en la Argentina desde 1976*. Buenos Aires: Abuelas de Plaza de Mayo, 1990.

———. *Los niños desaparecidos y la justicia*. Buenos Aires: Abuelas de Plaza de Mayo, 1988.

Aguinis, Marcos. *Un país de novela: Viaje hacia la mentalidad de los argentinos*. Buenos Aires: Planeta, 1988.

Aguirre, Luis Pérez. "The Consequences of Impunity in Society." In *Justice, Not Impunity*, 107–20. Geneva: International Commission of Jurists, 1992.

Americas Watch. *The State Department Misinforms: A Study of Accounting for the Disappeared in Argentina*. An Americas Watch Report. New York: Americas Watch, 1983.

Amnesty International. *Argentina—The Attack on the Third Infantry Regiment Barracks at La Tablada: Investigations into Allegations of Torture, "Disappearances," and Extrajudicial Executions*. New York: Amnesty International, 1990.

———. *Argentina: The Military Juntas and Human Rights: Report of the Trial of the Former Junta Members, 1985*. London: Amnesty International, 1987.

———. *"Disappearances": A Workbook*. New York: Amnesty International, 1981.

———. *The Missing Children of Argentina: A Report of Current Investigations*. New York: Amnesty International, 1985.

———. *Report of an Amnesty International Mission to Argentina, 6–15 November 1976*. London: Amnesty International, 1977.

———. *Testimony on Secret Detention Camps in Argentina*. London: Amnesty International, 1980.

Amorín, Carlos. *Sara Buscando a Simón*. Montevideo: Ediciones de Brecha, 1996.

Andersen, Martin Edwin. *Dossier Secreto: Argentina's Desaparecidos and the Myth of the "Dirty War."* Boulder, Colo.: Westview Press, 1993.

Angel, Raquel. "Una fecha marcada a sangre y fuego—Memoria de un día trágico." *Madres de Plaza de Mayo,* March 1986, 4–5.

Arditti, Rita. "Genetics and Justice: The Grandmothers of Plaza de Mayo Enroll Scientists in Their Struggle for Human Rights." *Woman of Power,* fall 1988, 42–44.

Arditti, Rita, and M. Brinton Lykes. "Recovering Identity—The Work of the Grandmothers of Plaza de Mayo." *Women's Studies International Forum* 15 (1992): 461–71.

Arizpe, Lourdes. "Foreword: Democracy for a Small Two-Gender Planet." In *Women and Social Change in Latin America,* edited by Elizabeth Jelin, xiv–xx. London: Zed Books, 1990.

Asamblea Permanente por los Derechos Humanos. *Las cifras de la guerra sucia.* Buenos Aires: Asamblea Permanente por los Derechos Humanos, 1988.

———. *Derechos humanos, democracia y el futuro de la APDH*. Buenos Aires: Asamblea Permanente por los Derechos Humanos, 1985.

Asociación Pro-Búsqueda de los Niños. "Los niños desaparecidos: Un reto de la posguerra." Presentation at the Thirteenth Congress of Federación Latinoamericana de Asociaciones de Familiares de Detenidos-Desaparecidos, San Salvador, November 20–25, 1995.

Australia, Commonwealth of. *Bringing Them Home: Report of the National Inquiry into the Separation of Aboriginal and Torres Strait Islander Children from Their Families*. Sydney: Human Rights and Equal Opportunity Commission, 1997.

Barki, Irene. *Pour ces yeux-lá . . . La face cachée du drame argentin: Les enfants disparus*. Paris: Éditions La Découverte, 1988.

Becker, Maria Josefina. "The Pressure to Abandon." *International Children's Rights Monitor* 5 (1988): 12–13.

Beckwith, Barbara. "Science for Human Rights—Using Genetic Screening and Forensic Science to Find Argentina's Disappeared." *Science for the People* 19, no. 1 (January/February 1987): 6.

Berra, Jorge Luis. *Banco Nacional de Datos Genéticos: La identificación de los niños desaparecidos en la Argentina*. Buenos Aires: Abuelas de Plaza de Mayo, n.d.

Bonaparte, Laura Beatriz. *Militares en la Argentina y su método de tortura interminable*. Copenhagen: Rehabilitation and Research Center for Torture Victims, 1984.

Bossert, Gustavo A. "Problemas jurídicos que se abren a partir de los avances científicos en materia de procreación." In *El derecho a la identidad: Los avances científicos, la regulación jurídica y los principios de la Convención sobre los Derechos del Niño (Ley 23.849),* edited by Alicia Pierini, 93–117. Buenos Aires: EUDEBA, 1993.

Bousquet, Jean-Pierre. *Las Locas de la Plaza de Mayo.* Buenos Aires: El Cid Editor, 1982.

Bouvard, Marguerite Guzmán. *Revolutionizing Motherhood: The Mothers of the Plaza de Mayo.* Wilmington, Del.: Scholarly Resources, 1994.

Boven, Theo van. *See* van Boven, Theo.

Brysk, Alyson. *The Politics of Human Rights in Argentina: Protest, Change, and Democratization.* Stanford: Stanford University Press, 1994.

———. "The Politics of Measurement: The Contested Count of the Disappeared in Argentina." *Human Rights Quarterly* 16 (1994): 676–92.

Bunster, Ximena. "Surviving Beyond Fear: Women and Torture in Latin America." In *Surviving Beyond Fear: Women, Children, and Human Rights in Latin America,* edited by Marjorie Agosín, 98–125. Fredonia, N.Y.: White Pine Press, 1993.

Camarasa, Jorge. *Los Nazis en la Argentina.* Buenos Aires: Editorial Legasa, 1992.

Camarasa, Jorge, Rubén Felice, and Daniel González. *El juicio: Proceso al horror.* Buenos Aires: Sudamericana/Planeta, 1985.

Carlotto, Estela Barnes de. "Prólogo." In *El derecho a la identidad: Los avances científicos, la regulación juridíca y los principios de la Convención sobre los Derechos del Niño (Ley 23.849),* edited by Alicia Pierini, 13–15. Buenos Aires: EUDEBA, 1993.

Carp, E. Wayne. "The Sealed Adoption Records Controversy in Historical Perspective: The Case of the Children's Home Society of Washington, 1895–1988." *Journal of Sociology and Social Welfare* 19, no. 2 (June 1992): 27–57.

Centro de Estudios Legales y Sociales. *Autoamnistía: Legalizar la impunidad.* Buenos Aires: Centro de Estudios Legales y Sociales, n.d.

———. *Terrorismo de estado: 692 responsables.* Buenos Aires: Centro de Estudios Legales y Sociales, 1986.

Cerda, Jaime Sergio. "The Draft Convention on the Rights of the Child: New Rights." *Human Rights Quarterly* 12 (1990): 115–19.

Chevance-Bertin, Marie Pascale. "Memóire pour l'impensable—le cas des enfants de disparus Argentins volés par des militaires ou des policiers." Presented at Université Paris VII, 1986–87.

Chevigny, Bell Gale, and Paul Chevigny. *Police Violence in Argentina: Torture and Police Killings in Buenos Aires.* An Americas Watch and Centro de Estudios Legales y Sociales Report. New York: Americas Watch; Buenos Aires: Centro de Estudios Legales y Sociales, 1991.

Chevigny, Paul. *Edge of the Knife: Police Violence in the Americas.* New York: New Press, 1995.

Chomsky, Noam, and Edward S. Herman. *The Washington Connection and Third World Fascism.* Vol. 1 of *The Political Economy of Human Rights.* Boston: South End Press, 1979.

Ciancaglini, Sergio, and Martín Granovsky. *Nada más que la verdad: El juicio a las juntas.* Buenos Aires: Planeta, 1995.

Cohen Salama, Mauricio. *Tumbas anónimas: Informe sobre la identificación de restos de víctimas de la represión ilegal.* Buenos Aires: Equipo Argentino de Antropología Forense and Catálogos, 1992.

Comisión de Familiares de Paraguayos Detenidos Desaparecidos en la Argentina. *Semillas de Vida/Ñemity Ra.* Asunción, Paraguay: Comisión de Familiares de Paraguayos Detenidos Desaparecidos en la Argentina, n.d.

Commission Argentine des Droits de l'homme. *Argentine: Dossier d'un génocide.* Paris: Flammarion, 1978.

Conte, Laura J. de. In "Identidad, Filiación, Apropiación, Adopción y Restitución." In *Filiación, identidad, restitución: 15 años de lucha de Abuelas de Plaza de Mayo,* edited by Estela Barnes de Carlotto, Alicia Lo Giúdice, Victor Penchaszadeh, and Juan Carlos Volnovich, 91–101. Buenos Aires: El Bloque Editorial, 1995.

Cook, Blanche Wiesen. "Eleanor Roosevelt and Human Rights: The Battle for Peace and Planetary Decency." In *Women and American Foreign Policy: Lobbyists, Critics, and Insiders,* edited by Edward P. Crapol, 91–118. Wilmington, Del.: Scholarly Resources, 1992.

Defence for Children International. *Protecting Children's Rights in International Adoptions: Selected Documents on the Problem of Trafficking and Sale of Children.* Geneva: Defence for Children International, 1989.

Defensa de los Niños Internacional. *Venta y tráfico de niños en Argentina—Investigación.* Buenos Aires: Defensa de los Niños Internacional and Secretaría de Desarrollo Humano y Familia, Ministerio de Salud y Acción Social de la Nación, 1989.

Di Lonardo, Ana María, Pierre Darlu, Max Baur, Cristian Orrego, and Mary-Claire King. "Human Genetics and Human Rights—Identifying the Families of Kidnapped Children." *American Journal of Forensic Medicine and Pathology* 5 (1984): 339–47.

Diana, Marta. *Mujeres guerrilleras: La militancia de los setenta en el testimonio de sus protagonistas femeninas.* Buenos Aires: Planeta, 1996.

Dinamarca, Hernán, and Marisol Santelices. *¿Donde están?: La historia de los niños uruguayos desaparecidos.* Montevideo: Ediciones La República, 1989.

Dinnerstein, Dorothy. "What Does Feminism Mean?" In *Rocking the Ship of State: Toward a Feminist Peace Politics,* edited by Adrienne Harris and Ynestra King, 13–23. Boulder, Colo.: Westview Press, 1989.

"Doctrina de la Seguridad Nacional (DSN)." *FEDEFAM,* November 1984, 22–29.

Dolkart, Ronald H. "The Right in the Década Infame, 1930–1943." In *The Argentine Right: Its History and Intellectual Origins, 1910 to the Present,* edited by Sandra McGee Deutsch and Ronald H. Dolkart, 65–98. Wilmington, Del.: Scholarly Resources, 1993.

Duhalde, Eduardo Luis. *El estado terrorista argentino.* Buenos Aires: Ediciones El Caballito, 1983.

Elkin, Judith Laikin. "Quincentenary: Colonial Legacy of Anti-Semitism." *Report on the Americas* 25, no. 4 (February 1992): 4–7.

Equipo Argentino de Antropología Forense. *Breve reseña sobre el caso de la Familia Manfil.* Buenos Aires: Equipo Argentino de Antropología Forense, n.d.

Equipo Interdisciplinario de Abuelas de Plaza de Mayo. "Abuelas opinan sobre Dolto." *Psyche,* December 1986, 11–12.

———. *El secuestro-apropiación de niños y su restitución.* Buenos Aires: Abuelas de Plaza de Mayo, 1989.
Erikson, Erik H. *Childhood and Society.* 2nd ed. New York: W. W. Norton, 1963.
Familiares de Desaparecidos y Detenidos por Razones Políticas. *Abogados desaparecidos.* Buenos Aires: Familiares de Desaparecidos y Detenidos por Razones Políticas, 1988.
Fariña, Juan Jorge, and M. Brinton Lykes. "Cuestiones éticas y epistemológicas ante la experimentación psicológica con niños." In *Actas del Congreso Nacional de Etica.* Buenos Aires: Asociación Argentina de Investigaciones Eticas, Universidad de Buenos Aires, 1991.
Feijoo, María del Carmen, and Mónica Gogna. "Women in the Transition to Democracy." In *Women and Social Change in Latin America,* edited by Elizabeth Jelin, 79–114. London: Zed Books, 1990.
Feitlowitz, Marguerite. *A Lexicon of Terror: Argentina and the Legacies of Torture.* New York: Oxford University Press, 1998.
Filc, Judith. *Entre el parentesco y la política: Familia y dictadura, 1976–1983.* Buenos Aires: Editorial Biblos, 1997.
Fisher, Jo. *Mothers of the Disappeared.* Boston: South End Press, 1989.
Flores, María Teresa. In "Identidad, Filiación, Apropiación, Adopción y Restitución: Area Jurídica." In *Filiación, identidad, restitución: 15 años de lucha de Abuelas de Plaza de Mayo,* edited by Estela Barnes de Carlotto, Alicia Lo Giúdice, Victor Penchaszadeh, and Juan Carlos Volnovich, 140–46. Buenos Aires: El Bloque Editorial, 1995.
Frontalini, Daniel, and María Cristina Caiati. *El mito de la guerra sucia.* Buenos Aires: Centro de Estudios Legales y Sociales, 1984.
Fundación Servicio Paz y Justicia. *La impunidad juzgada: El caso argentino.* Buenos Aires: Fundación Servicio Paz y Justicia, 1992.
Galeano, Eduardo. "1983, Buenos Aires: Las abuelas detectives" and "1983, Lima: Tamara vuela dos veces." In *Memoria del fuego.* Vol. 3, *El siglo del viento,* 321–23. Mexico City: siglo veintuno editores, 1986.
———. *We Say No: Chronicles, 1963–1991.* Translated by Mark Fried et al. New York: W. W. Norton, 1992.
Gelman, Juan, and Mara La Madrid. *Ni el flaco perdón de Dios: Hijos de desaparecidos.* Buenos Aires: Planeta, 1997.
Giberti, Eva. *La adopción.* Buenos Aires: Sudamericana, 1987.
Goñi, Uki. *Judas: La verdadera historia de Alfredo Astiz—el infiltrado.* Buenos Aires: Editorial Sudamericana, 1996.
González Janzen, Ignacio. *La Triple A.* Buenos Aires: Editorial Contrapunto, 1986.
Graham-Yooll, Andrew. *A Matter of Fear: Portrait of an Argentinian Exile.* Westport, Conn.: Lawrence Hill, 1982.
Guest, Iain. *Behind the Disappearances: Argentina's Dirty War against Human Rights and the United Nations.* Philadelphia: University of Pennsylvania Press, 1990.
Guillermoprieto, Alma. *The Heart That Bleeds: Latin America Now.* New York: Vintage Books, 1995.

Gurvich, Marta. "The Dirty War's Family Secrets." *In These Times,* April 28, 1997, 27–30.
Hagelin, Ragnar. *Mi hija Dagmar.* Buenos Aires: Sudamericana/Planeta, 1984.
Hammarberg, Thomas. "The UN Convention on the Rights of the Child—and How to Make it Work." *Human Rights Quarterly* 12 (1990): 97–105.
Harff, Barbara. "Recognizing Genocides and Politicides." In *Genocide Watch,* edited by Helen Fein, 27–41. New Haven: Yale University Press, 1992.
Harper, Charles. "From Impunity to Reconciliation." In *Impunity: An Ethical Perspective,* edited by Charles Harper, viii–xviii. Geneva: WCC Publications, 1996.
Herman, Judith Lewis. "Crime and Memory." *Bulletin of the American Academy of Psychiatry Law* 23 (1995): 5–17.
———. *Trauma and Recovery.* New York: Basic Books, 1992.
Herrera, Matilde, and Ernesto Tenembaum. *Identidad: Despojo y restitución.* Buenos Aires: Editorial Contrapunto, n.d.
Hillel, Marc, and Clarissa Henry. *Of Pure Blood.* New York: McGraw-Hill, 1976.
Hoeffel, Paul Heath, and Juan Montalvo (pseud. of César Chelala). "Missing or Dead in Argentina." *New York Times Magazine,* October 21, 1979, 44–45 ff.
Janeway, Elizabeth. *Powers of the Weak.* New York: Alfred A. Knopf, 1980.
Jonassohn, Kurt. "What Is Genocide?" In *Genocide Watch,* edited by Helen Fein, 17–26. New Haven: Yale University Press, 1992.
Joyce, Christopher, and Eric Stover. *Witnesses from the Grave: The Stories Bones Tell.* New York: Ballantine Books, 1992.
Kaplan, Jacob. *L'Affaire Finaly.* Paris: Les Editions du Cerf, 1993.
Kaplan, Temma. "Female Consciousness and Collective Action: The Case of Barcelona, 1910–1918." *Signs* 7 (1982): 545–66.
Kaufman, Edy, and Beatriz Cymberknopf. "La dimensión judía en la represión durante el gobierno militar en la Argentina (1976–1983)." In *El antisemitismo en la Argentina,* edited by Leonardo Senkman, 235–73. Buenos Aires: Centro Editor de América Latina, 1989.
Kisilevsky, Marcelo. "Testimonio de una lucha contra el olvido y la impunidad: Diálogo con Berta Schubaroff." *Nueva Sión,* January 19, 1990, 8–9.
Kordon, Diana, et al. *La impunidad: Una perspectiva psicosocial y clínica.* Buenos Aires: Sudamericana, 1995.
Lechner, Norbert. "Some People Die of Fear: Fear as a Political Problem." In *At the Edge: State Terror and Resistance in Latin America,* edited by Juan E. Corradi, Patricia Weiss Fagen, and Manuel Antonio Garretón, 26–35. Berkeley: University of California Press, 1992.
Lernoux, Penny. *Cry of the People: The Struggle for Human Rights in Latin America—The Catholic Church in Conflict with U.S. Policy.* New York: Penguin Books, 1991.
Lewis, Paul. "The Right and the Military Rule, 1955–1983." In *The Argentine Right: Its History and Intellectual Origins, 1910 to the Present,* edited by Sandra McGee Deutsch and Ronald H. Dolkart, 147–80. Wilmington, Del.: Scholarly Resources, 1993.

Lifton, Betty Jean. *Journey of the Adopted Self: A Quest for Wholeness.* New York: Basic Books, 1994.

———. *Lost and Found: The Adoption Experience.* New York: Harper and Row, 1988.

Liwski, Norberto Ignacio, and Horacio David Pacheco. *Acerca de las reservas argentinas a la Convención Internacional de los Derechos del Niño—Ley Nacional 23.849.* Buenos Aires: Sección Argentina de Defensa del Niño Internacional, 1991.

Lo Giúdice, Alicia. "La cajita: Subjetividad y traumatismo." Paper presented at Pensar la Niñez: Primer Encuentro Psicoanalítico Interdisciplinario. Buenos Aires, November 1992.

Lombardi, Alicia. "Las Madres de Plaza de Mayo: Un enfoque feminista." Paper presented at the fourth conference of the Asociación de Trabajo y Estudios de la Mujer. Buenos Aires, 1985.

López Faura, Norma. "El derecho a la identidad biológica en la adopción." Paper presented at the Second Interdisciplinary Adoption Symposium in the Southern Cone. Buenos Aires, November 5, 1994.

Madres de Plaza de Mayo. *Nuestros hijos.* 2 vols. Buenos Aires: Editorial Contrapunto, 1987.

Martín-Baró, Ignacio. "Political Violence and War as Causes of Psychosocial Trauma in El Salvador." *International Journal of Mental Health* 18 (1989): 3–20.

———. "War and the Psychosocial Trauma of Salvadoran Children." In *Writings for a Liberation Psychology,* edited by Adrianne Aron and Shawn Corne, 122–35. Cambridge, Mass.: Harvard University Press, 1994.

Martínez, Juan Carlos. *La Abuela de Hierro.* Buenos Aires: Fundación Servicio Paz y Justicia, 1995.

Mellibovsky, Matilde. *Círculo de amor sobre la muerte.* Buenos Aires: Ediciones del Pensamiento Nacional, 1990.

Méndez, Juan E. *Truth and Partial Justice in Argentina: An Update.* An Americas Watch Report. Washington, D.C.: Americas Watch, 1991.

Méndez de Díaz, María Elena, Nora Miselem Rivera, and Jamileth Díaz Guerrero. *La adopción: El tráfico de menores en Honduras.* Tegucigalpa: Centro de Estudios de la Mujer-Honduras, 1992.

Mignone, Emilio F. *Derechos humanos y sociedad: El caso argentino.* Buenos Aires: Centro de Estudios Legales y Sociales/Ediciones del Pensamiento Nacional, 1991.

———. *Witness to the Truth: The Complicity of Church and Dictatorship in Argentina, 1976–1983.* Translated by Philip Berryman. Maryknoll, N.Y.: Orbis Books, 1988.

Morandini, Norma. *Catamarca.* Buenos Aires: Planeta/Espejo de la Argentina, 1990.

Navarro, Marysa. "The Personal Is Political: Las Madres de Plaza de Mayo." In *Power and Popular Protest: Latin American Social Movements,* edited by Susan Eckstein, 241–58. Berkeley: University of California Press, 1989.

Noriega, Jorge. "American Indian Education in the United States: Indoctrination for Subordination to Colonialism." In *The State of Native America:*

Genocide, Colonization, and Resistance, edited by M. Annette Jaimes, 371–402. Boston: South End Press, 1992.

Nosiglia, Julio E. *Botín de guerra.* Buenos Aires: Cooperativa Tierra Fértil, 1985.

Nunca Más: The Report of the Argentine National Commission on the Disappeared. New York: Farrar, Straus, and Giroux, 1986.

Organización de los Estados Americanos, Comisión Interamericana de Derechos Humanos. *Informe sobre la situación de los derechos humanos en Argentina.* Washington, D.C.: Organización de los Estados Americanos, 1980.

Paoletti, Alipio. *Como los Nazis, Como en Vietnam.* Buenos Aires: Edición Cañón Oxidado, 1987.

Partnoy, Alicia. *The Little School: Tales of Disappearance and Survival in Argentina.* Pittsburgh: Cleis Press, 1986.

Penchaszadeh, Victor B. "Abduction of Children of Political Dissidents in Argentina and the Role of Human Genetics in Their Restitution." *Journal of Public Health Policy* 13 (1992): 291–305.

———. "Genetic Identification of Children of the Disappeared in Argentina." *Journal of the American Medical Women's Association* 52, no. 1 (winter 1997): 16–27.

———. In "Implicaciones Sociales y Científicas de Nuestra Lucha." In *Filiación, identidad, restitución: 15 años de lucha de Abuelas de Plaza de Mayo,* edited by Estela Barnes de Carlotto, Alicia Lo Giúdice, Victor Penchaszadeh, and Juan Carlos Volnovich, 32–35. Buenos Aires: El Bloque Editorial, 1995.

Pérez, Mariana Eva, and Yamila Grandi. *Algún día . . . .* Buenos Aires: Abuelas de Plaza de Mayo, 1990.

Price Cohen, Cynthia. "United States Signs the Convention on the Rights of the Child." *International Journal of Children's Rights* 3 (1995): 281–82.

Read, Peter. *The Stolen Generations: The Removal of Aboriginal Children in New South Wales, 1883 to 1969.* New South Wales, Ministry of Aboriginal Affairs. Sydney: Government Printer, 1982.

Ríos, Alcira E. "La pericia immunogenética en los casos de los menores víctimas de desaparición forzada." Paper presented to the National Commission on the Right to Identity, ca. 1996.

Rock, David. *Argentina, 1516–1987: From Spanish Colonization to Alfonsín.* Berkeley: University of California Press, 1987.

Rodríguez, Andrea. *Nacidos en la sombra: La historia secreta de los mellizos Reggiardo Tolosa y el Subcomisario Miara.* Buenos Aires: Sudamericana, 1996.

Rosenberg, Tina. *Children of Cain: Violence and the Violent in Latin America.* New York: William Morrow, 1991.

Rosenthal, Morton M. "Argentinian Jews in Danger." *ADL Bulletin,* November 1976, 4–5.

Ruddick, Sara. *Maternal Thinking: Towards a Politics of Peace.* Boston: Beacon Press, 1989.

Salaberry, Mariela. *Mariana: Tú y nosotros—Diálogo con María Ester Gatti.* Montevideo: Ediciones de la Banda Oriental, 1993.

Salinas, Juan. *AMIA: El Atentado. Quiénes son los autores y por qué no están presos.* Buenos Aires: Planeta, 1997.

Seoane, María, and Héctor Ruiz Núñez. *La Noche de los Lápices.* Buenos Aires: Planeta-Edición Definitiva, 1992.

Shirer, William L. *The Rise and Fall of the Third Reich: A History of Nazi Germany.* New York: Simon and Schuster, 1960.

Shumway, Nicolas. *The Invention of Argentina.* Berkeley: University of California Press, 1991.

Silletta, Alfredo. *El grito de los inocentes: Tráfico y venta de niños en la Argentina—Adopciones ilegales, robo y prostitución infantil.* Buenos Aires: Corregidor, 1996.

Simpson, John, and Jana Bennett. *The Disappeared and the Mothers of the Plaza.* New York: St. Martin's Press, 1985.

Snow, Clyde Collins, and María Julia Bihurriet. "An Epidemiology of Homicide: *Ningún Nombre* Burials in the Province of Buenos Aires from 1970 to 1984." In *Human Rights and Statistics,* edited by Thomas B. Jabine and Richard P. Claude, 329–63. Philadelphia: University of Pennsylvania Press, 1992.

Sommer, Susana E. *De la cigüeña a la probeta: Los peligros de la aventura científica.* Buenos Aires: Planeta, 1994.

Sonderéguer, María. "Aparición con vida (El movimiento de derechos humanos en Argentina)." In *Los nuevos movimientos sociales.* Vol. 2, *Derechos humanos. Obreros. Barrios,* edited by Elizabeth Jelin, 7–32. Buenos Aires: Centro Editor de América Latina, 1985.

Stallings, Barbara. *Banker to the Third World: U.S. Portfolio Investment in Latin America, 1900–1986.* Berkeley: University of California Press, 1987.

Sternbach, Nancy Saporta, Marysa Navarro-Aranguren, Patricia Chuchryk, and Sonia E. Alvarez. "Feminisms in Latin America: From Bogotá to San Bernardo." In *Rethinking the Political: Gender, Resistance, and the State,* edited by Barbara Laslett, Johanna Brenner, and Yesim Arat, 240–81. Chicago: University of Chicago Press, 1995.

Stewart, George A. "Interpreting the Child's Right to Identity in the UN Convention on the Rights of the Child." *Family Law Quarterly* 26 (1992): 221–33.

Stover, Eric. "Scientists Aid Search for Argentina's 'Desaparecidos.'" *Science,* October 4, 1985, 56–57.

Suárez-Orozco, Marcelo M. "The Treatment of Children in the 'Dirty War': Ideology, State Terrorism, and the Abuse of Children in Argentina." In *Child Survival: Anthropological Perspectives on the Treatment and Maltreatment of Children,* edited by Nancy Scheper-Hughes, 227–46. Dordrecht: D. Reidel, 1987.

Thoolen, Hans. Introduction to *People Matter: Views on International Human Rights Policy,* by Theo van Boven, 5–12. Amsterdam: Meulenhoff, 1982.

Timerman, Jacobo. *Prisoner without a Name, Cell without a Number.* New York: Vintage Books, 1982.

Tribunal Permanente de los Pueblos. *La impunidad juzgada: El caso argentino.* Buenos Aires: Fundación Servicio Paz y Justicia, 1992.

Ulla, Noemí, and Hugo Echave. *Después de la noche: Diálogo con Graciela Fernández Meijide.* Buenos Aires: Editorial Contrapunto, 1986.

United Nations. *Convention on the Prevention and Punishment of the Crime of Genocide.* New York: United Nations, 1991.

———. *United Nations Convention on the Rights of the Child.* New York: United Nations, 1990.

Utpba (Unión de Trabajadores de Prensa de Buenos Aires). *La construcción de la noticia: Estudio de un caso de manipulación de la información.* Buenos Aires, 1994. (Booklet and film).

van Boven, Theo. *Prevention of the Disappearance of Children.* N.p.: UN Economic and Social Council, Commission on Human Rights, 1988.

Varela-Cid, Eduardo, and Luis Vicens. *La imbecilización de la mujer.* Buenos Aires: El Cid Editor, 1984.

Veiga, Raúl. *Las organizaciones de derechos humanos.* Buenos Aires: Centro Editor de América Latina, 1985.

Verbitsky, Horacio. *The Flight: Confessions of an Argentine Dirty Warrior.* Translated by Esther Allen. New York: New Press, 1996.

———, ed. *Rodolfo Walsh y la prensa clandestina 1976–1978.* Buenos Aires: Ediciones de la Urraca, 1985.

"Verdad y ley para los niños recuperados: Un diálogo con Francoise Dolto." *Psyche,* October 1986, 4–6.

Walker, Richard H., ed. *Inclusion Probabilities in Parentage Testing.* Arlington, Va.: American Association of Blood Banks, 1983.

Walsh, Rodolfo. "Escuela de Mecánica de la Armada/Historia de la guerra sucia en la Argentina." In *Rodolfo Walsh y la prensa clandestina 1976–1978,* edited by Horacio Verbitsky, 13–36. Buenos Aires: Ediciones de la Urraca, 1985.

Weisbrot, Robert. *The Jews of Argentina: From the Inquisition to Perón.* Philadelphia: Jewish Publication Society of America, 1979.

Welty-Domon, Arlette. *Sor Alicia: Un sol de justicia.* Buenos Aires: Editorial Contrapunto, 1987.

Weschler, Lawrence. *A Miracle, a Universe: Settling Accounts with Torturers.* New York: Penguin Books, 1990.

Wiesenthal, Simon. *The Murderers among Us: The Wiesenthal Memoirs,* edited by Joseph Wechsberg. New York: McGraw-Hill, 1967.

Wynia, Gary W. *Argentina: Illusions and Realities.* New York: Holmes and Meier, 1986.

Yerushalmi, Yosef Hayim. *Zakhor: Jewish History and Jewish Memory.* New York: Schocken Books, 1989.

NEWSLETTERS

Chain of Life—A Progressive Adoption Newsletter. P.O. Box 8081, Berkeley, CA 94707.

Informaciones. Newsletter of the Grandmothers of the Plaza de Mayo. Buenos Aires, 1986–94.

Testimonios. Bulletin of the Familiares de Desaparecidos y Detenidos por Razones Políticas.

INTERVIEWS

Grandmothers of the Plaza de Mayo

Aguilar, Elsa Pavón de, Buenos Aires, December 19, 1993.
Argañaraz, Otilia Lescano de, Buenos Aires, November 5, 1993.
Baamonde, Emma Spione de, Buenos Aires, November 4, 1993.
Califano, Delia Giovanola de, Buenos Aires, October 29, 1996.
Carlotto, Estela Barnes de, Cambridge, Mass., October 30, 1989; Buenos Aires, December 16, 1993, and December 22, 1994.
Lanzillotto, Alba, Buenos Aires, October 26, 1993.
Lemos, Haydée Vallino de, Buenos Aires, November 5, 1993.
Mariani, María Isabel Chorobik de, La Plata, December 9, 1994.
Marizcurrena, Raquel Radío de, Buenos Aires, November 25, 1993.
Miranda, Amelia Herrera de, Buenos Aires, November 1, 1993.
Navajas, Nélida Gómez de, Cambridge, Mass., October 30, 1989; Buenos Aires, November 9, 1993.
Oesterheld, Elsa Sánchez de, Buenos Aires, November 10, 1993.
Pérez, Argentina Rojo de, Buenos Aires, November 28, 1993.
Quesada, Nya, Buenos Aires, November 22, 1993.
Roisinblit, Rosa Tarlovsky de, Buenos Aires, November 17, 1993.
Santander, Elena, Buenos Aires, October 27, 1993.
Schubaroff, Berta, Buenos Aires, November 18, 1993.
Segarra de, Antonia Acuña , Buenos Aires, December 7, 1993.
Torres, Sonia, Córdoba, December 2, 1993.
Waisberg de, Reina Esses, Buenos Aires, October 25, 1996.

Found Children

Lavalle Lemos, María José, Buenos Aires, December 22, 1994.
Logares Grinspon, Paula Eva, Buenos Aires, December 20, 1994.
Sfiligoy, Tatiana, Buenos Aires, December 17, 1993.

Others

Abdala, Lita, Buenos Aires, November 1, 1996.
Amorín, Carlos, telephone, May 4, 1998.
Antokoletz, María Adela, Buenos Aires, December 8, 1994.
Bianchedi, Marcelo, Buenos Aires, December 15, 1994.
Borón, Atilio H., Cambridge, Mass., March 19, 1996.
Careaga, Ana María, Buenos Aires, December 26, 1994.
Di Lonardo, Ana María, Buenos Aires, December 15, 1993, and October 31, 1996.
Doretti, Mimí, telephone, August 16, 1994.

Galiñanes, Arturo, Buenos Aires, November 18, 1993.
Gatti, María Ester, telephone, December 22, 1994.
Laborde, Adriana Calvo de, Buenos Aires, December 27, 1994.
Lo Giúdice, Alicia, Buenos Aires, December 14, 1993.
Meijide, Graciela Fernández, Buenos Aires, December 13, 1994.
Mignone, Emilio F., Buenos Aires, December 16, 1994.
Penchaszadeh, Victor B., New York, May 18, 1995.
Pérez, Mariana Eva, Buenos Aires, November 28, 1993.
Pierini, Alicia, Buenos Aires, December 6, 1993.
Ríos, Alcira E., Buenos Aires, December 27, 1994, and November 5, 1996.
Santucho, Miguel Hernán, Buenos Aires, October 31, 1996.
Snow, Clyde, telephone, January 24, 1996.
Stover, Eric, Boston, August 9, 1994.
Waisberg, Tania María, Buenos Aires, October 30, 1996.

INDEX

Indexer: Ruth Elwell
Compositor: Impressions Book and Journal Services, Inc.
Text: 10/13 Sabon
Display: Gill Sans
Printer and binder: Edwards Brothers, Inc.